50
political ideas
you really need to know

Ben Dupré

Quercus

Contents

Introduction

'Politics is supposed to be the second oldest profession,' joked Ronald Reagan in 1977. 'I have come to realize that it bears a very close resemblance to the first.' With apologies to the man who was to become 40th president of the USA (and to logic), it may be that the second oldest profession is in fact older than the first. For behaving politically is, arguably, inseparable from being human. Aristotle's definition of human beings as *zōa politika* (political animals) is based on his view that people express themselves most fully and characteristically within the context of the Greek city-state, or *polis* – the word from which 'politics' is derived. The polis, then, is the natural habitat of political animals, where they interact cooperatively to establish the laws and build the institutions on which social order and justice depend. And if humans are essentially political, it follows that life without politics is impossible.

The *polis* may be a product of civic collaboration, but its animating force is conflict. If people did not habitually disagree about things, there would be no need for politics. In a world of complete concord – or overwhelming oppression – politics could not thrive, because disagreement would be either absent or obliterated. We need to live politically because there is no general agreement about how the good things in life should be shared out; about who should have authority over whom, and how it is decided. As Mao Zedong shrewdly observed, politics is war without bloodshed: a means of resolving conflict without recourse to violence. The only common agreement, in a politically open society, is an agreement to tolerate difference, so politics is the art (or perhaps science – views differ) of compromise.

As disagreement is the essence of politics, it would be an injustice to the subject if I were to seek to justify the particular selection of 50 political ideas covered in this book. Indeed, given that finality is not the language of politics (as Disraeli observed), I will not even pretend that the treatment of each is definitive. I will merely thank my publishers (first Richard, now Slav) for their continuing support and my family for demonstrating that a sound political settlement does not depend on reason or equal division of labour. *Amor vincit omnia*.

Ben Dupré
Oxford 2010

01 Liberty

In the liberal democracies of the West, liberty is widely held to be the most basic of human rights: an ideal that is worth fighting for and, if need be, dying for. The great value attached to liberty is a measure of the many bitter struggles that have been fought to win it: against churches that were willing to kill to defend their orthodoxies; against the absolute power of monarchs; against the oppression of women and political dissidents; against slavery, prejudice, ignorance, and a thousand things besides.

Since the great American and French revolutions in the latter half of the 18th century, liberty has stood pre-eminent as the defining principle of liberalism. According to John Locke, a political theorist whose work inspired the Founding Fathers of the United States, the provision of liberty is the ultimate justification of a state's legal constitution: 'The end of law is not to abolish or restrain, but to preserve and enlarge freedom.' The freedom to hold whatever political and religious views one wishes; to express such views without fear or restraint; to decide for oneself where and in what manner to live one's life: such are the prizes of liberty.

According to the US Declaration of Independence of 1776, liberty, in company with life and the pursuit of happiness, is one of the natural and inalienable rights endowed upon all humans equally. It is a right that should not be limited without the strongest cause, yet neither can it be unlimited or absolute. As the English social philosopher and historian R.H. Tawney observed in *Equality* (1938), 'Freedom for the pike is death for the minnows.' Unfettered freedom – or licence – inevitably infringes the liberty of others. But where should we draw the line? Governments typically respond to external threats, such as war and terrorism, by

timeline

1644	1690	July 1776	July 1789
Milton's *Areopagitica* attacks government censorship	Locke's *Two Treatises of Government* published	US Declaration of Independence	Fall of the Bastille

restricting civil liberties; and the erosion of liberty that results is often, in the view of critics, no less insidious than the dangers that supposedly justified it.

Positive and negative freedom No modern account of liberty can ignore the seminal contribution made by the 20th-century political philosopher Isaiah Berlin. His analysis is constructed around a key distinction between two concepts of liberty: positive and negative freedom.

We commonly think of freedom as existing where there is no external restriction or coercion: you are free so long as there is no obstacle preventing you from doing what you want to do. This is what Berlin calls 'negative freedom'. In considering the circumstances in which it is permissible for society to curtail such freedom,

Berlin supports the 'harm principle' associated particularly with the Victorian philosopher John Stuart Mill. This stipulates that individuals should be left free by the state to act in any way that does not damage the interests of others. In this way an area of individual freedom can be defined, a private space that should remain sacrosanct and immune to outside interference. Freedom in this sense is always a compromise between individuals living together in society. 'What freedom means,' wrote the British dramatist Tom Stoppard in 2002, 'is being allowed to sing in my bath as loudly as will not interfere with my neighbour's freedom to sing a different tune in his.'

Now imagine a person who has liberty in this negative sense but lacks the wealth, education or other resources, mental or physical, to act upon it. Is such a person

The new price of liberty

The price of liberty, proverbially, is eternal vigilance. The original point was that civil liberties should be under constant scrutiny, lest they be eroded by the surreptitious action of government and lost. Today, in an extraordinary inversion, it is citizens themselves who have become the objects of eternal vigilance, as intelligence and law-enforcement agencies use ever more sophisticated technology to watch over us. Our movements are monitored by drones, satellites and a million surveillance cameras; our physical characteristics are biometrically analysed; our computer data is mined and profiled; our phone calls are routinely tapped; our emails are scanned. Big Brother is indeed watching.

1859	**October 1958**	**September 2001**
Publication of John Stuart Mill's *On Liberty*	Isaiah Berlin gives lecture entitled 'Two Concepts of Liberty'	George W. Bush delivers 'war on terror' speech before Congress

> **❝Those who have ever valued liberty for its own sake believed that to be free to choose, and not to be chosen for, is an inalienable ingredient in what makes human beings human.❞**
>
> **Isaiah Berlin, 1969**

fully free? Suppose that there is some course of action that you should take, and would take if you were not prevented by want of the necessary material means or by a deficiency in character or vision. What you lack in this case is what Berlin calls *positive* freedom: a form of empowerment or autonomy that allows you to fulfil your potential or to meet your destiny.

The problem, for Berlin, with this positive kind of freedom is precisely that it presupposes that there is some such 'destiny' – that there is some right path that you should follow, if only the 'better side' of your nature prevailed. It is as if there is something essential in human nature that determines what is right for humans to do, and that the free person is the one who expresses this essence. But who is to say what this destiny or essence is? Berlin's fear is that once those in authority – typically the visionaries and the zealots – take a view on how things should be, they will take it upon themselves to encourage the supposed 'better side' of others (and suppress their worse side) in what they consider to be their best interests. Such paternalistic government may soon turn to tyranny, setting a particular goal for society and prioritizing a certain way of life for its citizens. It is a short step then for the powerful to assume the right 'to ignore the actual wishes of men or societies, to bully, oppress, torture in the name, and on behalf,

Free and daring speculation

'Give me the liberty to know, to utter, and to argue freely according to conscience, above all liberties.' English poet John Milton's tirade against censorship, delivered in his *Areopagitica* of 1644, is one of the most eloquent of all pleas for freedom of speech and expression. John Stuart Mill takes up the cause in his *On Liberty* (1859), where he warns of the dangers of a culture of prejudice and intellectual repression in which questioning and criticism of received opinion is discouraged and 'the most active and inquiring

intellects' are afraid to enter into 'free and daring speculation on the highest subjects'. In a similar spirit German philosopher Immanuel Kant had earlier protested that the intellect needs liberty in order to achieve full maturity: 'Nothing is required for enlightenment except freedom; and the freedom in question is the least harmful of all, namely, the freedom to use reason publicly in all matters.' The case was put most pithily by English writer George Orwell, who defined liberty simply as 'the right to tell people what they do not want to hear'.

of [people's] "real" selves'. Berlin's own deep distrust of positive freedom was fuelled by the enormities of the 20th century, especially the totalitarian horrors of Stalin's Soviet Union, but others have taken a more benign view of its potential for personal transformation and self-realization.

The defence of liberty The realization and defence of liberty have rarely gone smoothly. The United States, self-proclaimed torch-bearer of liberty, was sullied by legalized slavery for nearly a century after it won its independence, and the practice continued informally well into the 20th century. Meanwhile in France, another great bastion of liberty, the 'serene and blessed liberty' proclaimed by a Parisian newspaper at the Fall of the Bastille in 1789 had been transformed, in the space of four years, to Robespierre's Reign of Terror, in which all political opposition was crushed and an estimated 17,000 suspected counter-revolutionaries were guillotined.

In 1795 the radical writer and activist Thomas Paine wrote that 'he that would make his own liberty secure must guard even his enemy from oppression', but few since have taken much notice of his words. The French revolutionaries' excuse for sweeping aside civil liberties was the threat of counter-revolution at home and the menace of foreign armies abroad. Sadly, subsequent governments, despite their claims to love liberty, have tended to copy the French model, forgetting the warning of the fourth US president,

> **'Those who would give up essential Liberty, to purchase a little temporary Safety, deserve neither Liberty nor Safety.'**
> **Benjamin Franklin, 1755**

James Madison: 'The means of defence against foreign danger historically have become the instruments of tyranny at home.' In September 2001, in the wake of the 9/11 Islamist attacks, Madison's successor George W. Bush declared a war on terror –'civilization's fight . . . the fight of all who believe in progress and pluralism, tolerance and freedom'. The war was supposed to usher in 'an age of liberty', but over the following years its casualties included civil liberties and human rights, as repressive legislation was enacted and so-called enemy combatants were abused, tortured and 'extraordinarily rendered' in defiance of international law.

the condensed idea
The struggle for freedom

02 Justice

We can all recognize the stark injustice of children slaving in sweatshops or starving where food is readily available; of people dying of AIDS for want of exorbitantly priced medicines or suffering torture and imprisonment without trial. A sense of justice, or more particularly a consciousness of injustice, appears to come naturally, almost instinctively, to humans: it may not be easy to define what justice is, but we seem to know it – or the lack of it – when we see it.

Beneath this sensitivity to injustice there is often an awareness of incongruity, of a dislocation between what people suffer and what we feel they deserve or have a right to expect. This association between justice and the idea of balance or proportion is very ancient, going back at least to Plato and Aristotle. In the case of justice as administered by law, it is symbolized by the figure of Justice personified, holding up a pair of scales.

The Greeks on justice In Plato's highly distinctive theory, presented most fully in *The Republic*, he draws a parallel between justice in his ideal state and moral excellence in individuals. Just as justice in the state resides in the three classes of citizens (rulers, guardians, producers) achieving a proper balance, or social harmony, in the performance of their duties, so the moral well-being of an individual depends on a proper balance, or inner harmony, between the three parts of the soul (reason, emotions, appetites). The logic of Plato's notion of justice as harmony readily leads to the view that the good of the state is inseparable from, or perhaps identical to, the realization of justice within it. The elevation of justice to the position of cardinal or supreme political virtue has been more or less explicit in much subsequent political theory. Thus for the Roman Cicero, for instance, in his capacity as political theorist, justice is 'the crowning glory', 'the sovereign mistress and queen of all the virtues'.

timeline

*c.*375 BC	*c.*350 BC
Plato sets forth doctrine of justice as harmony	Aristotle argues that a key aspect of justice is treating like cases alike

Developing the notion of balance or proportion, Aristotle identifies the essence of justice as people 'getting their due'. Justice is done, in life as in law, when there is a fitting congruence between the fate that a person suffers and the fate they deserve to suffer; a proper balance between what a person gets and what they ought to get. Generally, this variety of justice – so-called 'distributive justice' – concerns the fair or just distribution, within a community or society, of the necessarily limited resources, benefits and burdens (including rights and obligations). Both the good governance of a state and its stability depend crucially on the presence (and the visible presence) of justice of this kind. This was clearly understood by the French Enlightenment philosopher Denis Diderot, who commented that 'Justice is the first virtue of those who command, and stops the complaints of those who obey.'

> **'Justice is the constant and perpetual will to render to others what is due to them.'**
> **Emperor Justinian, 6th century** AD

Without fear or favour As well as carrying a pair of scales, Justice personified is blindfolded: she is required not only to be balanced in her judgements but to be even-handed and blind to differences such as 'party, friendship [and] kindred' (in Joseph Addison's phrase). Impartiality demands that all differences that lie beyond people's control, such as the colour of their skin or the place of their birth, be disregarded. Justice is not blind to all differences, however: being even-handed does not mean treating everyone equally. We may all agree, in principle, that like should be treated alike, but no two people are the same, so what is due to them is different. The demand of justice is that everyone who is similarly placed in morally relevant respects should be treated equally; in other words, equal treatment is required *unless* there are good reasons for departing from it.

The difficulties, of course, arise when we move beyond this measure of consensus. First, we may wonder what equality consists of. There is a huge gulf between equality of opportunity and equality of outcome. Even if life's opportunities were equally accessible to all, differing talent and luck would still ensure that people ended up occupying a very wide range of positions in society. Then there is the question of what count as morally relevant reasons for departing from an equal

1971
John Rawls sets out his theory of justice as fairness

2009
Amartya Sen argues for a pluralistic understanding of justice

The fable of the flute

Three children are squabbling over who should get to keep a flute. Anne claims the instrument on the grounds that she is the only one of the three who knows how to play it. The second child, Bob, says that he should have it, because he is so poor that he has no other toys to play with. Finally, Carla claims that the flute should be hers, because it was she who made it. So who should have the flute? On the face of it, each of the three children has a plausible claim, so arbitrating fairly between them will require careful negotiation and close scrutiny of all the relevant circumstances. In the end, the decision will depend on the relative weight given to the needs of the three children and to such matters as artistic expression and the relief of poverty.

The tale of the flute is told by the Nobel prize-winning Indian economist and philosopher Amartya Sen in his acclaimed book *The Idea of Justice* (2009). The crucial point about the fable, for Sen, is that there is no answer that is absolutely and objectively 'right'; a decision that is fair and acceptable to all cannot be reached at the level of principle alone, in the absence of public debate and reasoning. While justice in the abstract is hard to define and harder to apply, injustices in the real world are palpable, urgent and often curable; these can be removed, and justice in the world thereby incrementally enhanced, if we engage in public debate and make 'comparisons of actual lives'. In Sen's view, justice is not an abstract or monolithic set of principles; rather, there is a host of competing principles underpinning a plurality of competing versions of justice. 'What moves us is not the realization that the world falls short of being completely just, which few of us expect, but that there are clearly remediable injustices around us which we want to eliminate.'

> **'Justice is the first condition of humanity.'**
> **Wole Soyinka,**
> **Nigerian writer, 1972**

distribution of the good and bad things in society. Is it just and fair that my superior skills, or greater intelligence, or appetite for hard work bring me a larger share of life's rewards? Or is it the business of a just society to even out the inequalities that would otherwise arise from our differing natural endowments?

John Rawls and justice as fairness The most significant contribution to the debate over justice in the second half of the 20th century was made by the US political philosopher John Rawls. In *A Theory of Justice* (1971) Rawls agrees

> **❝We don't begin by asking what a perfectly just society would look like, but asking what remediable injustices could be seen on the removal of which there would be a reasoned agreement.❞**
>
> **Amartya Sen,** *Guardian,* **July 2009**

that any conception of social justice must comprise the notion of impartiality – that if the principles on which a social system is based are biased towards a particular group (a social class, perhaps, or a political party), that system is automatically rendered unjust.

The most influential aspect of Rawls's account is his answer to the question of what counts as a morally sufficient reason for departing from equal treatment. He argues that people placed behind an imaginary 'veil of ignorance', which conceals all personal interests and allegiances, will endorse what he calls the 'difference principle' in order to safeguard their own future (unknown) interests. According to this principle, inequalities in the distribution of scarce goods or resources (money, power, healthcare etc.) are justified only if they result in society's worst-off members being better off than they would otherwise have been. Tax cuts for the wealthy, for instance, would be justified, and just, provided that they resulted in an improvement in the fortunes of the least well-off. Clearly, Rawls's difference principle can be used to justify very large disparities between the least and most advantaged members of society. His conception of social justice remains the focus of intensive debate and criticism, both positive and negative.

the condensed idea
The crowning glory of the virtues

03 Equality

Whatever their inner convictions, few politicians today would stand up and argue the case for inequality. Alongside its revolutionary companions, liberty and fraternity, equality is now all but sacrosanct, an assumed component of a just society. Writing to George Washington in 1784, Thomas Jefferson remarked that the constitutional basis of the United States was 'the natural equality of man'. Equality's position as a cornerstone in political and social thinking has remained undiminished ever since.

Equality as an Enlightenment ideal has its origins in the political theorizing of John Locke and others in the second half of the 17th century. A hundred years later, in 1776, the idea that there are certain natural and inalienable rights, including 'Life, liberty and the pursuit of happiness', that belong to *all* men and to all men *equally* was enshrined in the US Declaration of Independence. Thirteen years later just such an ideal became the inspiration for the Declaration of the Rights of Man and of the Citizen issued by the French revolutionaries; and with it came their rallying cry: 'Liberty, Equality, Fraternity'.

The generally unimpeachable position of equality today may blind us to the extent to which its appeal is modern and localized and its realization imperfect. The idealized equality promoted by Enlightenment thinkers was in many respects a secularly inspired reaction to the so-called 'equality before God' – and the implicit and vast inequality between men (and women) – that had dominated human affairs over the preceding millennia. Even today, in non-Western countries where governance is theocratic, military or otherwise non-democratic, inequalities based on birth, caste and gender (among many other things) are the norm, and equality, as understood in the Western liberal tradition, is not even an aspiration.

timeline

1690

Locke's *Two Treatises of Government* published

1776

Inalienable human rights proclaimed in US Declaration of Independence

Equality of opportunity The perplexing issue at the centre of discussions of equality is well described by the Austrian-born political theorist and economist Friedrich Hayek in his influential *The Constitution of Liberty* (1960):

> From the fact that people are very different it follows that, if we treat them equally, the result must be inequality in their actual position, and that the only way to place them in an equal position would be to treat them differently. Equality before the law and material equality are therefore not only different but are in conflict with each other.

No two people are the same. To claim that everyone is equal, Hayek argues, is simply untrue – whimsical and ideologically driven wishful thinking. There is a huge spectrum of talents with which people are endowed, so if they enjoy 'equality before the law' – the same basic legal and political rights, as the classical liberal minimally requires – they will inevitably end up in very different social and economic situations. The kind of equality that a liberal like Hayek wants is equality of *opportunity*, which demands that there are no artificial obstacles, such as birth, race or gender, standing in the way of people making the most of their natural gifts and achieving their full potential. It is not, however, the business of a just state to intervene thereafter, interfering with people's rights and liberties in order to even out the inequalities of condition (wealth, status, power etc.) that are bound to arise. Equality, thus conceived, demands a level playing field but does not pretend that all players are equally gifted or try to ensure that they are equally rewarded in the exercise of their talents.

Towards equality of condition

Equality, then, as conceived by the liberal, is essentially meritocratic. The state's

Just deserts

In his essay 'The Idea of Equality' (1927), English writer Aldous Huxley expressed the inevitable tension between treating people equally and treating them as they deserve. 'The brotherhood of men does not imply their equality,' he noted. 'Families have their fools and their men of genius, their black sheep and their saints . . . A man should treat his brothers lovingly and with justice, according to the deserts of each. But the deserts of every brother are not the same.' Humans are not clones – no two can ever be identical; and fairness, which is often linked with equality, seems to demand that they should be treated equitably and according to their merit – but not equally, unless their merit is equal.

1960
Friedrich Hayek's *The Constitution of Liberty* published

1989
Communist regimes collapse in Soviet Union and Eastern Europe

2007
Free-market capitalism battered by global 'Credit Crunch'

responsibility is limited to providing a framework of equal rights and liberties that enable individuals to combine their native wit and hard work to rise to positions of eminence – that is, to positions of inequality. Such a conception sanctions the formation of elites, but ones based not on birth or wealth, as in the past, but on accomplishment: in effect, 'aristocracies' of merit.

Problems arise immediately, however. It is naive to suppose that removing humanly imposed barriers such as race and gender would be sufficient to allow supposedly natural talents to express themselves. Few modern states would consider that justice could be served by such minimal intervention. It is clear that a myriad factors limit the *effective* liberty that people have to fulfil themselves: deprived upbringing, poor education, lack of welfare provision – all contribute to producing societies that are riven by deep structural inequalities. All except the most dyed-in-the-wool libertarians would accept that the state needs to take *some* positive steps to weed out inequalities and to level the playing field. There is little agreement over the degree of intervention, however, and huge clouds of political dust have

Chimera or poison?

Even where equality has been recognized in principle as an ideal, its unattainability in reality has remained a commonplace in literature and political thought. In Anthony Trollope's *The Prime Minister* (1876), the duke of Omnium (the prime minister of the title) bemoans the fact that 'a good word signifying a grand idea has been driven out of the vocabulary of good men. Equality would be a heaven, if we could attain it.' In *Animal Farm* (1945) English writer George Orwell's tyrannical pigs cynically proclaim that 'All animals are equal but some animals are more equal than others', while in the same author's *Nineteen Eighty-Four* (1949), the mysterious Trotsky-like figure Emmanuel Goldstein observes that 'no advance in wealth, no softening of manners, nor reform or revolution has ever brought human equality a millimetre nearer'. Among philosophers there has never been any consensus over the possibility or desirability of equality. Plato reflects a common view among his Greek contemporaries when he sneeringly derides democracy as a 'charming form of government' that dispenses 'equality to equals and unequals alike'. And to German philosopher Friedrich Nietzsche, lauding his heroic *Übermensch* ('superman') driven by the will to power to rise above the shackled masses, the very idea of equality is loathsome: 'The doctrine of equality! . . . there exists no more poisonous poison: for it *seems* to be preached by justice itself, while it is the *termination* of justice.'

been thrown up in heated debate over such measures as public systems of education and welfare and the alleviation of poverty through redistributive taxation.

At the heart of such debate is the contention that the social and economic differences between individuals are due (or substantially due) to factors such as family, culture and background that lie beyond their control; and if these cannot be controlled and hence are not a proper subject for blame or merit, the liberal's merit-based justification for inequalities of condition is significantly undermined. The idea of the just society is shifted leftwards on the political spectrum, towards a model in which resources are allocated according to need rather than merit, and where it is the task of the state to eradicate structural inequalities and to bring about a greater equality of social and economic conditions.

> **It is better that some should be unhappy, than that none should be happy, which would be the case in a general state of equality.**
> Samuel Johnson, in Boswell's *Life of Samuel Johnson*, 1791

This concern with creating equality of condition, associated particularly with socialist political theory, came to be realized in the 20th century with the spread of communism. Inspired by Marx's maxim 'to each according to his need', communist regimes set out to create a state of uniformity among their citizens through programmes of social engineering and centralized economic management. Such attempts generally met with dismal failure, and the collapse of communism from 1989 onwards seemed to vindicate the liberal view of equality and to bear out US economist Milton Friedman's famous remark (1980): 'A society that puts equality – in the sense of equality of outcome – ahead of freedom will end up with neither equality nor freedom.' But any triumphalism was short-lived, dampened by the traumas to global capitalism in the decades that followed. In his novel *Le Lys rouge* (1894) the French writer Anatole France sarcastically observed how 'the majestic equality of the law . . . forbids the rich as well as the poor to sleep under bridges, to beg in the streets, and to steal bread'. In the economically chastened world of the early 21st century such a remark had a renewed piquancy: it was clear that the debate over equality was far from over.

the condensed idea
All animals are equal . . .

04 Human rights

Human rights are deeply rooted in our political consciousness. Today it is generally taken for granted that there are good things that people are entitled to have and bad things that they can expect or aspire to avoid. A wide, and ever-widening, range of such entitlements and immunities are supposed to belong to everyone, everywhere and at all times, purely as a consequence of our humanity – of the dignity and respect that are due to us as human beings.

Under the terms of the Charter by which the United Nations was established in 1945, every member state committed itself to 'promoting and encouraging respect for human rights and for fundamental freedoms for all without distinction as to race, sex, language, or religion'. Despite a depressingly patchy record of compliance on the ground, over the following decades the UN's lofty ambitions, backed up by a number of subsequent covenants and agreements, saw human rights enshrined not only in international law but also within the legal and constitutional arrangements of many of the world's countries. Meeting standards on human rights set by the international community has become a yardstick by which the legitimacy of governments is measured, while the demand for such rights has become a rallying cry for opposition groups worldwide. Meanwhile a myriad non-government organizations, from Amnesty International to Human Rights Watch, have sprung up to lobby for recognition of rights and to campaign against abuses everywhere that cause exploitation, oppression, persecution and loss of human dignity.

Beyond life and liberty The modern origins of human rights (though not the name) are to be found most prominently in the works of the English political theorist John Locke. Writing in the immediate aftermath of England's Glorious

timeline

1690	1776	1789
John Locke's *Two Treatises of Government* published	US Declaration of Independence	French revolutionaries' Declaration of the Rights of Man and of the Citizen

Revolution of 1688, in which the absolutist king James II was overthrown, Locke argues that there are certain rights that self-evidently belong to individuals by virtue of their humanity; these are natural, in the sense that they are the products of man's essential nature, and hence they are inalienable (they cannot be renounced) and universal (they belong to all people equally). The three principal rights named by Locke – life, liberty and property – were famously echoed in Thomas Jefferson's drafting of the US Declaration of Independence (1776), where he asserts as self-evident truths that 'all men are created equal; that they are endowed by their Creator with certain unalienable rights; that among these are life, liberty and the pursuit of happiness'. The rights claimed by Locke are mainly negative: he asserts, in defiance of political absolutism, the individual citizen's right to be free from the arbitrary authority and interference of the state. The legitimacy of government, in this view, depends on its capacity to uphold these rights, and it is the citizen's prerogative to overthrow the government if it fails to do so.

Nonsense upon stilts

Philosophically, the most heated debate over rights has focused on their source or basis. Locke's belief that they were the products of natural law – that they flowed from man's essential nature – was elaborated by the French Enlightenment *philosophes*, notably Montesquieu, Voltaire and Rousseau, whose views found final expression in the revolutionary Declaration of the Rights of Man and of the Citizen of 1789, which proclaimed that 'men are born and remain free and equal in rights' and that 'the aim of every political association is the preservation of the natural and imprescriptible [inalienable] rights of man'. The philosophical dismantling of the concept of natural law was begun in the middle of the 18th century by the Scottish philosopher David Hume, who objected to the idea that anything prescriptive and based on value (such as rights) could be inferred from something descriptive and based on fact (such as the nature of the world and of the human beings in it). Perhaps the most scathing dismissal came from the Utilitarian philosopher Jeremy Bentham. 'Natural rights is simple nonsense,' he wrote in 1795, 'natural and imprescriptible rights, rhetorical nonsense – nonsense upon stilts.' His view is that a right is 'the child of law', i.e. a matter of human convention, and that rights are justified, like anything else, if they tend to promote utility, or human happiness.

1945
Charter of the United Nations signed

1948
Universal Declaration of Human Rights

The continuing struggle

While human rights are held to be universal, their realization on the ground has been anything but. Genocide, ethnic cleansing, war crimes, torture, people trafficking, imprisonment without trial and a thousand other abuses have been widely perpetrated in all parts of the world. Even the supposed bastions of human rights, in Europe and America, have been guilty of cynically casting them aside under the pretext of emergency or threat to national security. Structural problems in the international order, and the vast inequalities in prosperity between states that result from them, have given rise to a whole new generation of rights, relating to such matters as development, the environment and use of natural resources. Meanwhile the forces of globalization have spawned an array of gigantic multinational corporations and financial institutions. Often with budgets far in excess of that of a small nation, the loyalties of these behemoths are usually to investors and shareholders, not to the local population or to any other outside interest. The new threat posed by such giants was highlighted in 2003 by Jean Ziegler, special investigator of the UN Commission on Human Rights:

> The growing power of transnational corporations and their extension of power through privatization, deregulation and the rolling back of the State . . . mean that it is now time to develop binding legal norms that hold corporations to human rights standards and circumscribe potential abuses of their position of power.

Since the great revolutions of the 18th century the development of civil society in the West has essentially been a story of the expansion of rights beyond the political sphere envisaged by Locke and Jefferson into social and economic areas. While initially the upholding of rights required restraint and non-interference on the part of the state, the focus moved increasingly to positive rights that typically called upon those in authority to take some form of affirmative action. From the middle of the 19th century, industrialization fuelled by virtually unbridled capitalism inflicted shocking poverty and hardship on working people, and it was in part to counter such exploitation that various welfare rights began to be implemented, albeit far from uniformly or universally. Since that time a new generation of positive welfare rights has come to encompass rights to a whole range of social and work-related benefits, including trade union representation, social security, minimum wage, paid leave, education, healthcare and much else besides.

More heat than light From the outset, this expansion of rights met with fierce resistance. Differing views on the nature and scope of rights reflected differing conceptions of the role of the state in shaping society. Those with socialist leanings would argue for state intervention to create greater equality and to protect the welfare of citizens. Free-market liberals, on the other side, would counter that welfare rights were not fundamental (they did not represent basic human needs) and that they threatened to undermine capitalism as the most efficient means of allocating resources. This ideological rift became all the more apparent in the decades following the formal birth of human rights, named as such, in the aftermath of the Second World War.

The document that has done more than any other to put human rights permanently at the forefront of political debate is the Universal Declaration of Human Rights, adopted by the General Assembly of the United Nations in Paris on 10 December 1948. Directly motivated by the atrocities of the recently ended war, this formal expression of the primacy of human rights reasserted the commitments contained in the UN's founding Charter, signed three years earlier, and elaborated the theoretical basis for those rights: 'All human beings are born free and equal in dignity and rights. They are endowed with reason and conscience and should act towards one another in a spirit of brotherhood.'

> **Recognition of the inherent dignity and of the equal and inalienable rights of all members of the human family is the foundation of freedom, justice and peace in the world.**
> Universal Declaration of Human Rights, 1948

Alongside civil and political rights, such as freedom of assembly, thought and expression, the Declaration also set forth a range of social and economic rights, including rights to work, education and participation in the cultural life of the community. From the beginning there was disagreement between the Western democracies and the Soviet bloc over the priority that should be accorded to these different kinds of rights, and the issue remained highly charged throughout the Cold War years. A more recent but equally persistent complaint has been that the idea of human rights as promulgated by international bodies such as the UN is culturally biased in the Western liberal tradition and fails to take sufficient account of regional differences. With conflict at the most basic level of definition and widespread abuse on the ground, it is certain that human rights are destined to remain at the epicentre of political activism.

the condensed idea
Life, liberty and . . . ?

05 The social contract

The state presumes to control our lives in all sorts of ways. Those wielding power within the state take our money in the form of taxes; they make wars in our name; they fine or imprison us if we break rules that they impose; they monitor our movements and tell us what to eat and where to smoke . . . and a thousand things besides.

How is this exercise of power legitimate? What justification is there for the existence and organization of the state and for the distribution of resources, rights and duties within it? Faced with these most basic questions, a long line of political theorists, from Thomas Hobbes in the 17th century to John Rawls in the 20th, have suggested that the best way to explain the legitimacy of the state is to suppose that its institutions and structures were established on the basis of a tacit agreement or 'social contract' between its members.

Why do people make contracts? Why do they enter into agreements that leave them open to penalties if they do things that they might otherwise choose not to do? Provided that a contract is fair, people feel that it is worth taking on some obligation or giving up some freedom in order to receive something more valuable in return. In general, while they might not otherwise choose to be bound by the terms of a contract, they judge that their interests are better served if they are restricted in this way than if they are not. In the case of the social contract proposed by Hobbes and others, our acceptance of the state and its right to limit what we do is one side of a bargain; the payback is not experiencing the chaos and anarchy that would occur in its absence.

timeline

1651

Thomas Hobbes's *Leviathan* argues the case for absolute sovereignty

1690

John Locke's *Two Treatises of Government* published

Hobbes and Leviathan To evaluate the terms of a contract properly, it is necessary to consider what life would be like if the contract were not in place: only then is it possible to judge whether the contract represents a bargain worth having. In a similar vein, theorists attracted to the idea that the organization of society can be understood in terms of an implicit social contract have tended to start by considering how things would stand in the absence of the kind of rules and regulations by which the rights and liberties of citizens are usually constrained.

> **Man is born free; and everywhere he is in chains. One thinks himself the master of others, and still remains a greater slave than they.**
>
> Jean-Jacques Rousseau, 1762

One of the first and greatest social-contract theorists, the English political philosopher Thomas Hobbes, began his great treatise *Leviathan* (1651) with an evocation of a hypothetical pre-social condition of mankind which he called the 'state of nature'. Hobbes's vision of the human condition unrestrained by social forces is unremittingly bleak and pessimistic. He assumes that, in the state of nature, humans will act in isolation, concerned only with their own pleasure, interest and preservation; their prime motivation 'a perpetual and restless desire of power after power, that ceaseth only in death'. Constantly at loggerheads and

The noble savage and the sleep of reason

While Thomas Hobbes sees the power of the state as a necessary means of curbing people's selfish and bestial nature, the French philosopher Jean-Jacques Rousseau, though clearly greatly influenced by Hobbes's ideas, shares none of his bleakness. In his best-known work, *The Social Contract* (1762), Rousseau considers that human vice and other ills are the *product* of society – that the 'noble savage', naturally innocent and content in the 'sleep of reason' and living in sympathy with his fellow men, is corrupted by education and other social influences. This vision of lost innocence and non-intellectualized sentiment proved inspirational for the Romantic movement that swept Europe towards the end of the 18th century.

1762
The 'noble savage' appears in Jean-Jacques Rousseau's *The Social Contract*

1971
John Rawls develops idea of justice as fairness in *A Theory of Justice*

in competition with one another, there is no possibility of trust or cooperation; and with no basis of trust, there is no prospect of creating prosperity or enjoying the fruits of civilization: 'no arts; no letters; no society; and which is worst of all, continual fear, and danger of violent death'. And hence, Hobbes famously concludes, in the state of nature 'the life of man [is] solitary, poor, nasty, brutish, and short'.

It is clearly in everyone's interest to work together in order to escape the hellish scene painted by Hobbes, so why do people in the state of nature not agree to cooperate? The answer is simple: because there is always a cost to pay in complying with an agreement and always something to be gained from not doing so. If self-interest is the only moral compass, as Hobbes suggests, you can be sure that someone else will always be ready to seek an advantage by non-compliance, so the best you can do is to break the contract first, before they do. And of course everyone else reasons in the same way, so there is no trust and any prospective agreement quickly unravels: long-term interest is always sure to give way to short-term gain, apparently leaving no way out of the cycle of distrust and violence.

> **By art is created that great Leviathan, called a commonwealth or state, which is but an artificial man . . . and in which, the sovereignty is an artificial soul.**
>
> **Thomas Hobbes, 1651**

How, then, can individuals mired in such wretched discord ever reach an accommodation with one another and so extricate themselves? The crux of the problem, for Hobbes, is that 'covenants, without the sword, are but words'. What is needed is an external power or sanction that *forces* all people to abide by the terms of a contract that benefits them all. People must willingly restrict their liberties for the sake of cooperation and peace, on condition that everyone else does likewise; they must 'confer all their power and strength upon one man, or upon one assembly of men, that may reduce all their wills, by plurality of voices, unto one will'. The solution, then, is joint submission to the absolute authority of the state (what Hobbes calls 'Leviathan') – 'a common power to keep them all in awe'.

Locke on government by consent Writing nearly half a century after Hobbes, another great English philosopher who used the idea of the social contract to explore the basis of government was John Locke. Hobbes refers to Leviathan – the power of the state – as 'that *mortal* God', indicating that sovereignty is ceded to the state by human convention, rather than by divine dispensation, which would have been the orthodox view at the time. In this regard Locke agrees with Hobbes, but his conception of the state of nature – the condition of mankind before the existence of society, without government or law – is considerably less bleak than Hobbes's. Accordingly, the contract that Locke envisages between people and sovereign is markedly less draconian. Whereas Hobbes requires the state's power to be unlimited and absolute in order to stave off the horrors of the 'war of all against all', Locke makes the case for what is essentially constitutional monarchy. In his view, the people consent to make over their power to the sovereign on condition that he uses it for the common good, and they reserve the right to withdraw that consent if the sovereign fails in his contractual duties. The forceful overthrow of the government by the people, by rebellion if necessary, remains a legitimate (albeit final) remedy.

Behind the veil of ignorance The most prominent and influential social-contract theorist of the second half of the 20th century was the US political philosopher John Rawls. In A *Theory of Justice* (1971) Rawls introduces a thought experiment which is clearly in the tradition of Hobbes's state of nature. To stress the centrality of the notion of impartiality in social justice, Rawls introduces what he calls the 'original position', a hypothetical situation in which individuals are placed behind a 'veil of ignorance', which obscures all personal interests and allegiances: 'No one knows his place in society, his class position or social status, nor does anyone know his fortune in the distribution of natural assets and abilities, his intelligence, strength, and the like.' Placed behind the veil and ignorant of what society has in store for us, we are obliged to play safe and to ensure that no one group is given an advantage at the expense of another. As in Hobbes, it is purely rational self-interest that drives decision-making behind the veil. It is the fact that, when placed in this position, we contract into certain social and economic structures and arrangements that makes them just and hence socially stable and robust.

the condensed idea
The price of social order

06 Democracy

Over the last century democracy has become widely regarded as the ideal system of government: a pre-eminently legitimate form that provides a political and social structure within which people can live happy, fulfilled and responsible lives. One of the reasons that US president Woodrow Wilson felt in 1917 that it was important to make the world safe for democracy was that it alone had the potential to release 'the energies of every human being'.

Since that time the spread of democracy across the globe has been spectacular. By the year 2000 it was estimated that roughly half the world's population enjoyed political institutions that provided historically high levels of democratic government. Indeed, democracy is now held in such high repute that it is easy to forget just how poorly regarded it was until relatively recently. For most of the last two and a half millennia almost every political theorist was energetically opposed to democracy, in principle and in practice.

The Greeks on democracy A generally dim view of democratic government dates back to its infancy in Athens, the Greek city-state that is generally credited with being the 'cradle of democracy'. (The word itself comes from the Greek meaning 'rule by the people'.) The system of government developed by the Athenians over the course of the fifth century BC was arguably the purest form of direct democracy that has ever been realized. The first step was taken in 507 BC by the popular leader Cleisthenes. The centrepiece of his reforms was the *ecclesia*, or assembly, which was open to all eligible citizens (Athenian males over the age of 18). Meeting regularly to debate the important business of state, this body would reach decisions by a show of hands on the basis of a majority of those present.

timeline

507 BC	1651	1690
Cleisthenes introduces democratic reforms in Athens	Hobbes discusses balance between state power and individual liberty	Locke identifies popular consent as the basis of state authority

In Thucydides' history of the Peloponnesian war, the virtues of democratic Athens are majestically proclaimed in a funeral oration delivered in 430 BC by the Athenian leader Pericles. He picks out many of the qualities that later advocates would stress, including a constitution that 'favours the many, not the few' and which demands liberty, equality before the law and political preferment gained on the basis of merit, not wealth or class. Pericles' enthusiasm was not shared by many of his contemporaries, however, nor by Greece's two most influential philosophers, Plato and Aristotle. Writing in the following century, in the wake of Athens's calamitous defeat in 404 by totalitarian Sparta, they scornfully dismiss democracy as inherently unruly, corrupt and unstable. In Aristotle's influential classification of political constitutions, democracy is the perverted form of 'polity', an ideal constitution in which the many govern in pursuit of the common good. In a democracy, by contrast, those in control – the lower strata of society – rule in their own interest and can therefore be expected to appropriate the wealth and property of the better-off citizens.

Democracy under fire The fear that democracy is inherently anarchic has since troubled proponents and opponents alike. A friend of democracy himself, Thomas Jefferson revealed his misgivings that it is 'nothing more than mob rule'. In a notably backhanded compliment in *The Social Contract* (1762), Jean-Jacques Rousseau states that a people of gods, if it existed, would govern itself democratically, but 'so perfect a government is not for men'. The reality – in a world where people are people, not gods – is that 'there is no government so subject to civil wars and intestine agitations'.

Unrepresentative democracy

However they might choose to describe themselves, few pre-20th century regimes would today qualify as full democracies simply because their franchises were so limited. In Athens, where women, resident foreigners and slaves were excluded from the enfranchised *demos* (people), some scholarly estimates suggest that as few as one in ten of the total population was eligible to vote. The situation was even more restricted in 19th-century Britain, where stern property requirements meant that even after the Great Reform Act of 1832, only about seven percent of the adult population were able to vote; universal suffrage was not achieved until 1928, when the vote was finally extended to all adult women.

1787	1789–99	1989–91
The Constitution defines the mechanisms of US democratic government	Radical democracy seen for the first time during French Revolution	Communist regimes collapse in Soviet Union and Eastern Europe

Democracy's tendency towards anarchy was generally premised on the supposed incompetence of the people to participate responsibly in the process of government. Victorian philosopher John Stuart Mill, though naturally sympathetic to democratic principles, was nevertheless concerned at the 'collective mediocrity' of the masses, who no longer 'take their opinions from dignitaries of Church or State, from ostensible leaders, or from books'. Winston Churchill reputedly joked that the best argument against democracy was a five-minute conversation with the average voter, while in the 1920s the US satirist H.L. Mencken dismissed it as 'a pathetic belief in the collective wisdom of individual ignorance'. Democracy's inadequacies even made it onto celluloid, in the 1949 film version of Graham Greene's *The Third Man*. At the climax of the drama the amoral Harry Lime, played by Orson Welles, sneeringly observes that Switzerland had 500 years of democracy and peace and only managed to produce the cuckoo clock.

> **❝Democracy substitutes election by the incompetent many for appointment by the corrupt few.❞**
> **George Bernard Shaw,**
> *Man and Superman*, **1903**

Probably the most persistent anxiety among early-modern theorists – one that again picks up on the concerns of the Greek philosophers – was the so-called 'tyranny of the majority'. Mill and others feared that the majority would abuse its position of power to trample underfoot the rights of minorities, vindicated (as they believed) by a system that seemed to legitimize the realization of their desires and aspirations.

Emergence of representative democracy The anxieties expressed by America's Founding Fathers were one part of a serious and long-running debate over democracy and popular sovereignty that arose in the welter of ideas generated by Enlightenment thinkers. A central question that set the direction for much subsequent theorizing – and a counterpoint to concerns over the prospect of tyranny exercised *by* the majority – was posed in 1651 by Thomas Hobbes, writing in the immediate aftermath of the English Civil War. How, he asked, should the sovereign power of the state, justified by the need to protect (among other things) the rights of individuals, be constrained in order to prevent its misuse to curtail those same rights? John Locke, writing four decades later, argued that the bestowal of such authority on the government by the governed, and the concomitant limitation of their own liberties, must only be done with the consent of the governed. Debate on the proper relationship between people and state thus resolved itself into an argument on the appropriate balance between might and right; between the claims of the state on one side and the rights of the individual on the other.

Hastened by two bloodily won revolutions, first in America and then in France, it would take many decades to bring forth the fruit of this debate: a version of democracy that was both constitutionally based and representative. Much refined and elaborated over the years, this theory – the 'grand discovery of modern times', according to James Mill, father of John Stuart Mill – provided a definitive answer to Hobbes's fundamental question over the limitation of power. By stipulating a range of political mechanisms, including regular elections and competition between parties and candidates, the representative system ensured that governors remained accountable to the governed and hence that the latter retained ultimate authority and control over the political process.

If all else fails . . .

Today the near-universal conviction that democracy is preferable to any of its rivals is such that in many political contexts 'democratic' has become virtually synonymous with 'legitimate'. The word has such a totemic quality that many repressive and authoritarian regimes have nevertheless chosen to style themselves as such. So, for instance, the former East Germany – a hard-line one-party state – was officially known as the 'German Democratic Republic'. In truth, the recent success of democracy is explained in part by the dismal failure of the alternatives. Speaking before the House of Commons in 1947, Winston Churchill famously observed that 'Democracy is the worst form of government except all those other forms that have been tried from time to time.' Within half a century democracy's chief rival as the basis of political organization, communism, had been swept aside in Russia and Eastern Europe.

the condensed idea
Rule – or tyranny – of the many

07 Monarchy

In the 21st century there is no widespread sympathy for a system of government in which supreme political authority is vested in a single person, usually for no better reason than that their father had earlier enjoyed a similar privilege. Those brought up to value competence and good character more highly than blue blood and good breeding are generally less than enthusiastic about kings, queens, emperors and sultans who inherit the right to rule, rather than earning it.

Less than a quarter of the world's sovereign states – 44 out of roughly 200 – currently have monarchical governments. Of these, the United Kingdom and 15 others are Commonwealth realms, which share a single monarch, Queen Elizabeth II. In all but a few cases – notably Saudi Arabia, Oman, Qatar, Brunei and Vatican City – the political authority of the monarch is either nominal or severely limited by law; real power lies elsewhere, usually with some form of parliament, while the monarch's role is primarily symbolic and ceremonial. This situation is relatively recent, however. For most of human history, monarchy was the dominant form of government, and monarchs exercised power that was often vast and virtually unrestricted.

Origins of monarchy Like any other political system, a monarchy evolves over time, consolidating its position as it develops its peculiar governmental structures and institutions. At the same time, it weaves its own fabric of foundational and dynastic myths, thereby creating a logic that claims to explain its legitimacy and helps to sustain it from generation to generation. However, at the inception of a monarchy, there must be some more immediate social need or emergency that provides a justification both of a monarchical system and of a particular incumbent.

timeline

1651	1688	1690
Hobbes's *Leviathan* argues for the absolute power of the sovereign	Glorious Revolution brings constitutional monarchy to England	Locke's *Two Treatises of Government* argue for government by popular consent

In ancient times conflict and war were all but ubiquitous, as a means of acquiring and defending fertile land and in order to win and secure trade routes, among other things. As the survival and prosperity of a community usually depended on martial success, skill as a warrior and as a leader of men in battle was the commonest cause of an individual being elevated to a position of authority that might develop into kingship. In arid climes, survival might also depend on efficient and orderly allocation of agricultural land and fresh water, so the ability to construct and manage essential infrastructure such as irrigation systems is thought to have been a factor in the establishment of monarchies in ancient China, Egypt and Babylonia. Given the overriding importance of particular skills and personal charisma, it is likely that most early monarchies were initially based on some kind of election, presumably from an established aristocratic elite.

From martial might to absolute power Martial prowess continued to be the prime qualification for monarchy, from Alexander the Great in the Hellenistic world and Augustus, the first Roman emperor, through to Charlemagne and the warrior kings of medieval Europe. Throughout the Middle Ages, kings were usually expected to lead their armies into battle in person, and success on the battlefield could help to strengthen the position of strong leaders, such as Edward I and Henry V of England, against the intrigues of ambitious nobles and the rival pretensions of the church. Such stability as there was depended on a code of honour that existed between monarch and aristocrats, binding them together in a delicate system of privileges and obligations.

> **Above all things our royalty is to be reverenced ... Its mystery is its life. We must not let in daylight upon magic.**
> Walter Bagehot, *The English Constitution*, 1867

From the Renaissance into the early modern period, the trend was towards consolidation, as European monarchs sponsored voyages of discovery and encouraged new forms of trade, set up bureaucracies to assist in government and levying taxes, and raised ever larger armies to extend their territories and to win glory and prestige. Great 16th-century monarchs such as the Holy Roman Emperor Charles V (Charles I of Spain) and Henry VIII and Elizabeth I of England were energetic in unifying their realms and strengthening their control over them. Centralization of power reached its peak in the reign of the French

1789
French Revolution ends absolute monarchy of Bourbons in France

1917–22
Imperial monarchies swept away in wake of First World War

king Louis XIV, the 'Sun King', who came to epitomize the notion of absolute monarchy. Enjoying unlimited autonomy over his kingdom, independent of the influence of both nobility and church, in 1655 he reputedly signalled the identification of king and state in his famous declaration '*L'état, c'est moi*' ('I am the state').

Casualties of war and revolution The so-called Age of Absolutism came to an abrupt end in 1789, when the French Revolution terminated the absolutist pretensions of the Bourbon dynasty in France, but the seeds of its dissolution had been planted long before. Shortly after the execution in 1649 of Charles I of England, who had sought to justify his autocratic behaviour by appeal to divine favour, a non-theistic case for absolutism was made by Thomas Hobbes. He argued that undivided sovereignty vested in the person of an all-powerful monarch was the only defence against the anarchy of the times. This view, however, was later countered by John Locke, who argued that sovereign power is granted by popular consent and may likewise be withdrawn if it is not exercised in the common interest. The English Bill of Rights (1689) prohibited the king from acting outside the law thus dealing a fatal blow to the claim that royal authority was divinely ordained and hence could not lawfully be challenged.

The supremest thing upon earth

Since earliest times monarchs have sought to base their legitimacy on sacred right. Some, including Egyptian pharaohs and Roman and Japanese emperors, were themselves venerated as gods, while others claimed to be appointed by God as his representatives on earth. The idea that a monarch derived the right to political power, absolute and unlimited, directly from God (not from the people and not through the church) was formulated in the Middle Ages as the divine right of kings; according to this doctrine, the monarch was answerable to God alone, and opposition to his rule (i.e. rebellion) was treason against God and liable to punishment by damnation. The Stuart king James I pushed the doctrine to its limit in a speech to Parliament in 1610, in which he claimed that 'The state of monarchy is the supremest thing upon earth; for kings are not only God's lieutenants upon earth, and sit upon God's throne, but even by God himself they are called gods.' The divine right was the theoretical counterpoint to the quarrel between James's son, Charles I, and the English parliament, which led to the Civil War and the eventual execution of Charles. Briefly revived by Charles II, the divine right was finally snuffed out in the Glorious Revolution of 1688.

> **The chief objection to one-person rule is the frequent descents of autocrats into megalomania, to which is added, when the post is hereditary, incompetent heirs.**
>
> Anthony Quinton, 1995

The voice of the people, when it was audible at all, did not inevitably call for democracy or the fall of kings – the emperorship of Napoleon, after all, was a nationalist-based monarchy that claimed legitimacy through popular assent. Nevertheless, change was in the air, and a series of revolutions in the 19th and early 20th centuries, precipitated by popular unrest and defeat in war, led to the toppling of monarchical regimes in the Russian, Austro-Hungarian, German and Ottoman empires.

Monarchy today For the most part, those monarchies that have survived into the 21st century have done so by following what Trotsky once called the 'English formula': they have adapted themselves to a system of government in which the monarch 'reigns but does not rule'. By 1867 the functions of the British monarchy had been eroded to the point where the English economist Walter Bagehot could sum up the three entitlements of a constitutionally constrained sovereign as 'the right to be consulted, the right to encourage, the right to warn'.

By the end of her reign in 1901, Victoria had reinvented the role of the British monarchy and so established the pattern for viable 20th-century royalty. Direct political power was replaced by significant symbolic influence, as the king or queen became an emblem of national unity: the focus of patriotism, the cement of social cohesion, a unifying figure representing a country's ambitions and aspirations. Henceforth, the lack of real political power would generally be accounted one of monarchy's chief recommendations. The advantage of a head of state who is 'above politics' – in a way that an elected president never can be – was noted by British prime minister Margaret Thatcher, speaking in 1985: 'Those who imagine that a politician would make a better figurehead than a hereditary monarch might perhaps make the acquaintance of more politicians.'

the condensed idea
Ruling or reigning?

08 Tyranny

In the course of more than 2,500 years of use the word 'tyranny' has taken on so much unsavoury baggage that it is now firmly established in the lexicon of political rhetoric. As a term of abuse in political debate or attack, it readily conjures up a picture of oppressive and arbitrary government.

As is often the case with such rhetoric, fine distinctions in meaning are blurred, usually deliberately. Indeed, in this polemical use, tyranny is hardly distinguishable from its close cousins, despotism and dictatorship. When in 1940, at the lowest point of the Second World War, Winston Churchill denounced Hitler's Germany as 'a monstrous tyranny, never surpassed in the dark, lamentable catalogue of human crime', he doubtless wished to call to mind a host of unpleasant characteristics, including the harshness of the Nazi leader's rule and the illegality of the manner in which he had acquired it.

The Greeks and tyranny The later meaning of 'tyrant' – that of usurper, or one who illegally seizes power within a state – is close to its original meaning. In the Greek 'age of tyrants' – the seventh and sixth centuries BC – the word 'tyrannical' described, initially at least, the means by which political power was acquired: it was neutral with respect both to the character of the ruler and to the quality of his rule. Indeed, many of the early Greek tyrants were regarded with affection as champions of the people – of the many and the poor against the few and the rich, as it was commonly put – and several appear to have enjoyed popular support in displacing ruling aristocracies. The best known of the early tyrants, Pisistratus of Athens, was fondly remembered for his prosperous and law-abiding period of rule; a golden age in which the city flourished and became a cultural centre renowned throughout Greece.

timeline

7th century BC	7th–6th century BC	c.546–510 BC	mid–4th century BC
The word 'tyrant' first used by the Greek poet Archilochus	Age of tyrants in Greece	Tyranny of Pisistratus and his sons Hipparchus and Hippias	Definitive Greek account of tyranny given by Aristotle

A number of later tyrants, however, including Pisistratus' own sons, were not so enlightened. Over time, as they increasingly abused their power, the image of tyranny deteriorated, and the stain became indelible in the philosophies of Plato and Aristotle, who were in agreement that the tyrant was the very worst form of ruler. Tyranny appears in Aristotle's influential classification of the types of political constitution, which is based on two criteria: the number of people who rule (one, few or many), and in whose interest they rule (their own or the common interest). Within this system, tyranny appears as the corrupt or deviant version of monarchy, and a tyrant is a ruler who rules in his own interest.

Many of the points that Aristotle makes about tyranny are made by comparing and contrasting it with the concept of despotism, which the Greeks regarded as a characteristically Asiatic form of government. While despotism, like tyranny, is most strongly opposed to liberty (which the Greeks associated particularly with themselves), there are several important points of contrast. First, a despot, however all-encompassing his power, rules in accordance with existing law and is thus in some sense constitutionally established; a tyrant, by contrast, seizes control and rules arbitrarily, on the basis of his own will and whim. As a consequence, the subjects of a despotism can be said to cede power willingly, and therefore cannot be described as being coerced, or ruled by force; unlike those living beneath a tyrant, they tacitly consent to the system of government in which they live and thus do not act under the influence of fear. It

The despotism of liberty

Tyranny does not entail loss of liberty, not directly at any rate, yet in political rhetoric it is the sternest duty of liberty's champions to oppose tyranny. Living up to his family motto ('Rebellion to tyrants is obedience to God'), Thomas Jefferson declared in 1787 that 'The tree of liberty must be refreshed from time to time with the blood of patriots and tyrants. It is its natural manure.' The most dazzling displays of verbal gymnastics, in this connection, were given by the French revolutionaries. Pondering whether the use of terror did not make despots of the revolutionaries, Robespierre claimed in 1794 that terror was justified if used to 'daunt the enemies of liberty'. 'The government of the Revolution,' he concluded, 'is the despotism of liberty over tyranny.'

1775–83	1789–99	1922–45	1929–53
American Revolution fought to overthrow 'absolute Tyranny' of Britain	French Revolution fought to overthrow despotism of French kings	Fascist tyrannies of Mussolini and Hitler in Italy and Germany	Joseph Stalin rules as effective dictator of Soviet Union

The tyranny of the majority

'The one pervading evil of democracy,' wrote Lord Acton in 1878, 'is the tyranny of the majority.' He goes on to describe a form of tyranny, posing a threat to democracy alone, in which the rights of minorities are trampled underfoot by the majority, acting under the belief that realizing the 'will of the people' is legitimized by the democratic process. His concern was shared not only by a range of political theorists, from Edmund Burke to Alexis de Tocqueville and John Stuart Mill, but also by the Founding Fathers of the United States. An anxious Thomas Jefferson likened democracy to mob rule, in which 'fifty-one percent of the people may take away the rights of the other forty-nine', while John Adams, future second president, writing in 1787, was alarmed at the idea of all branches of government coming under the control of the majority: 'Debts would be abolished first; taxes laid heavy on the rich, and not at all on others; and at last a downright equal division of everything be demanded and voted.' In 1833 the fourth president, James Madison, wrote disapprovingly of 'the sweeping denunciation of majority governments as the most tyrannical and intolerable of all governments', but it was precisely to reduce the danger of such a tyranny that he introduced the separation of powers and the elaborate system of checks and balances that are so prominent in the US Constitution, for which he was largely responsible.

is for this reason that despotisms, unlike tyrannies, are typically long-lasting and stable and are not marked by problems of succession.

Where law ends The idea that tyranny consists in an individual or group acting illegally, first in the acquisition of power and then in its use, has persisted in subsequent characterizations. This has sometimes been elaborated into the view that thirst for power is the tyrant's original motivation and that the exercise of power unrestrained by the rule of law is the ultimate cause of his corruption. In an address to the House of Lords in 1770, William Pitt the Elder, echoing a sentiment expressed earlier by John Locke, observed that 'Unlimited power is apt to corrupt the minds of those who possess it; and this I know, my lords, that where laws end, tyranny begins.'

> **'Wherever law ends, tyranny begins.'**
> **John Locke,** *Two Treatises of Government,* **1690**

In the fact of its operation without restraint of law, tyranny is largely indistinguishable from dictatorship, at least as conceived in modern times (a *dictator* was originally a Roman magistrate who was given extraordinary powers for a fixed term during an emergency and remained accountable within the law).

Modern autocrats, from Napoleon to Stalin and Hitler, who rose to power in part through personal charisma and claimed legitimacy by appeal to the popular will, were denounced by their opponents indiscriminately as dictators and tyrants. The usual orientation of tyranny towards power is exposed by English writer George Orwell in *Nineteen Eighty-Four* (1949): 'Power is not a means, it is an end. One does not establish a dictatorship in order to safeguard a revolution; one makes the revolution in order to establish the dictatorship.'

The totalitarian state The peculiar horrors and sheer scale of 20th-century tyrannies prompted some to the view that they differed not merely in degree but in kind from earlier regimes and therefore required a new terminology. The name 'totalitarianism' was first coined with reference to the fascist dictatorship of Mussolini's Italy, then applied to Nazi Germany. After the war, following the defeat of Germany and Italy, it became a key term in the rhetoric of the Cold War liberals and was used almost exclusively with reference to the Soviet Union under Stalin.

> **Of all tyrannies a tyranny sincerely exercised for the good of its victims may be the most oppressive.**
>
> **C.S. Lewis, 1949**

Certainly the scale of ambition of these regimes to control and direct every aspect of individual and social behaviour sets them apart from anything that had gone before. Typically the apparatus of state was highly centralized around a single party under a single charismatic leader, and an elaborate, technologically sophisticated bureaucracy was developed to manage social and economic activity and to coordinate the secret police and other agencies used to monitor, terrorize and eliminate dissidents, real or imagined. What was perhaps most distinctive about the Nazi and Soviet systems was the extent to which ideology was used, in reaction to the supposed decadence of liberal democracy, in an attempt to bring about a utopian transformation of society. Be that as it may, the picture of total, all-embracing state control, infusing every sphere of life, was itself part of the totalitarian mythology, mediated through propaganda and censorship; the actual effectiveness of the total state, and even its existence as such, have been seriously questioned in recent decades.

the condensed idea
Monarchy corrupted

09 Utopianism

'I want to gather together about twenty souls,' wrote D.H. Lawrence in a letter of January 1915, 'and sail away from this world of war and squalor and found a little colony where there shall be no money but a sort of communism as far as necessaries of life go, and some real decency.' In yearning for escape to a simpler and more decorous place, the novelist sets himself in a long tradition of visionaries and mystics (and not a few cranks) who have dreamt up brave new worlds where the faults and foibles of mankind are cured and hope is renewed.

Such dreams of earthly paradise – such utopias – have rarely existed outside the minds of their creators. In most cases this is a cause for relief, not regret, as Evelyn Waugh observed in his wartime novel *Put Out More Flags* (1942): 'The human mind is inspired enough when it comes to inventing horrors; it is when it tries to invent a Heaven that it shows itself cloddish.' In the 20th century, in particular, massively ambitious and massively misguided attempts to reform societies on ideological lines, fully confirming Waugh's pessimism, displayed mankind's capacity to turn utopian dreams into living nightmares.

More's *Utopia* The name 'utopia' was originally coined by the English scholar and statesman Sir Thomas More. In *Utopia*, written in Latin and published in 1516, his imaginary paradise is an island where men and women live together as equals in an early version of a communist society. Education is provided by the state and religious intolerance is forbidden; everything is held in common and gold, not especially prized, is used to make chamber pots. The modern implication of 'utopian' – that a scheme or project is both idealistic and unattainable – is present in More's account. At the beginning of *Utopia* there is

timeline

1516	1649	1888
Thomas More coins the name 'utopia'	Communist-style Diggers active in wake of English Civil War	Edward Bellamy's technocratic vision of the future *Looking Backward* is published

a short prefatory verse which explains that the ideal state he describes, 'Utopia' (from the Greek meaning 'no place'), might also warrant the name 'Eutopia' (meaning 'good place'). As open criticism was dangerous in More's day, *Utopia* allowed him to draw an oblique contrast with many dysfunctional aspects of society and politics in contemporary Christian Europe. Many subsequent writers have followed More's example in using utopias as a way of criticizing society's ills without openly antagonizing dangerous people in high places.

Utopian ideas and the promise of change often hold a special appeal to subordinate social and political groups, who lack a voice within established power structures. Dominant groups, on the other hand, typically prefer continuity and wish to preserve the status quo. Many utopians, like More, have seen a remedy in removing inequalities in wealth and the greed and envy that flow from them and hence have proposed as an alternative some kind of egalitarian, communist system. Such radical remedies usually have a better prospect of success in times of extreme social turmoil. For instance, at the time of the English Civil War, a number of radical groups emerged, one of the more eccentric of which was the Diggers, or True Levellers, whose visionary leader, Gerrard Winstanley, insisted that God's earth was a treasury common to all and that the institution of property was a consequence of the Fall. In April 1649 a

Floating fancies

Readiness to embrace utopianism and the possibility of social improvement has historically been a significant fault line between conservatives on the one hand and socialists and liberals on the other. In his *Reflections on the Revolution in France* (1790), Edmund Burke, great prophet of modern conservatism, writes disdainfully of those who, neglecting the 'institutions of their forefathers', are swept along on the latest 'floating fancies or fashions' and concoct grand schemes to cure the ills of society. Deeply suspicious of such social panaceas, founded as they believe on unwarranted assumptions about the perfectibility of mankind, conservatives are portrayed by their opponents as cynical and contemptuous of human endeavour and aspiration. In response, the conservative may note how frequently, as a matter of historical record, hell has been reached by roads paved with good intentions. As US satirist Ambrose Bierce put it, in his *Cynic's Word Book* (1906), a conservative is 'a statesman enamoured of existing evils, as distinguished from the Liberal, who wishes to replace them with others'.

1890	1891	1932	1949
Publication of William Morris's pastoral idyll *News from Nowhere*	Oscar Wilde's essay 'The Soul of Man under Socialism' published	Aldous Huxley publishes his dystopian classic *Brave New World*	George Orwell's totalitarian nightmare *Nineteen Eighty-Four* published

> **'Without the Utopias of other times, men would still live in caves, miserable and naked ... Out of generous dreams come beneficial realities. Utopia is the principle of all progress, and the essay into a better future.'**
>
> **Anatole France, *c.*1900**

party of Diggers, intent on restoring the people's right to common land, started digging the commons at St George's Hill, Surrey, and a number of other colonies sprang up, though all were short-lived.

Victorian hope, Edwardian angst A frequent criticism of utopias today, both literary and other, is that they (unlike dystopias) are dull and lifeless – that a picture of perfection is a static and desiccated vista, from which the energizing sap of human passion, conflict and fallibility has been extracted. A very different view was widespread in the 19th century, however, when the quest for utopias, fuelled by the progress of science, was seen as the key to progress. This buoyant optimism was articulated by Oscar Wilde in his essay 'The Soul of Man under Socialism' (1891), in which he argues for a socialist world where the benign application of technology has replaced the drudgery of work. 'A map of the world that does not include Utopia is not worth even glancing at,' he protests, 'for it leaves out the one country at which Humanity is always landing. And when Humanity lands there, it looks out, and seeing a better country, sets sail. Progress is the realization of Utopias.'

Towards the end of the century, however, a note of alarm at the remorseless advance of science was already audible. Reacting in horror to the technocratic vision of the future offered by the US novelist Edward Bellamy, who imagined a world that was classless and egalitarian, yet heavily industrialized and bureaucratic, the English socialist artist and author William Morris provided a strong antidote in his *News from Nowhere* (1890). His pastoral idyll offers a world that has been scrubbed clean of industrial grime and where men and women are free and equal.

These signs of anxiety intensified in the early decades of the 20th century. While the optimistic Victorians dreamed of utopias that were egalitarian and inclusive, the anxious Edwardians devised utopias that were elitist and exclusive. For the science-fiction writer H.G. Wells, the objective was not so much to make a better world for people to live in, but to make a better people to live in the world. To calm fears that decent folk would be overwhelmed by the 'people of the abyss' – the ever-growing working poor – new 'sciences' were emerging that seemed to promise ready solutions. Social Darwinism, a damaging perversion of Charles Darwin's theory of evolution by natural selection, proposed that the lessons of the 'survival of the fittest' should be applied to races and societies; in the name of human improvement, measures to assist those afflicted by poverty or otherwise 'unfit' were criticized as attempts to correct 'natural' inequalities of class and wealth and hence to interfere with the necessary biological 'weeding out' of weak and unworthy elements. At the same time, eugenics promised a proactive way of improving and purifying the human stock, by all means including compulsory sterilization.

Dystopian visions

One positive legacy of the disastrous utopian experiments of the 20th century was what are arguably the two greatest dystopian classics. In Aldous Huxley's *Brave New World* (1932), social stability is gained at the cost of an anodyne existence induced by drugs and brainwashing within a eugenically manipulated caste system. George Orwell's *Nineteen Eighty-Four* (1949) is a totalitarian nightmare in which the abiding image is 'a boot stamping on a human face – forever'.

Brave new worlds The belief that human character itself lay within the scope of utopian transformation paved the way for the horrors of the 20th century. 'The trouble with kingdoms of heaven on earth is that they are liable to come to pass,' the British commentator Malcolm Muggeridge observed in 1968, 'and then their fraudulence is apparent for all to see.' The truth of his remark had been cruelly borne out over the preceding half-century, as the hideous consequences of eugenics and race policy were seen in Nazi Germany; the communist utopia of Marx and Engels was translated into agricultural collectivization and the gulags of Stalin's Russia; and the Great Leap Forward regressed into the oppressive sterility and stricture of Mao's Cultural Revolution.

the condensed idea
Earthly paradise – or hell on earth

10 Revolution

Revolution – the idea of transforming the world, of curing its ills at a stroke – has long exercised a power fascination. It was the prospect of a radical break with the past precipitated by the French Revolution that exhilarated the Romantic poet William Wordsworth: 'Bliss was it in that dawn to be alive, but to be young was very heaven.' Another admirer of the French revolutionaries, the Welsh dissenting minister Richard Price, caught the mood of the times, and of revolutionary zeal in general, when he exalted 'the love for liberty catching and spreading, a general amendment beginning in human affairs; the dominion of kings changed for the dominion of laws'.

In its fullest modern sense, revolution is, in Karl Marx's phrase, 'the forcible overthrow of all existing social conditions'. Such an upheaval entails a radical transformation from one state of affairs to another. There must be an existing system – some kind of *ancien régime*, or 'old order' – which is sufficiently dysfunctional and unpopular to provoke discontent and disaffection and hence to make itself vulnerable to revolutionary activity. Nevertheless, the *ancien régime* must also be established and coherent as a system of political and social institutions, with some semblance of legitimacy, at least to the extent that it provides a focus for the energies of the revolutionaries. Otherwise a protest will lack sufficient coherence in motivation and direction to be recognizable as a revolution, rather than as a more or less spontaneous uprising or riot.

No less important, however, is that a revolution must be a transformation *into* something: a process, constructive as well as destructive, that not only sweeps away the old but which puts something new and supposedly better in its place. It is this promise of a new beginning – the hope of a *novus ordo seclorum* ('new order

timeline

for the ages'), in the words of the motto on the Great Seal of the United States – that is the ultimate justification for revolution and for its usual high cost in human life and suffering. And it is because revolutions purportedly have this constructive function that they are typically programmatic in nature: they are ideological, in that they are underpinned by a specific framework or scheme of ideas; and utopian, in the sense that they hold out the prospect of a better future.

The locomotives of history Just as it was for Wordsworth and Price, this model of radical revolution was brought scintillatingly to life by the French Revolution of 1789. Consciously supported on the pillars of Enlightenment rationalism, this was the first truly secular revolution, which set itself against a system of absolute monarchy and ecclesiastical dominance that had lasted for hundreds of years. From this time onwards, it would be an article of faith for radicals, and a cause of alarm for conservatives, that revolution was an inevitable force of social and political change. According to this view, radical upheavals were the necessary steps by which societies progressed towards a fairer and more productive state; they were the best, indeed only means of sweeping aside the outmoded and unjust institutions of the existing social order and the individuals who benefited from it. In the middle of the 19th century this conception of revolution as an irresistible and progressive force was given its definitive statement by the most influential figures in the history of revolutionary thought, the German émigré and political theorist Karl Marx and his lifelong collaborator Friedrich Engels.

> ‘After a revolution, you see the same men in the drawing room, and within a week the same flatterers.’
>
> George Savile, Lord Halifax, English politician and essayist, 1750

First set forth in *The Communist Manifesto* of 1848, the cornerstone of Marxist theory is the contention that the 'history of all hitherto existing society is the history of class struggles'. According to this distinctive understanding of history, the development of human societies is determined by progression through a sequence of modes of economic production (feudalism, capitalism, socialism). Each of these works to the benefit of a particular social class; and as each mode develops, conflict intensifies between the dominant class, which enjoys the benefits of the established

1917
Russian Revolution overthrows
Romanov tsarist dynasty

1989–91
Collapse of
communist Eastern
Europe and the Soviet
Union

The Kitchens of the future

Among the reasons why radical, progressive revolution seems doomed to failure are its intrinsic tendency towards utopianism – to reach for the unattainable – and its insatiable appetite for snake oil. In his *Reflections on the Revolution in France* (1790), the most important early critic of revolution, Edmund Burke, censures the willingness of the headstrong revolutionary to be 'delivered over blindly to every projector and adventurer, to every alchemist and empiric'. One manifestation of this is a head-in-the-clouds drive towards moral perfectionism and the unhappy consequence for revolutionary idealists that 'by hating vices too much, they come to love men too little'.

Karl Marx himself was consistently reluctant to draw up utopian blueprints for societies established according to his precepts: 'It is not our task to write recipes for the kitchens of the future,' he wrote in 1867. Unfortunately, Stalin, Mao and others who defiled his name in the 20th century were less scrupulous in this regard. Suffering from the pathological tendency, identified by political theorist Alexis de Tocqueville in 1856, to consider 'the citizen as an abstract proposition apart from any particular society', these revolutionary masters of central planning and social engineering concocted wildly utopian schemes that brought misery and death to tens of millions.

but increasingly obsolete mode, and the rising class, which is destined to usurp its position of dominance. This conflict finally reaches a crisis, or revolution, in which the oppressive and outmoded class is forcibly overthrown. The French Revolution, for Marx, was such a transition, in which the feudal overlords were displaced by the more productive capitalist class. In due course it would be the turn of the latter – the property-owning bourgeoisie – to be overturned by the working class, or proletariat, who would set up a classless, socialist society and thus bring to an end the process of political change. Thus, according to this analysis, revolutions are the driving force behind historical progress – 'the locomotives of history', in a metaphor Marx used later.

> **The most radical revolutionary will become a conservative on the day after the revolution.**
>
> Hannah Arendt, German-born US political theorist, 1970

All change and no change Alongside this positive assessment of revolution as a progressive force that brings permanent and beneficial change, there has always been a bleaker and more pessimistic view. Many before and since have shared George Bernard Shaw's gloomy perspective, expressed in 1903: 'Revolutions have never lightened the burden of tyranny: they have only shifted

> **❝Revolution: an abrupt change in the form of misgovernment . . . Revolutions are usually accompanied by a considerable effusion of blood, but are accounted worth it – this appraisement being made by beneficiaries whose blood had not the mischance to be shed.❞**
>
> **Ambrose Bierce,** *The Cynic's Word Book,* **1906**

it to another shoulder.' In recent decades, in particular, there has been a strong revisionist tendency, primarily among conservative historians, to dismiss the positive aspects of revolutions, treating them as ill-starred and often bloody cul-de-sacs, rather than as significant turning points on the path of progress.

Corroboration for this downbeat assessment was found especially in the collapse of the communist governments of Eastern Europe and the Soviet Union between 1989 and 1991. This seemed to confirm that major revolutionary upheavals, of which the Russian Revolution of 1917 stood as the paradigmatic case, produced transient change, not the permanent transformation predicted by Marxist theory. Indeed, one of the commonest criticisms of revolution is that, as a matter of historical fact, it has changed very little, and even where there has been some measure of change, it has almost never gone as expected. In both the French and the Russian revolutions, a short-lived period of idealistic optimism was followed by a split between moderates and extremists, brought on by internal and external pressures, and then a process of radicalization, in which all power was funnelled into the hands of a few. Thus, in France, a decade of bloodshed and war effected the substitution of the absolute power of Napoleon Bonaparte for the absolute power of Louis XVI; while in Russia it took very much the same amount of time for the feudal autocracy of the Romanovs to be replaced by the horrifying despotism of Joseph Stalin.

the condensed idea
The juddering locomotives of history

11 Anarchism

In the cartoonist's imagination, the anarchist is a dark and seedy figure, hooded and bearded, a social outcast armed with a spherical Orsini bomb, bent on bringing indiscriminate death to those unlucky enough to fall in his path of destruction. While a few anarchist attacks in the past did something to justify the caricature, no other set of political views can have been the cause of greater confusion and misunderstanding than those that are grouped together under the name of anarchism.

The aim of anarchists is, naturally enough, to bring about or realize anarchy. But what precisely is meant by this? Before the 19th century the word was used almost exclusively in a negative sense, as a term of political disapprobation or abuse. In the French Revolution, for instance, it was applied to a group of extreme radicals called the *Enragés*, who were accused by their opponents of promoting a catalogue of social calamities that included neglect of government and public morality, disregard of the law and abuse of property.

> **❝Anarchy is order; government is civil war.❞**
> **Anselme Bellegarrigue, French anarchist (attributed), 1848**

But while this strongly negative sense is deeply rooted, it is not the only meaning of the word. Derived from the Greek meaning 'without authority' or 'without rule', 'anarchy' also has a neutral sense, signifying no more than the absence of government or authority. Several leading anarchists delighted in playing on this ambiguity and the apparent paradox that resulted from it, thereby (inadvertently or not) reinforcing the stereotype. Be that as it may, the popular image in fact does scant justice to a line of political thought that takes a markedly sympathetic and optimistic view on human potential and which continues to have a significant influence on modern politics.

timeline

1793	1840	1845
William Godwin's *Enquiry Concerning Political Justice* is published	Pierre-Joseph Proudhon declares that 'Property is theft'	Max Stirner's *The Ego and His Own* published

Liberation and spontaneous order

The characteristic shared by anarchists is a deep distrust of authority. They deny that anyone can legitimately exercise power over another, and their aim, therefore, is freedom from all forms of coercion and control. They believe that institutionalized power, embodied in the oppressive machinery of the state, is invariably exercised in the interest of those who wield it and in a manner that exploits others. The kind of freedom craved by anarchists was succinctly expressed by the US anarchist Emma Goldman, writing in 1910: anarchism, she claims, 'stands for the liberation of the human mind from the dominion of religion; the liberation of the human body from the dominion of property; liberation from the shackles and restraints of government'.

The justification for the anarchist claim that the state is illegitimate and is not entitled to expect the obedience of its citizens is that such a demand is a violation of individual autonomy. People, it is claimed, are essentially reasonable and able to run their affairs together in a peaceful and productive manner, without the threat of the state's bludgeon. Inverting the familiar claim that the power of the state is needed to curb people's selfish or violent instincts, the anarchist claims that people are naturally good and that this innate human sympathy is subverted and corrupted by the injustice inherent in the hierarchical power structures of the state. Anarchy, then, leads not to chaos, as is commonly supposed, but to a kind of spontaneous and natural order.

The urge for destruction

The caricature of the anarchist as a crazed loner bent on destruction and carnage is based mainly on a variant known as revolutionary anarchism which became dominant around the turn of the 20th century. Associated originally with the figure of Mikhail Bakunin, this doctrine held that the impact of the state on its citizens is so baneful that it warrants forcible removal, by any means including violence. The underlying idea is that new life emerges from annihilation, or, as Bakunin put it, 'the urge for destruction is also a creative urge'. It resulted in a spate of terrorist attacks on high-profile leaders and politicians, whose assassinations were intended to highlight the vulnerability of the state and so to inspire the masses to revolution (by serving as 'propaganda of the deed'). Victims included French president Sadi Carnot (1894), Spanish prime minister Antonio Cánovas del Castillo (1897), Italian king Umberto I (1900) and US president William McKinley (1901).

Property is theft The person usually credited with giving the first fully developed account of anarchism – though he did not use the name – is the Englishman William Godwin (husband of Mary Wollstonecraft and father of Mary Shelley), who was both a radical and an extreme individualist. In his *Enquiry Concerning Political Justice* (1793), Godwin starts from the premise that 'Perfectibility is one of the most unequivocal characteristics of the human species.' He then sketches an ideal society in which people live together harmoniously in small, self-governing communities; where men and women associate on a basis of equality and work together in the common interest, without the corrupting influence of laws and institutions imposed by the 'brute engine' of government.

Godwin's communitarian vision of a decentralized society left a significant impression on perhaps the most influential figure in the history of anarchism, the French social theorist Pierre-Joseph Proudhon. The first person to consciously call himself an anarchist, Proudhon repeatedly plays on the apparent paradox implicit in his views, provocatively contrasting the orderly anarchy he envisages with the existing social order – the 'unity and centralization', which is in fact 'nothing but chaos, serving as a basis for endless tyranny'. 'Although a firm friend of order,' he protests, 'I am (in the full force of the term) an anarchist.'

Proudhon's reputation was built in part on his first book, *What is Property?* (1840), and on the answer he famously gave to that question: 'Property is theft.' He was not in favour of communism, however. Just as Godwin had condemned 'accumulated property' as a source of exploitation, Proudhon attacks property rights which allow landlords to exploit their tenants by extracting profit from their labour in the form of rent. But he was not opposed to personal 'possession' of the means of production: he regarded it as a basic right of a free person to have access to the tools and land necessary to make an adequate living. Proudhon's proposed social arrangement, known as mutualism, was essentially a federal system of small, autonomous associations of workers and producers engaged in a free and fair exchange of goods; the system was based on mutual benefit and on the principle of need, not profit.

> We reject all privileged, licensed, official, and legal legislation and authority . . . convinced that it could only turn to the benefit of a dominant and exploiting minority, and against the interests of the vast enslaved majority.
>
> **Mikhail Bakunin**

Anarcho-syndicalism Rejection of centralized authority does not imply any specific political direction, so it is no surprise that there have been almost as many versions of anarchism as there are anarchists to devise them. At one pole, the extreme individualism of the German philosopher Max Stirner, set forth in *The Ego and His Own* (1845), rejects not only state control but all other restraints, social and political, on individual freedom and autonomy. In his vision of life as a 'union of egoists', self-interest alone is the guiding principle. At the other extreme, the non-violent communitarianism of Proudhon hardened, in the next generation, into the full-scale collectivism of his Russian follower Mikhail Bakunin, a revolutionary activist who called for the overthrow of the state by violent means; and then into anarchist communism, which was championed by another Russian, the prince-turned-revolutionary Peter Kropotkin.

Direct action

Since the countercultural revolution of the 1960s anarchism's central values, including its emphasis on spontaneity and direct action, have inspired new waves of support, especially among the young. Green politics have been influenced by radical eco-anarchists, who argue that environmental protection is incompatible with existing political structures and a world order dominated by the materialist values of the West. Rejecting traditional political channels, opponents of globalization and free-market capitalism have adopted anarchist-inspired tactics of direct action in highly publicized demonstrations against global institutions such as the International Monetary Fund, the World Bank and the World Trade Organization.

In the early decades of the 20th century – the high-water mark of anarchism as a force in practical politics in both Europe and America – these various strands combined to inspire anarcho-syndicalism. This doctrine identified and empowered trade unions (syndicates) as engines of social revolution, committed to the militant overthrow of capitalism and the organs of the state. Unlike most versions of anarchism, anarcho-syndicalism came to exuberant life in eastern Spain during the Civil War. Railways and factories in Catalonia were seized and run by committees of workers, while anarchist communes were set up by peasants, who worked the land in common and shared out food and other essentials equitably among families. This real-life experiment in anarchy was short-lived, however, as the Spanish anarchists suffered the same fate as their comrades throughout Europe, driven to the point of extinction by the rise of fascism and communism.

the condensed idea
Order out of disorder

12 Secularism

'The mixing of government and religion can be a threat to free government . . . When the government puts its imprimatur on a particular religion, it conveys a message of exclusion to all those who do not adhere to the favoured beliefs. A government cannot be premised on the belief that all persons are created equal when it asserts that God prefers some . . . When the government arrogates to itself a role in religious affairs, it abandons its obligation as guarantor of democracy.'

In a landmark decision given in 1992, the US Supreme Court ruled that prayer-giving at a public school graduation ceremony was a violation of the First Amendment to the US Constitution. In giving his opinion, quoted above, Justice Harry A. Blackmun echoed a concern shared two centuries earlier by the Founding Fathers: that infringement of the principle of secularism enshrined in the US Constitution – allowing religious differences to invade the public arena – presented a direct threat to the fundamental concepts of freedom, equality and democracy on which the nation had been built.

The wall of separation Composed of 16 of the most debated words in the English language, the Establishment and Free Exercise Clauses form the first part of the First Amendment, which was adopted, together with the rest of the Bill of Rights, in 1791. The text states that 'Congress shall make no law respecting an establishment of religion, or prohibiting the free exercise thereof.' By forbidding Congress from declaring an official religion and by guaranteeing freedom of religious expression, the Founding Fathers laid the foundations of the 'wall of separation' (as Thomas Jefferson called it) that divides the proper spheres of faith and politics. Though its precise interpretation is hotly contested, on any reading the provision prevents religion and the state from interfering with one another and aims (in the

timeline

14th–15th century	early 1700s	1789–90
Beginnings of humanist movement in Renaissance Europe	Europe ravaged by wars of religion	*Laïcité* (secularism) established in France

> ❝I contemplate with solemn reverence that act of the whole American people which declared that their legislature should "make no law respecting an establishment of religion, or prohibiting the free exercise thereof", thus building a wall of separation between Church and State.❞
>
> **Thomas Jefferson, 1802**

words of another Supreme Court judge, Arthur Goldberg) to 'promote and assure the fullest possible scope of religious liberty and tolerance for all'.

As the school prayer ruling demonstrates, the separation of church and state is jealously guarded in the United States. To the extent that secularism consists in keeping divine authority out of the management of worldly affairs, the USA is certainly among the most secular nations on earth. In view of this, it may seem unexpected to find President Bill Clinton, in a speech made in 1995, commenting – surely accurately – that 'in this highly secular age the United States is clearly the most conventionally religious country in the entire world, at least the entire industrialized world'. However, the apparent paradox quickly evaporates if secularism is distinguished from related concepts such as atheism and humanism, with which it is sometimes confused. In the meaning that Clinton has in mind, secularism is not hostile or opposed to religion at all; rather, it refers to a particular understanding of the proper place of religion in the constitution and operation of a state.

The European secular myth America's success at achieving a markedly secular religiosity is exceptional, as becomes clear when comparisons are drawn with Europe, the supposed cradle of secularism, where the situation is in many respects the reverse of that in the USA. Most European countries are in reality both less religious and less secular than the USA (at least in the Clintonian sense), but this is not necessarily how things appear to Europeans themselves. In an open letter to teachers written in 2007, the new French president Nicolas

1791	**1802**	**1992**	**1990s**
US First Amendment requires separation of state and religion	President Thomas Jefferson makes first reference to 'wall of separation'	US Supreme Court gives landmark ruling (*Lee vs. Weisman*) on school prayer	Yugoslav Wars in Balkans fuelled by religious and ethnic tensions

Europe's troubled soul

Indications of Europe's troubled secular identity, now and in the past, are everywhere to be seen: rows over Muslim headscarves and other symbols of religious affiliation; protests against discriminatory blasphemy laws; 'balanced treatment' for creationism and evolutionary theory in schools . . . the list goes on and on. On a grander scale, the European Union, a global presence that so often belies its name, has been searching its soul, or perhaps reinventing it, in its efforts to countenance the eastward expansion of the EU and in particular integration of Turkey, a country that straddles east and west and where greater democratic freedom has apparently been accompanied by an increasingly public demonstration of its Muslim culture and religion. In another revealing episode, in the early 2000s the EU came to blows over the preamble to the constitutional treaty. In its original draft the preamble made mention of both God and Europe's Christian values, but the final compromise wording referred to 'inspiration from the cultural, religious and humanist inheritance of Europe'. Perhaps the saddest indication of the equivocal nature of European secularism is the fact that in the last decade of the 20th century a vicious war motivated as much by religious differences as ethnic ones could rage in the Balkans, in the very heart of Europe.

Sarkozy asked rhetorically: 'Faced with the risk of a confrontation between religions which would open the door to a clash of civilizations, what better defence do we have than a few great universal values and secularism?' Sarkozy's image of Europe, armed with liberal Western values, as a bastion against the encroachments of religious zealotry is typical of a certain patrician superiority that looks in supercilious alarm to east and west: one way it sees the threatening fundamentalisms of Asia, the other the bland fervour of American religiosity. But the picture is seriously distorted.

Europe's perception of itself as a bulwark against dangerous religious forces from outside is hard to recognize in reality. Most obviously, those forces are no longer external, if indeed they ever were. To suppose otherwise is to ignore centuries of immigration and demographic change which have produced a rich potpourri of religious and cultural influences; in particular, the wave of Muslim immigration into Europe over recent decades is merely the latest phase of a very ancient process. Furthermore, the view that secularism is some kind of crowning achievement of the European Enlightenment is itself based on a semi-mythical narrative of secularization. Beginning in the Renaissance, when scientific explanation first started to displace theologically inspired accounts of mankind's place in the world, this creation myth reaches its bloody climax in the religious wars of the 17th century. At this point of crisis (so the story goes), the destructive sectarian passions released by the Protestant Reformation were finally calmed by a happy combination of Enlightenment rationalism and the progressive forces of the scientific revolution. In this supposed secular transformation political theology based on divine revelation at last gave way to political philosophy based on human reason. Religion was removed to its own protected and private sphere, while an open and liberal public arena was created in which freedom of expression, toleration of difference, and (in due course) democracy blossomed.

> 'The fact that we have freedom of religion doesn't mean we need to try to have freedom from religion.'
> **Bill Clinton, 1993**

Embraced as both the origin and the justification of Europe's modern secular identity, this story is substantially flawed. The immediate legacy of the 17th-century religious wars was not a Europe of modern secular states but a patchwork of confessional, territorial ones; usually the only freedom allowed to religious minorities who found themselves in the wrong confessional territory was the 'freedom' to move elsewhere. With the exception of ostentatiously secular France (where a revolution saw secularism, or *laïcité*, paid for in the blood of its citizens), to this day no European country has been entirely or consistently secular. The United Kingdom has an established church, as do the Lutheran countries of Scandinavia, while other nations, such as Poland, Ireland and Italy, remain essentially Catholic. Where strict secularism has prevailed for a time, as for instance in the Soviet Union and Eastern Europe, the result has generally been intolerance and profoundly illiberal government. Based on a mixture of fantasy and bad history, the story of European secularism – paradoxically, the inspiration for a more successful and impressive version in North America – is an often unsatisfactory tale, with no happy ending in view.

the condensed idea
Separating church and state

13 Republicanism

'The true and only true definition' of a republic, wrote John Adams, future second president of the USA, in 1787, is 'a government, in which all men, rich and poor, magistrates and subjects, officers and people, masters and servants, the first citizen and the last, are equally subject to the laws.'

Few since have shown such confidence in saying what a republic is, or what republicanism – the doctrine of those who favour the establishment of republics – involves. Adams's fellow republican (though personal enemy), the radical Thomas Paine, carped at those who were quick enough to 'abuse something which they called republicanism; but what republicanism was, or is, they never attempt to explain.' While republicanism was to remain a somewhat flexible bundle of ideals, stubbornly resistant to codification, it was Paine himself who memorably anticipated Adams in highlighting the rule of law as the pre-eminent republican principle, declaring in his revolutionary pamphlet *Common Sense* (1776) that 'In America *the law is king*. For as in absolute governments the king is law, so in free countries the law *ought* to be king.'

What all free men deserve Today the word 'republic' is loosely applied to any state that does not have a monarch, sometimes with the added qualification that it must have an elected head of state, usually a president. It is true, as a matter of historical fact, that many, probably most, republics have been set up in place of monarchies, frequently by violent means. Such, of course, was the case in 18th-century North America, where Britain's disgruntled colonists reluctantly came to see a complete break from the British Crown as the only solution to their grievances; and a few years later in France, where the Bourbon dynasty was brought to a bloody end in the turmoil of the French Revolution.

timeline

510 BC	27 BC	1649–60
Expulsion of Etruscan kings marks creation of the Roman republic	Roman republic comes to formal end as Augustus becomes emperor	English republic ('Commonwealth') set up following execution of Charles I

Paine himself was clearly no friend of monarchs: 'The nearer any government approaches to a republic,' he wrote in *Common Sense*, 'the less business there is for a king.' Often in republican folklore, it is a particular overbearing monarch – such as George III, Paine's 'Royal Brute' – who is identified as the bogeyman, the agent of oppression. But it was not monarchy per se that was objectionable to Paine or Adams, but what it generally stood for: absolute power, arbitrarily exercised, usually in its own, not the public, interest. Indeed, not all early American republicans thought that monarchy was necessarily incompatible with republicanism. In 1775 Adams stated that 'the British constitution is . . . nothing more or less than a republic, in which the king is first magistrate'; the grievance, for Adams and others, was that Britain – 'an empire of laws, and not of men', in which the office of monarch was 'bound by fixed laws, which the people have a voice in making' – chose not to allow their American cousins a similar liberty, denying them 'the basic rights guaranteed to all Englishmen, and which all free men deserved'.

The Roman republic

According to tradition, the Roman republic was established in 510 BC, following the expulsion of Tarquin the Proud, the last of the decadent Etruscan kings, in a revolt led by the republican hero Lucius Brutus. The constitution introduced after the fall of the kings was democratic in the sense that sovereignty was notionally vested in the people, but in practice power was concentrated in the hands of a broad-based oligarchy of 50 or so noble families, who reserved for themselves the main magistracies (political offices) and controlled the main debating chamber, the Senate.

There were, however, numerous constitutional barriers to prevent abuses of power. For instance, all offices were fixed-term, and even the highest offices, the two consulships, were strictly circumscribed by law and subject to veto by the tribunes of the people. While these various safeguards proved suggestive to later republicans, so too was the republic's ultimate fate. The constitutional pillars of the republican system were steadily eroded by corruption and abuse, and the whole edifice finally collapsed, to be bloodily replaced in 27 BC by the highly autocratic imperial regime initiated by Augustus.

1775–83

American Revolution leads to birth of USA

1789–9

French monarchy violently replaced with radical republic

In a letter written in 1780, another of the Founding Fathers, Alexander Hamilton, sheds further light on the centrality of equality before the law in republican thinking. 'The obedience of a free people to general laws,' he observes, 'however hard they bear, is ever more perfect than that of slaves to the arbitrary will of a prince.' It is not ill treatment as such that is despised so much as the fact that such treatment may be inflicted at the whim of another. The republican goal is not merely freedom from oppression but freedom from the fear or threat of it. The idealized republican is a free man – citizen not subject, master of his own destiny, at liberty to live his life according to common laws and to look others in the eye without fear or deference.

Duty and civic virtue The central feature of republican mythology – the suppression of tyranny – found its chief archetype in the Roman republic (see box page 53). (The word 'republic' comes, aptly enough, from the Latin word for 'state' or 'public affairs', *res publica*; the English word 'commonwealth' is close in meaning.) The fascination that Rome's republic held for later republicans, including those who framed the US Constitution, lay as much in the indomitable spirit of its great heroes as in the detail of its constitutional arrangements. In

Setting a course between tyrannies

'Republican government', wrote Thomas Paine in the *Rights of Man* (1791), 'is no other than government established and conducted for the interest of the public, as well individually as collectively.' This might suggest that democracy is the natural form of government for a republic. Paine himself felt that representative democracy was best suited to republicanism, but he recognized that this was not necessarily so. Most early republicans, indeed, were very wary of pure or direct democracy, believing it to be little better than mob rule and a recipe for anarchy and the abuse of property and other basic rights. It was to protect the upright citizen from the tyranny of the masses, as well as the tyranny of despots, that the architects of the US Constitution favoured the separation of powers and incorporated numerous checks and balances. In the resultant mixed constitution, sovereignty was divided up between several bodies, so preventing any one of them from enjoying absolute and unchecked power.

particular, they were much impressed with the dutifulness (*pietas*) shown by its champions – the tyrant-slaying Brutuses, the invincible Scipios, the austere Catos, all of whom showed unstinting and selfless devotion to public service.

Roman *pietas* was a model for the civic virtue that became the hallmark of American republicanism, where the essential quality in the upstanding citizen was a willingness to step forward in the service of the state and to place the common good before any selfish or partisan interest. Such active participation generally meant having a significant stake in society and a degree of education that would allow reasoned deliberation among independent-minded and intellectual equals. One consequence, following the assumptions of the time, was that women and unpropertied workers (and of course slaves) had to rely on the virtuous (male, white) elite for their protection.

Uneasy partners Now and in the past, liberalism and republicanism have often been coupled together, but it is not always or necessarily an easy marriage. The kind of public-spirited republicanism that values selfless participation in civil society does not sit easily with the brand of liberalism that sees the role of the state as essentially limited to that of mediator, whose function is merely to protect the rights of individuals and to arbitrate in cases where interests conflict. Traditional republicanism also goes hand in hand with a certain social conservatism and austerity, but these, too, are far removed from the economic individualism and wealth creation beloved of classical liberalism. Today, the rhetoric of individual rights appears to have triumphed over that of communal duties, but the underlying tensions are far from resolved. In the case of the USA, this basic opposition is the creative force behind the political and cultural dynamics of the nation.

> **The republican is the only form of government which is not eternally at open or secret war with the rights of mankind.**
>
> **Thomas Jefferson, 1790**

the condensed idea
Where law is king

14 Capitalism

In the euphoria following the collapse of the state-run economies of the Soviet bloc from 1989, some commentators saw the triumph of liberal democracy and of the capitalist system of economic and social organization that underpinned it. The hubris of such claims became painfully apparent in the global meltdown of financial institutions in the first decade of the 21st century.

Though sometimes presented by its more fervent admirers as an ideology, capitalism is basically, or at least originally, a mode of production: a way of organizing economic activity. The essential activity of a capitalist system is the use of privately owned wealth to generate income. Everything that is needed to make goods – the 'means of production', namely the capital required to procure land, materials, tools, ideas and labour – is owned by individuals (capitalists), who use these means to make things that can be sold at a profit. The wealth thus generated steadily accumulates and is partly reinvested to sustain and expand the business. The other requirements for capitalism to thrive are a legal framework that provides, minimally, for contracts to be made; and a free or open market. It is the distinctive feature of capitalist systems, in contrast to command economies, that all decisions of production and distribution are left ultimately to the market, not to government.

The modern understanding of capitalism is inseparable from the analysis of the concept given in the mid-19th century by Karl Marx in *Das Kapital*. For Marx, the origin of capitalism is to be found in the class conflict between the bourgeoisie (capitalist class), who privately own the means of production, and the proletariat (working class), whose labour is exploited, in return for inadequate wages, in order to generate profit for their oppressors. Accumulation of wealth leads inevitably, in the Marxist view, to the concentration of power, not only

timeline

1776	1848	1854	1867–94
Principles of free trade set out in Adam Smith's *The Wealth of Nations*	Overthrow of capitalism predicted in Marx's *The Communist Manifesto*	First attested use of 'capitalism' (in Thackeray's *The Newcomes*)	Marx gives definitive critique of capitalism in *Das Kapital*

economic but also social and political, in the hands of the capitalist class, who thereby come to a position of dominance over the proletariat. This situation of oppression can only be brought to an end by revolution, in which the bourgeoisie will be forcibly overthrown and private property abolished.

Adam Smith and the free market Nearly a century before Marx's great work, the essential dynamics of the engine that drives capitalism – the free market – were brilliantly analysed by the Scottish economist Adam Smith. At the time he was writing his seminal *The Wealth of Nations* (1776), many of the conditions that would allow the burgeoning of free-market capitalism (not a term used by Smith himself) were already in place. The growth of trade at home and abroad had created an entrepreneurial spirit and a generation of merchants who brought to Britain much of the wealth that would nurture the new industries of the fledgling Industrial Revolution. At the same time a class of free wage labourers was forming, willy-nilly, from agricultural workers displaced en masse by the running-down of feudally managed estates. The final obstacle in the path of economic transformation – and a principal target of Smith's pioneering work – was the mass of monopolies and price controls still imposed by the state.

> **Capitalism is the astounding belief that the most wickedest of men will do the most wickedest of things for the greatest good of everyone.**
> **John Maynard Keynes (attributed)**

Smith's genius was to see that, in a market where enterprise, competition and motivation towards personal gain are given free rein, the dynamics of supply and demand will ensure that producers produce goods and services that consumers wish to buy, at a price that offers a reasonable but not excessive profit on their investment. The system so conceived is naturally self-regulating, in that variables such as cost, price and profit are determined as functions of the system as a whole and cannot be manipulated, without damaging the system, either by the parties to a transaction or by any third party (such as the government) outside it. The implication that politics and economics are essentially distinct and that politicians should not meddle in economic matters provided the theoretical justification for the classical liberal doctrine of laissez-faire – the idea that the state should refrain from attempting to plan or direct the course of markets.

1929	1933	1970s	1989	2007
Stock market crash in USA triggers Great Depression	Keynes criticizes free trade in his essay 'National Self-Sufficiency'	Monetarist policies gain favour in Europe and the USA	State-run (command) economies of Soviet bloc begin to collapse	Beginning of deep global economic downturn ('Credit Crunch')

Not intelligent, not beautiful

Full-blooded, libertarian, free-market capitalism requires that the state keeps its hands off: the system is self-regulating and optimal, so any regulation or intervention (for which read: interference) must, by definition, undermine efficiency. The most influential critic of this view was the great British economist John Maynard Keynes. Commenting on the 'decadent international but individualistic capitalism' that prevailed in the years after the First World War, he wrote acidly: 'It is not intelligent. It is not beautiful. It is not just. It is not virtuous. And it doesn't deliver the goods.' Keynes's own interventionist views appeared to be vindicated by the Great Depression of the 1930s, and for several decades his recommendation – that government spending should be used to boost demand in the economy, so increasing employment and overcoming recessionary pressures – was widely followed. The mood changed again in the 1970s, however, as Keynesianism fell out of fashion, to be replaced as the prevailing orthodoxy by monetarism, a doctrine chiefly associated with the US economist Milton Friedman. Reasserting the perfection of the free market, monetarists insisted that the state's role should be limited to controlling the money supply, in order to reduce inflation, and to removing monopolies, tariffs and other external restraints on the market. The age of deregulation, privatization and the 'small state', initiated by so-called 'neoliberals', notably Ronald Reagan and Margaret Thatcher, was brought to a juddering halt in the mid-2000s, when the global 'Credit Crunch' ushered in a phase of government intervention on a scale without historical precedent.

While Smith claimed that the free market was the most effective mechanism in coordinating economic activity, he allowed that the state had a role beyond that of merely facilitating commerce. There were things that could not be left to private entrepreneurs, who would have no interest in supplying facilities in which they could see no profit; to the state would still fall 'the duty of erecting and maintaining certain public works'. The question whether society's needs, such as transport and education, are best provided by the state or though private initiative has been the subject of fierce debate ever since.

Miracle or monster? Even capitalism's critics tend not to deny its capacity to generate economic growth. In a hundred years of ascendancy, wrote Marx in 1848, the bourgeoisie had 'created more massive and more colossal productive forces than have all preceding generations together'. The profit motive that stimulates entrepreneurs to accumulate wealth encourages them to expand

> **Advocates of capitalism are very apt to appeal to the sacred principles of liberty, which are embodied in one maxim: The fortunate must not be restrained in the exercise of tyranny over the unfortunate.**
>
> **Bertrand Russell, 1928**

their businesses, and this allows ever more refined division of labour (splitting manufacturing process into smaller, simpler tasks) and other efficiencies that contribute to overall economies of scale. But is bigger necessarily better?

Supporters like to claim that free-market capitalism is not only efficient but ethical. In seeking to show that ownership of capital and accumulation of wealth are morally acceptable, they generally give some variant of Adam Smith's suggestion that the market's 'invisible hand' guides individuals acting in their own interest to promote, unconsciously, a greater, collective good. Alternatively, they may invoke the 'trickle-down' effect, which alleges that the greater prosperity of those at the top filters down to the lower levels, leaving everyone better off (in essence, a variation on John Rawls's difference principle).

To opponents of capitalism, however, most of this seems like pie in the sky – a triumph of hope over experience. For Marx and his collaborator Friedrich Engels, a major impetus towards revolutionary communism was the appalling misery and hardship brought down on working people by the harshness of industrial capitalism; Engels, in particular, had seen working conditions deteriorate, as people were forced to work longer hours in squalid factories at tasks that became ever more tedious and repetitive. According to the Marxist analysis, it is the *essence* of capitalism to be exploitative, because workers' exertions are inadequately rewarded precisely in order to generate profit. 'The inherent vice of capitalism is the unequal sharing of blessings,' observed Winston Churchill in 1954: the wealth created by capitalism never has been, and never could be, shared between worker and employer; indeed, the gap between rich and poor has grown steadily wider. As for the trickle-down theory, this was magisterially dismissed by the economist J.K. Galbraith as 'horse-and-sparrow economics' – the idea that 'if you feed enough oats to the horse, some will pass through to feed the sparrows'.

the condensed idea
The triumph of greed?

15 Conservatism

'If it is not necessary to change, it is necessary not to change.' Or, as we might say in these rougher times: 'If it ain't bust, don't fix it.' This homely maxim, first credited (in its more refined form) to the 17th-century English statesman Viscount Falkland, reflects a very ancient human instinct that lies at the heart of conservative thought.

A dislike of change for change's sake; a reluctance to jeopardize what works for what might, in theory, work better; faith in the firm lessons of the past over airy promises for the future; a concern to preserve what is thought best in established society; in general, 'adherence to the old and tried,' as Abraham Lincoln put it, 'against the new and untried': all these are aspects of what is today one of the most significant political philosophies – conservatism.

Yet, while these various sentiments may reliably inform the spirit of conservatism, its precise nature is harder to define. Conservatism tends towards the reactionary – typically, it is opposed to political and social reform and counsels restraint when confronted with change – and for this reason it often takes its lead and much of its colour from what it is opposed to. It is little surprise, then, that self-styled conservatives have held a very wide range of beliefs, not all of them obviously compatible with one another.

Burke and the principle of conservation The word 'reactionary' was originally used as a direct translation of the French *réactionnaire*, meaning an opponent of the French Revolution, so it is fitting that the first great articulation of conservative thinking was prompted by the mighty political and social upheaval that erupted in France in 1789. In his *Reflections on the Revolution in France* (1790), the Irish-born politician and writer Edmund Burke expresses

timeline

1789–99	1790	1797
French Revolution prompts reactionary fears across Europe	Edmund Burke makes the first great statement of conservative values	Death of Edmund Burke

his disgust at the incendiary passions of the revolutionaries, whom he regards as ideological zealots, driven by idealism and theoretical abstractions to sweep aside all that had gone before.

Burke himself does not use the words 'conservative' or 'conservatism'. Indeed, these terms were not used (in their political sense) until the 1830s, more than three decades after his death, initially as a new designation for the British Tory party. Nevertheless, Burke is much concerned with what he calls the 'principle of conservation', and it is easy to see why later conservatives would look upon him as an inspirational figure. In a passage on the 'science of government', he urges the importance of experience as the supreme political virtue and then embellishes the point in a well-known metaphor:

The art of timely lopping

Conservatism is sometimes unjustly portrayed as merely reactionary, a form of antiquarianism that is fixated on the past for no better reason than that it is past. A better understanding was shown by the Victorian poet laureate Alfred, Lord Tennyson, who declared in his poem 'Hands all Round' (1882): 'That man's the true Conservative / Who lops the mouldered branch away.' 'But', he later added in conversation with the Scottish philosopher William Angus Knight, 'the branch must be a mouldered one, before we should venture to lop it off.'

> It is with infinite caution that any man ought to venture upon pulling down an edifice which has answered in any tolerable degree for ages the common purposes of society, or on building it up again without having models and patterns of approved utility before his eyes.

Institutes and laws, hallowed by time Conservatism sets great value on tradition and wisdom drawn from the customs and practices of previous generations. This accumulated store of knowledge, far exceeding the intelligence of any individual, is, in Burke's view, society's most precious asset, a sacred trust to be taken up by one generation and reverently passed on to the next. Seen in this light, society becomes far more than the sum of its current members and institutions; rather, it is a harmonious 'partnership not only between those who are living, but between those who are living, those who are dead, and those who are to be born'.

1830	**1832**	**1908**	**1980s**
The term 'conservative' first used to designate the British Tory Party	In *The Prelude* (published 1850) Wordsworth hails 'the Genius of Burke'	Publication of G.K. Chesterton's *Orthodoxy*	Reaganomics and Thatcherism define neoliberal agenda in USA and Europe

Critics tend to see conservatism's veneration for the past as unhealthy nostalgia, reflecting cynicism about how things stand in the present and pessimism about the prospects of improvement. Tradition, English writer G.K. Chesterton noted, is the 'democracy of the dead', which involves 'giving votes to the most obscure of all classes, our ancestors'; but enfranchising those unfortunate enough to be 'disqualified by the accident of death' surely suggests little confidence in the judgement of the living. Conservatism's supposedly dim view of human nature was, as it seemed to Victorian commentators, one of the principal characteristics that distinguished it from liberalism.

Liberalism's essentially optimistic view of human potential meant that its proponents were typically socially progressive and enthusiastic about social reform and improvement. The instinct of conservatism, in contrast, was to see people as essentially weak and selfish, and for this reason the principal object of a well-run society was to maintain order and stability. The contrast was neatly captured by Victorian Britain's greatest liberal prime minister, William Gladstone: 'Liberalism is trust of the people tempered by prudence. Conservatism is distrust of the people tempered by fear.'

The politics of reaction

If the core of conservatism is a disposition to preserve, it is inevitable that its precise nature evolves with its perception of which aspects of the established order are most under threat. For this reason the range of ideas and policies associated with conservatism has been enormously varied over time. For much of the 19th century, successive waves of liberal reform and social disruption caused by the processes of industrialization provided the greatest provocations to conservatives. Some of these issues, such as universal suffrage, carried on over into the 20th century, but increasingly conservative energies became focused on resisting the perceived threat of socialism and communism. The strongly neoliberal agenda of the Reagan–Thatcher era of the 1980s, in which the priorities were free markets, deregulation and minimizing the size of the state, was in many respects a classic conservative response to the lavish and costly welfare policies that had gone before. In the same way, the apparently odd coupling of Reaganomics (economically very hands-off) with extreme social conservatism (morally very hands-on) was a typical reaction to the youth counterculture that took hold in the 1960s.

❝Genius of Burke! . . .
. . . he forewarns, denounces, launches forth,
Against all systems built on abstract rights,
Keen ridicule; the majesty proclaims
Of Institutes and Laws, hallowed by time;
Declares the vital power of social ties
Endeared by Custom . . . ❞

William Wordsworth, *The Prelude*, 1832/1850

The standard of a statesman To a true conservative, the scepticism imputed by such critics – scepticism about the extent of our current knowledge and, in particular, about the capacity of present-day politicians to know the true consequences of their policies – looks both judicious and well founded. The conservative nature is deeply suspicious of the airy schemes of political planners and visionaries – the utopias, panaceas and 'floating fancies' (Burke's phrase) that are shown by bitter experience to turn dreams of social progress and improvement into nightmares of regression or repression.

In any case, the conservative would argue, the critic's picture of a hidebound reactionary, fossilized in an idealized past and unwilling to wake up to present realities, is little more than a caricature. The criticism made by the Victorian moralist Matthew Arnold – that 'the principle of Conservatism . . . destroys what it loves, because it will not mend it' – is unjust because the true spirit of conservatism goes far beyond an arid antiquarianism. Understanding that the secret of preservation is not stagnation, the conservative has a subtle attitude to change. 'There is something else than the mere alternative of absolute destruction or unreformed existence,' Burke observed. 'A disposition to preserve and an ability to improve, taken together, would be my standard of a statesman.' Everything else is vulgar in the conception, perilous in the execution.'

the condensed idea
A disposition to preserve

16 Liberalism

For complex historical reasons, the use of the word 'liberal' has come to have very different connotations on different sides of the Atlantic. In Europe, the word is generally a term of praise, applied to politicians who, typically, are socially progressive and concerned to protect civil liberties. In the USA, by contrast, the term is much more politically loaded and is often used as term of political abuse.

In fact, it would be truer to say that in the USA the term 'liberal' is used with both positive and negative connotations. In a speech given in 1960, Democrat presidential nominee John F. Kennedy explained the distinction precisely. When the Democrats' opponents applied the label 'liberal', they wished to suggest someone 'who is soft in his policies abroad, who is against local government, and who is unconcerned with the taxpayer's dollar'. Kennedy, however, was proud to say that he was a liberal, because in the mouth of a Democrat it meant 'someone who looks ahead and not behind, someone who welcomes new ideas without rigid reactions, someone who cares about the welfare of the people . . .'; in other words, someone who is progressive and cares about civil liberties – a liberal precisely in the European sense. So how was enlightened European liberal transformed into the bogeyman of the US conservative right: the tax-and-spend, 'bleeding-heart' liberal?

Classical liberalism While it may have given rise to highly contrasting responses, liberalism, as a modern political doctrine, has consistently focused on a single, if complex, idea: defence of the liberty and liberties of the individual against abuses of power, premised on a view of individuals as rational, autonomous agents, each of equal value and hence worthy of equal consideration.

timeline

1690	1775–83	1776	1789–99
John Locke's *Two Treatises of Government* published	American Revolution fought for 'Life, liberty and the pursuit of happiness'	Adam Smith's *The Wealth of Nations* argues the case for free trade	French Revolution fought for 'liberty, equality, fraternity'

The origins of such an outlook are usually traced to the works of the English philosophers Thomas Hobbes and John Locke. Shocked by the social turmoil and human suffering caused by decades of religious conflict in the first half of the 17th century, first Hobbes, then Locke, began to speculate on the basis and justification of government. Both agreed that the sovereign's power was justified only by the consent of the governed, and Locke argued that it was the function of the state to safeguard the natural rights and property of its citizens. Locke's *Two Treatises of Government* (1690) provided much of the theoretical inspiration for the two great transformative upheavals of the following century, the American and French revolutions; and it was largely in the course of these seismic events that the individual was finally liberated, following centuries of subservience to king and priest, from the grip of ancient custom and authority.

Locke's doubts about the state's ability to use its powers responsibly suggested that the scope of government should be strictly defined by constitutional limits agreed by the people. This insight in the political sphere was mirrored, in the economic sphere, in the work of the Scottish economist Adam Smith. In *The Wealth of Nations* (1776) Smith argued that the common good of the state would best be assured by allowing individuals to pursue their own interests in a free market, since by doing so they would necessarily serve the interests of others at the same time. The doctrine of laissez-faire, requiring that the state's involvement in the operation of markets be kept to a minimum, thus provided the economic counterpart of Locke's view and established the firm association of classical liberalism with free-market economics.

Neo, not new

In an interview published in 1975 US president Ronald Reagan signalled the conservative right's successful pilfering of classical liberalism's traditional trappings. The definition Reagan gives – 'a desire for less government interference or less centralized authority or more individual freedom' – looks like a textbook summary of classical liberalism, but in his view it is the 'basis of conservatism'. The adoption of common means, though never common ends, by (neoliberal) conservatism and (classical) liberalism has fuelled much political rhetoric and wrangling between left and right.

1859	1933	1979–80
John Stuart Mill's *On Liberty* published	Franklin D. Roosevelt launches New Deal to counter effects of Great Depression	Elections of Margaret Thatcher (1979) and of Ronald Reagan (1980) bring New Right 'neoliberal' policies to Britain and the USA

Against bigotry and dogma

Since its inception, liberalism's conjoined twin has been tolerance. Probably the most influential argument for the latter was made by John Stuart Mill, who based his case on human diversity, which he regarded as inherently valuable, and on respect for human autonomy – the capacity that allows individuals to make their own choices in life. In his essay *On Liberty* (1859), he argues that a person's 'own mode of laying out his existence is the best, not because it is the best in itself, but because it is his own mode'. A necessary adjunct to toleration of the views of others is rational flexibility with respect to one's own, as Bertrand Russell noted in an essay published in 1950: 'The essence of the liberal outlook lies not in *what* opinions are held, but in *how* they are held: instead of being held dogmatically, they are held tentatively, and with a consciousness that new evidence may at any moment lead to their abandonment.'

The liberal outlook, being essentially progressive, is most naturally opposed to a conservative world-view. It was not until the beginning of the 19th century that the name 'liberal' was first used of those who were characteristically open to new ideas and proposals for reform, first in matters of religion, then in politics. It was also in the 19th century that a full elaboration of classical liberalism was achieved, when the utilitarian philosophers Jeremy Bentham and John Stuart Mill applied the lessons of Smith's free-market economics more broadly to the political domain. They advocated representative democracy as the surest means of aligning the interests of government and governed and developed an elaborate system of individual rights that still lies at the core of modern liberal thinking.

Private power and the big state Historically, a common criticism of liberalism has been that its concern with limiting public power has sometimes made it blind to the effects of private power. In the course of the 19th century liberally minded policy-makers had played a significant role in transforming the political and economic climate of Europe; limited and constitutional government was now the norm and industrialization and free trade were generating enormous wealth. However, as both Smith and Mill had foreseen, free enterprise and capitalism, entirely unregulated, had the potential to generate great inequalities in the distribution of wealth, and by the end of the 19th century it had become clear that ordinary working people were being impoverished by an industrial and financial elite that exercised vast economic and political power.

The realization that laissez-faire policies could themselves produce such inequalities and thus undermine basic civil liberties brought about a dramatic U-turn in liberal thinking. The central aim of protecting the rights and autonomy of the individual, far from requiring the scope of government to be limited, seemed to demand a robust interventionism, in which the power of the state was expanded and harnessed to correct the injustices caused by unfettered capitalism. A generation of 'new' ('social' or 'welfare') liberals emerged who set out to correct social inequalities by regulating industry and introducing a range of economic and fiscal reforms. So it was that, while the end of liberalism remained the same, its choice of means was completely transformed.

Stagflation and the New Right

Among the most notable achievements of new liberal thinking was the sweeping welfare and social security initiatives introduced by US president Franklin D. Roosevelt's New Deal in the 1930s. Liberalism's new interventionist approach continued to flourish in the decades of unprecedented growth and prosperity that followed the Second World War. From the 1970s, however, economic stagnation, leading to high inflation and growing national debt, shattered confidence in continued progress.

Individualism and equality

The corollary to liberalism's commitment to one pillar of Enlightenment thinking – the sanctity of the individual – is a consistent devotion to another, the principle of equality. The first US president, George Washington, implies as much in a letter written in 1790: 'As mankind become more liberal, they will be more apt to allow that all those who conduct themselves as worthy members of the community are equally entitled to the protections of civil government.'

Such economic turmoil, casting a deep shadow over the liberal left's welfare and big-state policies, swept the 'New Right' to power in both the USA and Britain; and the leading disciples of what was confusingly known as 'neoliberalism', Ronald Reagan and Margaret Thatcher, eagerly embraced (in theory if not always in practice) the central dogmas of classical liberalism: contraction of the state and free trade. In the bitter political wrangling that ensued, New Right rhetoric mercilessly parodied liberalism as helter-skelter, tax-and-spend, politically correct gobbledygook, thus perpetuating the caricature that Kennedy had previously found so objectionable.

the condensed idea
In defence of the individual

17 Socialism

In the course of the last two centuries a bewildering array of widely divergent socialist ideas and programmes have been dreamt up: from the idealistic plans of the early utopian socialists; through the revolutionary schemes of Marx and Engels; to the more moderate proposals of social democrats. While many of these schemes remain dreams only, a few have come to transformative life: some bringing great advances in social justice and equality, others blighting lives and whole societies.

There have been many incarnations of socialism but its core values and basic aims have remained remarkably consistent. Socialists of all kinds are united in their determination to oppose the many perceived injustices brought about by capitalism. They seek to create a more just society by countering capitalism's tendency to concentrate wealth and power in the hands of the minority who win out in the dog-eat-dog world of competition and exploitation prescribed by the laws of the market.

The essence of capitalism is that the 'means of production, distribution and exchange' – the factories, mines, railways and other resources needed to produce goods and services – are privately owned and exploited by individuals (or individual firms) to generate wealth for themselves. Accordingly, for most of its history, socialism has held that the surest way to remedy the ills of capitalism is for the state to nationalize these productive resources (take them into public ownership) and to manage them on behalf of all society's members.

Early socialists Although many of the principles of socialism can be traced back much earlier, the first people to be called socialists emerged, mainly in France and Britain, in the 1820s and 1830s. Most of these early social radicals (often called, after Marx, 'utopian socialists') were moved by the savage

timeline

1825	1825	1848	1867–94
Death of Claude-Henri de Saint-Simon, founder of French socialism	Robert Owen's New Harmony settlement established in Indiana, USA	Marx's militant 'scientific socialism' set forth in The Communist Manifesto	Marx gives definitive critique of capitalism in Das Kapital

inequalities caused by industrialization, in which business entrepreneurs and factory owners accumulated fortunes on the backs of working people, who for the most part toiled long hours on pitiful wages in squalid and dangerous conditions. A common theme in many early socialist works is a vision of life as part of a community, in a society infused with a spirit of cooperation and inclusivity.

The founder of French socialism, the aristocrat Claude-Henri de Saint-Simon, while not going so far as to advocate full public ownership of productive resources, proposed that their use be centrally planned and managed by a group of enlightened industrialists, scientists and engineers whose expertise would be used to eradicate poverty and meet the various needs of the community. Another early socialist pioneer, Robert Owen, himself a successful industrialist, had boundless faith in fundamental human decency and was convinced that social harmony would follow if only people were treated humanely and sympathetically. Putting theory into practice, in 1825 he bought a plot of land in the US state of Indiana and organized a settlement named New Harmony, which was based on principles of cooperation and common ownership.

> ❝The inherent vice of capitalism is the unequal sharing of blessings; the inherent virtue of socialism is the equal sharing of miseries.❞
> **Winston Churchill, 1954**

Marx's scientific socialism The most influential critique of capitalism was given by Karl Marx and his lifelong collaborator Friedrich Engels, so it is no surprise that Marx's ideas have provided the principal theoretical basis for later socialist thought. According to his analysis, capitalism is not only unjust but irrational, in the sense that it is *essentially* wasteful and inefficient. He attributes these negative characteristics to the combination of market allocation and private ownership, and thus his solution calls for central economic planning and abolition of private property.

In *The Communist Manifesto* (1848) Marx takes a rather dim view of earlier socialists, largely dismissing them as naive idealists responsible for 'fantastic pictures of future society'. He contrasts their pipe dreams with his own hard-headed 'scientific socialism', which is founded on the notion of class struggle as the driving force behind historical progress. Marx's communism is a militant form of socialism that can be attained only through violent revolution; industrial

1914–18	**1917**	**1927**	**1989**
Socialist loyalties deeply split by First World War	Russian Revolution marks final split of moderate and revolutionary socialism	Stalin established as uncontested leader of the Soviet Union	Collapse of communist regimes in Eastern Europe begins

capitalism, together with the capitalist class (bourgeoisie) who profit from its exploitative returns, will, as a matter of historical necessity, be overthrown in spontaneous uprisings of the working class (proletariat). Government of capitalist oppression will be usurped by a 'dictatorship of the proletariat', but this phase is transitional and will be replaced, at the 'end of history', by full-blown economic and social communism. In this final state, government itself will have withered away and all class distinctions will have been obliterated, leaving people free from necessity and exploitation and at liberty to cultivate their natural gifts.

Ballot or bomb? A troubling matter for Marx's supporters was that his prediction of capitalism's inevitable and bloody demise appeared to be stubbornly falsified by events. In spite of the fact that the bourgeoisie's grip on power showed no signs of weakening, the conditions of working people had generally improved by the end of the 19th century. As the reality of social change without political revolution became increasingly apparent, many moderate socialists began to entertain the idea of evolutionary, rather than revolutionary, socialism – of reforming the state from within, rather than actively overthrowing it. A gulf was opening up between orthodox Marxists, who insisted on the necessity of violent struggle, and revisionists or gradualists, who believed that socialist ideals could be realized progressively and peacefully by constitutional and democratic means.

This growing schism finally became an open breach in the years up to and including the First World War. Hitherto socialism had sought to present itself as

If once you fail . . .

Socialism's opponents have often been quick to accuse its followers of being naive or otherworldly. Whatever truth there is in the charge, it should be acknowledged that related qualities – optimism and indefatigability – are their charm. In this respect, Robert Owen, one of the great pioneers of socialism, is a prime specimen. Reflecting his infinite trust in human nature, New Harmony – his experimental community established in Indiana, USA, in 1825 – was, as his son later recalled, an ill-assorted selection of humankind, 'a heterogeneous collection of radicals, enthusiastic devotees of principle . . . and lazy theorists, with a sprinkling of unprincipled sharpers thrown in'. The settlement's predictable failure after just two years took much of Owen's fortune with it, but his optimism was undiminished and he marched on, undeterred and forever hopeful, to found other experimental communities and to play a leading part in the trade union movement.

an international movement: Marx's call to arms in *The Communist Manifesto* was, after all, an appeal for the working men of the world to unite. Now, suddenly, workers and socialists alike were confronted with a stark choice of whether or not to support their national governments in the war effort – in a war, moreover, of a decidedly capitalist complexion. Most chose country over international socialism – a blow from which the latter never fully recovered.

Irrevocable split The decisive split between moderate and extreme socialists finally came in 1917, when the revolutionary Bolsheviks under Lenin seized power in Russia. Initial hopes that the Russian Revolution would start a wave of socialist revolutions were soon disappointed, as the violence of the communists was repudiated by moderates elsewhere. In the West, even die-hard revolutionary Marxists were moved to despair as the systemic corruption and brutality of Stalin's tyranny, socialist in name only, began to emerge.

The iron curtain that descended over Europe after the Second World War symbolized an equally unbridgeable divide between the socialist-communist regimes of the Soviet bloc and Western democratic socialists (by this time often known as social democrats). The futility of socialist attempts at realizing an egalitarian society by central diktat was summed up by an acerbic joke that was popular among eastern Europeans under communism: 'Under capitalism, man exploits man; under socialism, it's the other way round.' Such was the abuse of the term that, after the collapse of communism from 1989, socialism became, almost literally, the political ideology that dared not speak its name.

In the West social democratic parties, setting out on a non-Marxist route to socialist goals, aimed to mitigate the harsh effects of capitalism through welfare reforms and redistributive taxation. However, in the last quarter of the 20th century they too ran into problems, as their interventionist instincts and welfare policies were threatened by tough economic conditions and the rise of the small-state, laissez-faire neoliberals of the New Right. However, in the first decade of the 21st century a number of intractable problems, including the global 'Credit Crunch' and environmental concerns, served as a reminder that capitalism had problems of its own. Predictions of the death of socialism were looking very premature.

the condensed idea
The struggle for social justice

18 Communism

'The philosophers have only *interpreted* the world in various ways; the point is to *change* it.' In this famous remark, written in 1845, the radical socialist Karl Marx makes it clear that the goal of his work is to move beyond theory to action; his ultimate purpose is practical and revolutionary change.

Just three years later, Marx and his collaborator Friedrich Engels published *The Communist Manifesto*. Although its immediate impact was slight, this slim text – little more than a pamphlet – arguably did more than any other document to change the history of the 20th century.

In the opening words of the *Manifesto*, Marx conjures up the 'spectre of communism' which was haunting the 'powers of old Europe' in the first half of the 19th century. This menacing incubus was an upwelling of extreme socialists, who had mobilized on behalf of working people oppressed and impoverished in a transformation of industrial production that had brought great wealth to their capitalist employers. Their objectives were the violent overthrow of capitalist society and the abolition of private property. In the century after Marx's death in 1883, this spectre rose again in a wave of communist regimes, first in Russia, then in Eastern Europe, China and elsewhere. Bringing to life his ideas – or what passed for his ideas – in the real world, these regimes left a trail of human suffering that tarnished his name. When this 'sad, bizarre chapter in human history' (as Ronald Reagan called it) drew to a close in the years after 1989, Marx's vision of revolutionary struggle culminating in a classless socialist society seemed as bankrupt as the broken-down states that had usurped the name of communism.

Yet in the 21st century – especially in the wake of the global 'Credit Crunch' which exposed the evils of unbridled capitalism – perceptions have shifted. It may be true, as is sometimes suggested, that communism is destined to failure because

timeline

1818	1844	1848	1867–94	1883
Karl Marx born in Trier in the Rhineland	Marx meets lifelong collaborator Friedrich Engels in Paris	*The Communist Manifesto* published on behalf of the Communist League	*Das Kapital* (in three volumes) sets out Marx's theory of the capitalist system	Marx dies in London

it is based on a misunderstanding of human psychology. Still, it is possible, now that the toxic dust of real-world communist regimes has settled, to admire once again the fundamental decency of Marx's vision of a society in which each gives according to his ability and takes according to his need.

Towards the end of history Marx's ideas, intended from the outset both as a political doctrine and as a practical programme for action, are based on a highly distinctive economic theory of historical progress. According to Marx, the first priority for any society is to produce whatever is required to ensure its own survival. Such production can only be achieved with the 'mode of production' characteristic of the age – the combination of raw materials that are available, the tools and techniques that exist to process them, and the various human resources that can be called upon. The underlying structure imposed by these economic factors determines, in turn, the pattern of social organization within the society as a whole, and in particular, the relations between the various social elements, or 'classes'.

At each historical stage, Marx asserts, one class is dominant and controls the current mode of production, exploiting the labour of other classes in order to further its own interests. The various modes characteristic of past and present ages are, however, always unstable. Inherent 'contradictions' in the relations between the various social elements lead inevitably to tensions and upheavals, and eventually to conflict and revolution in which the dominant class is overthrown and replaced.

The mode of production in Marx's own day was industrial capitalism. This he believed to be a necessary stage of economic development, which in displacing feudalism had

The opium of the people

Karl Marx, a well-known atheist, believed that religion was a sop to the masses: a conservative force that the capitalist class exploited to keep the workers enslaved. It acted, in his view, like a painkiller – an opiate – that stupefied people and resigned them to their wretched conditions as part of God's plan. 'Religion is the sigh of the oppressed creature,' he wrote plaintively in 1843, 'the feelings of a heartless world, just as it is the spirit of unspiritual conditions. It is the opium of the people.'

1917	1927	1949	1991
Lenin begins to lay the theoretical foundation of Marxism–Leninism	Stalin becomes uncontested leader of the Soviet Union	Mao oversees foundation of People's Republic of China	Soviet Union collapses

brought a massive increase in productive output. However, the bourgeoisie, the dominant class under capitalism, had used their economic power to generate vast wealth for themselves by buying and selling commodities at a profit that was due to the labour of the working class (the proletariat). Such exploitation, Marx claimed, would necessarily escalate and bring about ever greater impoverishment of the proletariat. Eventually a crisis would occur when the working class, realizing that the gap between their own interests and those of the bourgeoisie was unbridgeable, would rise up, overthrow their oppressors, take control of the means of production, and abolish private property. To defend their interests against a bourgeois counter-revolution, they would establish 'a dictatorship of the proletariat'. This would be a transitional state, however, whose power would gradually 'wither away', to be replaced – at the 'end of history' – by fully realized communism: a stable, classless society in which there is true freedom for all.

Nothing to lose but their chains

Recognized now as one of the most momentous documents ever published, *The Communist Manifesto* made surprisingly little impact on its first appearance. A short tract of fewer than 12,000 words, written in collaboration with Friedrich Engels and published in 1848, it was originally intended as a platform for the largely ineffective, quarrelsome and short-lived Communist League. In the Manifesto's closing lines, Marx gives perhaps the most resounding and portentous rallying cry ever delivered:

> The Communists disdain to conceal their views and aims. They openly declare that their ends can be attained only by the forcible overthrow of all existing social conditions. Let the ruling classes tremble at a Communistic revolution. The proletarians have nothing to lose but their chains. They have a world to win.
>
> WORKING MEN OF ALL COUNTRIES, UNITE!

Lenin and the vanguard

Marx well understood the psychology of dominance and oppression. 'The ruling ideas of every epoch', he wrote in 1845, 'are the ideas of the ruling class': the prevailing 'ideology' – the system or scheme of ideas expressed in the media, in education etc. – always reflects the views of the dominant class, determining orthodox opinion, defending the status quo, and so serving to justify unequal relations of economic and political power.

In *What Is to Be Done?*, published in 1902, Vladimir Ilich Ulyanov – better known as Lenin, future leader of the Bolshevik Revolution in Russia – accepts Marx's analysis of ideology. He thinks, however, that Marx has not properly understood its implications in the motivation towards revolution. Marx's assumption had been that the workers would rise up spontaneously to overthrow their oppressors, but Lenin feared that the dominant ideology would induce a 'false consciousness' (Engels's phrase) that would blind them to their own interests and induce them in effect to connive in their own oppression. His concern seemed particularly plausible in the case of Russia, which was a desperately poor country that had progressed little beyond agrarian feudalism; it had barely entered the stage of industrial capitalism (as required by orthodox Marxism) and was very far from having developed an enlightened revolutionary proletariat. What was needed, in Lenin's view, was a vanguard party of professional revolutionaries – an elite group of radicalized intellectuals like himself – who would lead the workers to revolution and guide them in setting up a temporary dictatorship of the proletariat.

> **The history of all hitherto existing society is the history of class struggles.**
>
> **Karl Marx,** *The Communist Manifesto,* **1848**

Many of the problems for communism in its various 20th-century incarnations can be traced back to the fundamental loss of faith in the people that was reflected in Lenin's development of the vanguard theory and what became known as Marxism–Leninism. All communist regimes claimed to be democratic, but more or less implicit in this claim was the belief that the people were not yet ready or able to govern themselves. For this reason, real-world communist states became fossilized in what was supposed to be a transitional phase: political power remained concentrated in the vanguard, and the dictatorship was not of the proletariat but of the increasingly centralized communist party.

'The worst advertisement for socialism', wrote George Orwell in 1937, 'is its adherents.' And so it proved, to a tragic degree, in the world's experience of socialist/communist states in the 20th century. Here, if anywhere, the more things changed, the more they stayed the same. Capitalist class structures were replaced by rigid hierarchies, in which a new political class governed in its own interests. Command economies lumbered along inefficiently under the corrupt direction of huge and unaccountable central bureaucracies, producing not surpluses but bread queues and price riots. In almost every case, the classless paradise promised by Marx quickly degenerated into dystopian nightmare.

the condensed idea
Marx's unquiet spectre

19 Social democracy

The three pillars on which Marx's vision of an ideal future society is founded – collective solidarity over individualism, freedom over exploitation, and equality for all over sectional interest – have remained firmly at the core of socialist thinking. How these ends are to be attained, however, has been bitterly contested, producing deep rifts within socialism.

Marx himself insisted that the transition from capitalism to socialism could be brought about only by violent revolution of the working people, who would eventually, and inevitably, rise up and overthrow their capitalist oppressors, whereupon they would abolish private property and seize control of the means of production. While revolutionary Marxism long remained the orthodox socialist position, from early on it coexisted, with growing unease, alongside a less explosive view of how the shared ideals of socialism could be realized. Over time, a schism developed between orthodox Marxists and those who thought that a socialist society could come about otherwise than by revolution. The latter, subsequently known as social democrats, henceforth followed a peaceful, constitutional path to socialism that was necessarily at odds with the course of their revolutionary cousins.

Origins The evolutionary, non-revolutionary route to socialism has its origins as a political movement in doctrinal disputes that came to the fore in the fledgling Social Democratic Party of Germany (*Sozialdemokratische Partei Deutschlands*, or SPD), which formed from an already querulous alliance of existing socialist organizations in 1875. Foremost among the so-called revisionists, who favoured a more gradual, peaceful transition to socialism, was the German political theorist and activist Eduard Bernstein. Noting that the conditions of

timeline

1848	1875	1884	1899	1904
Marx's *Communist Manifesto* proclaims the core values of socialism	Formation of German Social Democratic Party (SPD)	Foundation of the British Fabian Society	Eduard Bernstein's *Evolutionary Socialism* argues for non-revolutionary change	Rosa Luxemburg attacks revisionists in *Reform or Revolution?*

working people, far from deteriorating, were generally improving, particularly through pressure exerted by recently formed trade unions, he began to question the inevitability, indeed the desirability, of the crisis of capitalism that Marx predicted and on which his revolutionary thesis depended. In a book known in English as *Evolutionary Socialism* (1899), he argued that the triumph of socialism would follow, not from some hypothetical cataclysm of class struggle, but from its success in alleviating the misery of the poor. In his view, the overturning of capitalism was no more than a means to certain socialist ends, the most important of which was winning justice for the disadvantaged in society; and the surest way of achieving these ends was to work within existing political structures and processes – not to overthrow and start from scratch, but to adapt and reform. In time, he believed, the extension of universal suffrage would allow workers to vote in socialist parties with a mandate to realize socialist objectives.

> **❛Free development of each is the condition for the free development of all.❜**
>
> **Karl Marx,** *The Communist Manifesto,* 1848

The efforts of Bernstein and fellow revisionists to advance socialism within a democratic context, trusting in electoral and parliamentary means, predictably provoked a furious reaction from orthodox, revolutionary socialists. The German revolutionary Rosa Luxemburg, for one, bitterly attacked the democratic approach in 1904, dismissing parliamentary politics as a 'historically determined form of the class rule of the bourgeoisie'. Deep differences in outlook, exacerbated by the First World War and cemented in place by the Bolshevik Revolution in Russia in 1917, took institutional form as communist (revolutionary socialist) parties sprang up all over Europe in opposition to diverse socialist (social democratic) groups united in their commitment to constitutional means.

The Swedish model Shortly before and after the Second World War a form of social democracy was established in Sweden that was to prove lastingly influential elsewhere. Enjoying a strong popular mandate and an almost unbroken hold on power between 1932 and 1976, the Swedish Social Democratic Workers' Party (SAP) set about realizing its promise to create a *folkhemmet* ('people's home'), the central feature of which was a 'cradle-to-grave' welfare system that would offer a place of security for all the country's citizens. Within a few decades

1917	**1932**	**1932**	**1989–91**	**1997**
Russian Revolution becomes symbol of Marxist revolutionary strategy	Swedish Social Democratic Party elected on pledge to create a 'people's home'	British Labour Party lays foundations of welfare state	Collapse of communist Eastern Europe and the Soviet Union	New Labour under Tony Blair embark on the Third Way

The Fabians

The revolutionary Marxist tradition never put down deep roots in Britain, where the preference of (largely) middle-class intellectuals for pragmatism and steady progress was marked by the foundation in 1884 of the Fabian Society. The Fabians' non-revolutionary gradualism was reflected in their name, derived from the Roman general Quintus Fabius Maximus, whose cautious delaying tactics against Hannibal in the Punic Wars earned him the nickname 'Cunctator' ('delayer'). The Fabians' brand of 'ethical' socialism adopted a middle course between utopian and revolutionary positions. Preferring indirect influence to activism, the society had a leading role in laying the theoretical foundations of the Labour Representation Committee (1900), which was renamed the Labour Party six years later. In spite of their relatively genteel origins, the Fabians were consistently progressive, being among the first to lobby for minimum wages, universal healthcare and a national system of education.

Swedish society had been transformed by a succession of bold measures, including unemployment insurance, family and housing allowances, health services, pension schemes, and an expanded and inclusive educational system.

Underpinning the SAP's social programme was a fresh approach to economics that was no less influential. Setting aside the central Marxist dogma of nationalization, the Swedish social democrats introduced a 'mixed economy' in which business and industry were left largely in private ownership but were subject to substantial government direction. Such regulation included a range of measures to counter economic fluctuations – first used to good effect during the Great Depression of the 1930s – such as job creation, investment in public works and services, and promotion of labour mobility. The cornerstones of Swedish social democracy were equality of wealth and income through redistributive taxation; pursuit of full employment through economic growth; provision of universal welfare; and promotion of workers' interests through collaboration with strong trade unions. Guided by these principles, the SAP was unprecedentedly successful in eradicating poverty and fostering strong social cohesion in Sweden.

Unsurprisingly, the Swedish example proved inspirational to social democratic parties in other countries. Not all such parties were so quick to jettison classical socialist dogma: the British Labour Party, for instance, elected to power in 1945, introduced a national healthcare system while also taking control of major industries and public utilities. Generally, however, the policy focus of postwar social democrats was effective intervention to mitigate the inequalities of wealth and power caused by capitalism, not abolition of capitalism as such. Over time, public ownership of the means by which prosperity was generated became less important than ensuring that certain social groups were not excluded from the benefits (such as healthcare and education) that such prosperity could provide.

Decline and the Third Way After decades of plenty that saw postwar social democratic governments lay the foundations of modern social-welfare programmes across Europe, a number of factors conspired to bring a change in fortunes. The challenge for progressive social democrats had always been to maintain a politically sustainable balance between income from taxation and investment in public services. For Sweden and Britain, among others, that balance went seriously awry in the 1970s and 1980s, as public borrowing spiralled out of control, traditional heavy industries went into decline, and delicate relationships between governments and trade unions became strained to breaking point. During this same period, in geopolitical terms, the end of the Cold War and the collapse of communism not only brought discredit on social democracy by association but also jeopardized its customary occupancy of the middle ground between Soviet communism and American individualism.

Even more menacing in the longer term, the forces of globalization, allowing rapid movement of capital and labour across borders, began to expose uncompetitive practices and to deprive national governments of the kind of control over their own economic destinies on which social democratic interventionism depended. In an online world populated by vast multinational corporations, the ambitions of social democrats looked increasingly obsolete. Faced with this danger, many social democrats began to contemplate a 'Third Way' – essentially a centre-left position, in which a sympathetic brand of capitalism would be allied to the socialist commitment to equality and welfare. In 1997 British New Labour under Tony Blair was elected in a landslide as pioneer and champion of the Third Way. But critics remained unconvinced, believing that the true price of salvaging social democracy – if indeed it had been saved at all – was the death of socialism.

the condensed idea
Evolution over revolution

20 Multiculturalism

Human beings have never been static. Over thousands of years, innumerable groups, ranging from single families to whole populations, have moved permanently from one area to another. In many cases, such movements are more or less involuntary: people may be forcibly uprooted and taken as slaves or prisoners, or compelled to flee the ravages of war or natural disaster. Other such migrations are undertaken freely, usually in search of living conditions that are more secure or offer greater economic opportunities.

Depending on the cause of their moving, migrants may or may not bring their physical belongings, but they always take with them their mental possessions: the language, culture, customs and history they shared with those they left behind. What becomes of this cultural baggage when they arrive in their new home depends, again, on why they moved in the first place. While slaves, by definition, are excluded from participating as equals in the societies into which they are introduced, voluntary migrants, by contrast, may interact with the host culture in a number of ways. At one extreme, they may attempt to assimilate themselves fully into the new culture, suppressing their native customs and taking on those of their hosts. At the other, they may live alongside or among their hosts, retaining much of their native custom and interacting with their new neighbours within the limits prescribed by their culture.

For most of human history, incoming groups have generally been expected, and sometimes obliged, to assimilate themselves, or 'blend in', with the dominant host culture. More recently, however, the view that cultural diversity is something to be cherished and celebrated, not suppressed and feared, has become widespread,

timeline

1820s	1908	1915
Beginning of great migration of Europeans to North America	Israel Zangwill's *The Melting Pot* plays in Washington DC	Horace Kallen's *Democracy Versus the Melting Pot* published

especially in Western liberal democracies. It is this attitude that informs the approach to cultural interaction known as multiculturalism.

The melting pot From the early 1800s, the biggest ever experiment in cultural integration got underway, as wave after wave of Europeans made their way across the Atlantic to start a new life in North America. In the century and a half between 1830 and 1980, over 35 million Europeans settled in the United States, at first mainly from Ireland and Germany, then increasingly from southern and eastern Europe. On arrival, the various incoming ethnic groups were generally left in little doubt about what was expected of them. They were to fulfil the promise proudly borne on the Seal of the United States – *e pluribus unum* ('out of many [comes] one'): they were to undergo a process of integration – 'Americanization' – in which their diverse customs and identities would be absorbed into the dominant American culture.

In search of social glue

With ever greater intensity in the wake of the Islamist attacks in the USA and Europe since 11 September 2001, critics of multiculturalism have focused on the issue of divided loyalties. Surveys have shown that the great majority of black and Asian people living in Britain – some immigrant, others born in the country – think of themselves as British; and as a matter of empirical fact, a wide variety of groups of different ethnic origins can and do live together in peace and as functional communities while retaining many of their native ways and customs. Yet there clearly has to be *some* common ground. With a plurality of groups comes a plurality of loyalties, and such loyalties are always divided to some degree. What happens when such allegiances pull in different directions? At what point does such division become incompatible with common citizenship? What amount of common culture, identity or history is sufficient to provide the 'glue' that holds a multicultural society together? Liberals may find such questions hard to ask, let alone answer, but robust answers are needed to ensure that enemies of pluralism are unable to exploit popular anxieties to open up social divisions.

1957	11 September 2001	2004
Earliest attested use of the term 'multiculturalism'	Islamist terrorists launch attacks against USA	Law on conspicuous religious symbols in schools passed in France

Vive la différence?

The assimilationist model of cultural integration has been most exhaustively elaborated in France, where the ideal of universal citizenship has been taken to imply that ethnic (and other) differences should be suppressed, at least in the public domain. Government action in pursuance of this view has provoked much heated debate – a controversy that has been stoked by the rhetoric of the political right, which habitually invites immigrants 'to love France or leave it'. President Nicolas Sarkozy has been notably unguarded in some of his comments. In 2006, a year before he was elected to the presidency, he showed little fondness for a conciliatory tone: 'When you live in France, you respect the rules. You don't have lots of wives, you don't circumcise your daughters, and you don't use your bath to slaughter sheep in.'

The meeting of different cultures is never a simple process, however: neither side remains unaffected, and the product is something new, distinct from the original ingredients. A recognition of this complexity was shown in the image popularly used in the US to describe the process of assimilation: a melting pot. The phrase was taken from the title of a hit play written in 1908 by the Jewish writer Israel Zangwill. The hero of the play, a Jewish immigrant who has survived a pogrom in his native Russia exclaims: 'Understand that America is God's Crucible, the great Melting Pot where all the races of Europe are melting and re-forming! . . . God is making the American.' Historically, assimilation has not always been a benign process – often it has been used to dominate subject peoples, by severing ancient ties and loyalties. In the American context, however, it was generally welcomed on both sides, in a spirit of hope and optimism.

Modern theoretical justifications of assimilation are often based on broadly liberal principles and on a particular understanding of equality as sameness. Social justice, it is argued, demands that everyone enjoys the same rights and opportunities. No discrimination on the basis of ethnic origin or culture, therefore, should be allowed, and the means by which rights are conferred and protected – citizenship – should be the same for all. In recent times, the case for assimilation has been most vigorously defended in republican, secularist France, where the debate has become most heated with respect to the wearing of religious symbols (notably the Islamic headscarf, or *hijab*) in schools.

The salad bowl At roughly the same time that Zangwill was singing the praises of the melting pot, a radically different approach to the issue of cultural diversity was being articulated by an immigrant US university lecturer and philosopher, Horace Kallen. He argued that an America in which ethnic, cultural and religious diversity was retained and celebrated would thereby be both enriched and strengthened. Initially a minority view, what Kallen called 'cultural pluralism' gathered support as the century wore on, and by the 1960s his approach – by that time often known as multiculturalism – had become the mainstream position, at least among US intellectuals. Accordingly, the popular image of the melting pot was increasingly displaced by other metaphors, such as a mosaic or (humorously) a salad bowl, in which the overall effect is achieved by parts or ingredients that retain their original character or flavour.

Like assimilation, multiculturalism is generally defended on liberal grounds. Firmly rejecting the assimilationist view of equality as sameness, advocates insist that a plurality of different ways of life should be tolerated or even encouraged, provided they do not adversely interfere with the lives led by others. Much of the theoretical underpinning of this view is drawn from the so-called 'identity politics' that have transformed other areas of political activism. Just as gays and feminists, for instance, no longer see equality with (respectively) heterosexuals and men as the criterion of success, in a similar way ethnic minorities, including immigrants, now demand that their native cultures and values are given equal recognition and allowed to express themselves in their own right and in their own terms.

Critics of multiculturalism commonly raise doubts over the liberal host society's supposed role as a neutral medium or matrix into which alien mores can be seamlessly embedded. At the most basic level, the coherence of this role is questioned, since the priority that liberal democracies give to neutrality is itself normative or morally prescriptive and thus bound to lead, not to the creation of a neutral public space in which minorities can express their cultural differences, but to a systematic neutering of minority cultures. Also, if multiculturalism implies a level of cultural relativism that precludes judgement of minority practices, the liberal host may find itself called upon to protect a range of customs, illiberal by its own lights, such as forced marriage and female genital mutilation. At the very least, the host will be required to show a degree of toleration that some of the newcomers would not wish to reciprocate. Apart from being morally questionable, such asymmetries, it is suggested, are bound to generate tensions between the elements that make up a modern multicultural society.

the condensed idea
Dealing with cultural diversity

21 Labour movement

'The labour movement was the principal force that transformed misery and despair into hope and progress. Out of its bold struggles, economic and social reform gave birth to unemployment insurance, old age pensions, government relief for the destitute, and above all new wage levels that meant not mere survival, but a tolerable life. The captains of industry did not lead this transformation; they resisted it until they were overcome.'

In a speech delivered in 1965, civil rights activist Martin Luther King Jr acknowledges the vital contribution of the labour movement in transforming the lives of ordinary working people. He has in mind the benefits brought to those who had struggled to make a living in the 1930s, in the desperate days of the Great Depression. However, his words are equally true of the efforts of other leaders who had championed the cause of working people over the preceding hundred years.

King focuses on one of the key facets of the labour movement: trade unionism. In this aspect, the movement's aim is to win improvements in matters such as pay and working conditions by means of collective action. But – as King also indicates – gains made in these areas were typically won in the teeth of fierce opposition from employers. The fight for recognition of workers' rights – most importantly, the right to unionize – dominated the early stages of the labour movement, and in some countries (notably Britain) the issue of basic rights shifted the focus beyond economics firmly into the realm of politics.

timeline

1848	1906	1917	1919
Marx's *Communist Manifesto* calls on the workers of the world to unite	Foundation of the British Labour Party	Revolution allows Russian unions freedom to organize	Comintern established to encourage global socialist revolution

The struggle for recognition The labour movement remains a somewhat nebulous concept, partly because it has always meant different things to different people. From early on, the struggles of ordinary working people acting collectively to improve their lot had a strong, even romantic appeal to radicals and revolutionaries, so the labour movement was subjected to much theoretical analysis and intellectualization. Most influentially, Marx's analysis of history as class struggle presents the working class (proletariat) as an idealized category – a homogenized group capable of concerted action against the capitalist class (bourgeoisie). Prior to, and then alongside, this process of abstraction, there were many actual labour movements: the innumerable actions of real people acting in groups to promote and protect their interests in the labour market and in the workplace. It is in the explosion of such initiatives in the first half of the 19th century, first in Britain and then in Europe and the USA, that the origins of the modern labour movement are usually found. Typically, such initiatives were extremely variable from place to place, while the groups responsible were often ad hoc and short-lived.

Embryonic union activity of this kind was a direct response to the new and often harsh world forged in the furnace of industrial capitalism. Collective bargaining, in which workers would appoint representatives to negotiate pay and other terms of employment, offered some defence against the exploitation of labour that was endemic in a system of largely unregulated industry and commerce. Predictably, employers who felt that their own interests were threatened by this new assertiveness fought

1906: annus mirabilis

In the history of the British labour movement, 1906 proved to be a pivotal year. Decades of political activism to win proper recognition of workers' rights culminated in that year in the foundation of the Labour Party, which first came to power in 1924 and would henceforth be the political vehicle of working-class aspirations. Also in 1906, the Trade Disputes Act gave British unions immunity to prosecution in the civil courts and protected their funds against claims for damages. This principle of legal abstention informed the conduct of British labour relations for more than half a century, until it was progressively undermined following the 1971 Industrial Relations Act. In popular memory, the most devastating blow to the British labour movement was delivered in 1984–5, when the Conservative government of Margaret Thatcher faced down the National Union of Miners in a bitter, protracted and socially divisive strike.

1936	1971	1984–5
Labour movement opposes fascism in Spain	British Industrial Relations Act proscribes unfair industrial practices	British National Union of Miners crushed by Thatcher's government

back, either taking matters into their own hands, or attempting (often successfully) to put legal barriers in the path of labour activism. In Britain, the most basic workers' right – the right to organize – remained a central issue throughout the 19th century, and was only satisfactorily resolved in the first decade of the 20th.

Towards a new world order An important legacy of the intellectualization of the labour movement was its lasting but ambivalent commitment to internationalism. The rallying cry of Marx's *Communist Manifesto*, calling on the working men of the world to unite, does not admit national distinctions, and the inevitable overthrow of the capitalist system, unconfined by borders, is assumed to lead to the establishment of a new socialist world order. In keeping with this vision, in 1919, within two years of the Russian Revolution, Soviet leader Lenin established the Communist International (Comintern), or Third International. The claimed purpose of this organization was to foment socialist revolution around the world, by spreading communist doctrine and coordinating opposition to bourgeois imperialism; and many revolutionary communist groups, seeing themselves as part of an international labour movement, accepted its leadership.

> **❝The strongest bond of human sympathy, outside of the family relation, should be one uniting all working people of all nations and tongues and kindreds.❞**
>
> **Abraham Lincoln, 1864**

The high point of the Comintern's international strategy came in the Spanish Civil War (1936–9), when the International Brigades, initially coordinated from Moscow and recruited largely from the ranks of communists and trade unionists, saw liberation of Spain from fascism as a duty of (in Stalin's words) 'progressive humanity'. But this show of solidarity was exceptional. Socialist and labour parties committed to change by reform from within, not by revolution, generally showed little enthusiasm for the Comintern and its internationalist ambitions. In practice, national labour movements intent on gaining rights and improved conditions for working people were usually obliged to focus their energies primarily on domestic politics and domestic issues. In any case, by the late 1920s it had become apparent that the main function of the Comintern, with Stalin pulling the strings, was to serve narrowly Soviet policy initiatives overseas.

From plenty to hardship The golden age of trade unionism, and of the labour movement generally, was the first three decades after the Second World War. The election of left-leaning, social democratic parties in many countries marked the beginning of unprecedented cooperation between government and labour, as capitalism mitigated by redistributive taxation and high social spending brought a transformation in welfare and living conditions. Mass-production methods became ubiquitous, giving extra bargaining power to large-scale general unions and contributing to sustained economic prosperity that brought higher wages, better working conditions and all manner of consumer goods to generations of newly affluent workers.

The bubble burst as massive and irreversible changes transformed the world order, economically and politically. Most significantly, in the last quarter of the 20th century, the forces of globalization brought mobility of capital and labour that made socialist goals such as full employment and cradle-to-grave welfare provision look unattainable. In the so-called post-industrial age, the growing realization of a global single market made the quest for international competitiveness paramount. As traditional heavy industries were squeezed by the inexorable growth of the service sector, old-style trade unionism was portrayed as rigid, archaic and out of touch. In a world where the buzzword was flexibility and cheap labour was readily available, unions found themselves increasingly marginalized and fragmented; where they were not frozen out completely, their bargaining power was much reduced, and concerted and centralized action all but impossible. Ideologically, too, the ground had shifted, as neoliberal theory demanded deregulation and the free play of market forces.

In the first decade of the 21st century, the labour movement looked more vulnerable than it had been for a century: union membership had plummeted; historical ties with political parties had been weakened; the capacity to mobilize resources was much diminished. Could the decline be reversed? In a major irony, what the labour movement needed, in a globalized world, was precisely what it had so signally failed to forge in the past: a system of international ties that would bind disparate national movements and allow them to pursue jointly common interests that they were now too weak to pursue on their own. What was less certain is whether there was still enough common ground to allow the workers of the world to answer the call that Marx had made more than a century and a half earlier.

the condensed idea
Workers in union

22 Feminism

For most of recorded history, women have been very clearly the second sex, their place firmly in the home. It is only in the last 150 years that laws formally stipulating women's subordinate position in Western societies have been removed from the statute books. Until that time, women had limited access to education, were barred from entering most professions, and were unable to vote or stand for elective office. For the most part, married women were considered unfit to conduct business on their own or to own property without restriction. Indeed, in certain respects wives were treated as the property of their husbands.

Feminism – belief in the social, economic and political equality of the sexes – is a relatively recent phenomenon. It is a testimony to the great strides that the feminist movement has made over the last two centuries that, in the West at least, many discriminatory practices that were once blithely taken for granted are now regarded as totally unacceptable. The task of realizing gender equality is still a work in progress, however. Much institutionalized discrimination may have been formally removed, but long-ingrained and often unconscious attitudes are harder to erase. Women still face all sorts of indignity and prejudice, from the 'glass ceiling' and lower pay at work, to unthinking assumptions about capacities and roles at home and in society. No country is free of sexism, and in some parts of the world discrimination on grounds of gender is still explicitly sanctioned by law.

First wave: struggle for the vote During the European Renaissance, there had been a long-running 'debate about women', which was often little more than a literary mock-battle in which the case for women – refutation of the charge that they are innately frivolous and inferior – was argued elegantly but to little effect.

timeline

1792	1869	1894	1918
Mary Wollstonecraft protests against subordination of women	Publication of J.S. Mill's *The Subjection of Women*	Earliest attested use of the term 'feminist' ('feminism' in following year)	Vote granted to British women over 30 (over 21, as for men, after 1928)

> **From the tyranny of man, I firmly believe, the greater number of female follies proceed . . . Let woman share the rights, and she will emulate the virtues of man.**
>
> Mary Wollstonecraft, 1792

In England, the person usually credited with injecting passion and urgency into this hitherto rather sterile debate was Mary Wollstonecraft, mother of Mary Shelley and (according to Horace Walpole) a 'hyena in petticoats'. In *A Vindication of the Rights of Woman* (1792), Wollstonecraft makes a spirited plea for justice and equality for the 'oppressed half of the species', railing in particular against a restrictive system of education and upbringing that produces in women a 'slavish dependence', a 'weak elegancy of mind', and no other ambition than to attend to their looks and please men. If only women were allowed the same opportunities as men, she insists, they would prove to be no less intelligent and no less able.

The clamour for change grew steadily louder in the decades after Wollstonecraft's death in 1797, and in the mid-19th century the cause of women gained an energetic supporter in John Stuart Mill. In *The Subjection of Women* (1869) Mill argued that 'the legal subordination of one sex to the other . . . ought to be replaced by a principle of perfect equality, admitting no power or privilege on the one side, nor disability on the other'. In the USA and Europe the drive for women's emancipation was given impetus by the struggle to abolish slavery, as female abolitionists noted that the political rights they were demanding for black people were in many respects superior to those they enjoyed themselves.

Up until the 1920s feminist energies were focused quite narrowly on the business of winning the right to vote. And as polite lobbying ran up against entrenched establishment opposition, it turned militant and sometimes violent. Suffragettes on both sides of the Atlantic launched an uncompromising campaign that included boycotts, demonstrations, arson and hunger strikes. Such activism, soon to become a hallmark of feminism, finally bore fruit as laws extending the franchise to women were passed in Britain (1918 and 1928) and the United States (1920).

1920	1949	1960s	1990s
19th Amendment to US Constitution prohibits disenfranchisement on basis of sex	Publication of Simone de Beauvoir's *The Second Sex*	Start of feminism's second wave	Start of feminism's third wave

The Feminine Mystique

In the boom years of the 1950s and 1960s, it appeared that middle-class women in the USA had never had it so good. Warm, cosy homes equipped with perfect husbands, model children and hundreds of ingenious gadgets meant that America's homemakers needed less effort than ever before to transform themselves into domestic goddesses. The flaw in this suburban idyll was pointed out by Betty Friedan in *The Feminine Mystique* (1963). The housewives of America had been reminded so often of their fairytale existence that they had come to believe it themselves, but a very different reality lay hidden just below the surface: the numbing tedium of suburban domesticity, the limited horizons, the lack of ambition and aspiration. It took Friedan's bestseller to wake them up – to raise their consciousness – but the women of America were ready for change.

Second wave: the women's movement Winning the vote was a major triumph for feminism, but in almost every area of life Western societies were still riddled with sex-based inequalities. At the first women's rights convention in the USA, held at Seneca Falls, New York, in 1848, a resolution was passed demanding that women be granted 'equal participation with men in the various trades, professions and commerce'; more than 70 years later it was painfully clear that little progress had been made towards this goal. The sense of common purpose created by the struggle for women's suffrage quickly dissipated, and the loss of focus, exacerbated first by world depression, then by world war, left the women's movement deflated and fragmented. Just as it had taken the fervour generated by the abolitionist movement to galvanize the so-called 'first wave' of feminism, so now it took a new period of hope and crisis in the 1960s – the era of civil rights, Vietnam, hippie culture and student protest – to kick-start the 'second wave'. All at once a thousand new initiatives, aimed at a thousand perceived injustices, sprang up everywhere. But this renewed and widespread activism brought to the surface differences and divisions that had long existed within feminism.

Liberal, or mainstream, feminists had tended to take a pragmatic line, aiming for strict equality with men in every area. The primary task, for them, was to eradicate any form of discrimination: to remove formal or informal barriers that stopped women breaking through the glass ceiling in the workplace; to provide adequate maternity-leave rights and childcare arrangements; to ensure that equal educational and training opportunities were available for women.

Alongside these liberal feminists, there had always been more radical voices. As early as 1898, the leading US anarchist Emma Goldman had scoffed at the idea that liberation could be won merely by winning the vote; a woman could gain true freedom only 'by refusing the right to anyone over her body; by refusing to bear children, unless she wants them; by refusing to be a servant to God, the state, society, the husband, the family'. Later feminists questioned whether strict equality with men was what they should be fighting for in any case. Was it right to measure progress in overturning the historical subordination of women by their success in gaining access to power and privilege in a patriarchally organized world – in a system that was founded on the assumption of male dominance? For many, outdoing men on their own terms, playing them at their own games, was not enough.

> **I didn't fight to get women out from behind vacuum cleaners to get them onto the board of Hoover.**
>
> **Germaine Greer**, Australian feminist writer, 1986

Third wave: global sisterhood As the 20th century drew to a close, a 'third wave' of feminism emerged, motivated in part by the perceived shortcomings of earlier feminists. The new movement represented a modulation of tone as much as a change in substance. In place of the rather earnest image of their predecessors, third wavers were self-consciously knowing, ironic, playful, abrasive, brash: strident 'girl power' took the place of flower power; the strutting confidence of Madonna displaced the soul-searching anguish of Joan Baez.

There was still substance behind the gloss, however. Arguably the most persistent fault of the predominantly white and well-heeled second wave, in spite of its pretensions to 'global sisterhood', was an inability to fully comprehend the needs and aspirations of black and Third World feminists, who too often felt patronized or marginalized. Effortlessly empathetic, the third wave embraced new voices and achieved a level of inclusivity and pluralism beyond anything that had gone before, thereby holding out the promise of a truly global feminism.

the condensed idea
Towards global sisterhood

23 Green movement

There is only one earth. For the foreseeable future, this planet will be our only home, and our survival will depend on its continuing ability to provide us with food and other resources and to deal with the waste products of our activities. The earth has met these needs for tens of thousands of years, but in the recent past the burden placed on it has increased dramatically. For every person on earth in the early 1700s, it is estimated that there are more than ten alive today, each one of whom makes (on average) a far greater demand on the finite resources available.

Concern over the impact of human activity on the environment grew in the course of the 19th century, as the processes of industrialization combined with a rocketing population to greatly magnify mankind's capacity to damage natural systems. Since that time, human ingenuity and technology have found new and more efficient ways to meet growing demands on increasingly depleted resources. So far, catastrophic effects have been averted, but the manifest strains on the earth make it clear that things cannot continue indefinitely on their present course.

Changing models: sustainability A single issue – climate change – has recently raised environmental concerns to a new level of intensity, but the beginnings of the modern green movement go back several decades, to the late 1960s. Concerns that were initially confined mainly to disparate groups of scientists and intellectuals spread rapidly, spawning a number of green parties and non-governmental organizations (NGOs) dedicated to promoting environmental issues

timeline

1700	1960s	early 1970s	1971
World population at an estimated 0.6 billion	First warnings that human activity might contribute to global warming	First attested use of 'green' in the sense of 'environmentalist' or 'ecological'	Greenpeace set up to campaign for protection of the environment

and lobbying for political action. Early activists were often quite narrowly focused in their concerns, targeting specific issues such as habitat loss, conservation and the use of nuclear energy, both civil and military.

The central insight shared by environmentalists was, and is, that our current energy-hungry lifestyles are unsustainable. In particular, the model of economic growth driven by ever-rising consumption, developed in the West and exported elsewhere, is unsustainable. Our relationship with nature has become unbalanced and dysfunctional: we behave as if the planet were something to be conquered and tamed, an asset to be exploited, a resource to be plundered. Confronted with this malaise, environmentalists are in broad agreement on the remedy: sustainable development. According to this model, all economic (and other) activity must take full account of its toll on the environment and so avoid environmental degradation and long-term depletion of natural resources. We save ourselves by saving the planet, and this calls for changes in attitude. 'We abuse land because we regard it as a commodity belonging to us,' wrote US ecologist Aldo Leopold in his influential A *Sand County Almanac* (1949). 'When we see land as a community to which we belong, we may begin to use it with love and respect.'

6 We do not inherit the land from our ancestors, we only borrow it from our children. 9
Native American proverb

Enlightened stewardship While environmentalists agree that our relationship with the planet is seriously awry, there is less consensus about what the proper relationship should be. Many pioneers in the green movement were motivated initially by the dangers posed to humans by their abusive and exploitative treatment of the planet. The threat was often expressed in terms of human well-being or survival, and the call for change was predicated on our moral responsibilities to our fellow humans and to future generations. Essentially human-centred, the favoured image was one of enlightened stewardship, in which a properly developed ecological consciousness, allied to prudence and self-interest, counselled respectful, sympathetic and of course sustainable management of our fragile planet.

6 That which is not good for the bee-hive cannot be good for the bees. 9
Marcus Aurelius, Roman emperor, *Meditations*, 2nd century AD

1972	1986	1992	2009	2010
First green party (Values Party) founded in New Zealand	Escape of radioactive material following accident at Chernobyl nuclear power plant	Sustainability discussed at first UN Earth Summit, in Rio de Janeiro, Brazil	UN Climate Change Conference in Copenhagen fails to reach significant agreement	World population at approximately 6.8 billion

> **❝Humanity has passed through a long history of one-sidedness and of a social condition that has always contained the potential of destruction . . . The great project of our time must be to open the other eye: to see all-sidedly and wholly, to heal and transcend the cleavage between humanity and nature . . .❞**
>
> **Murray Bookchin**, US anarchist and environmental pioneer, 1982

This kind of view informed the report of the 1987 World Commission on the Environment and Development (entitled *Our Common Future*), where sustainability was defined as 'development that meets the needs of the present without compromising the ability of future generations to meet their own needs'. The approach is pragmatic in that it recognizes that there is a better prospect of changing human behaviour than human nature. It is not suggested that 'the needs of the present' are simply misguided; indeed, the report goes on to anticipate 'the possibility of a new era of economic growth, based on policies that sustain and expand the natural environmental resource base'. The message, relatively positive and politically palatable, is not that we have to abandon all our existing aspirations but that we have to be smarter and more sympathetic in realizing them.

Deep ecology Alongside this pragmatic approach, there have always been more idealistic, less compromising voices within the green movement. From this perspective, the image of the sympathetic steward is firmly rejected as implying an unequal and exploitative relationship between humans and nature. The earth and all its teeming life are not valuable because they serve us or satisfy our needs; they are not worthy of consideration because they are beautiful or enrich our lives. Indeed, many of the species that share the earth with us are neither useful nor beautiful, yet they are still intrinsically valuable. Our moral obligations extend beyond our fellow humans, present and future, to encompass other forms of life and the planet itself. It is not enough to save the earth in order to save ourselves. We need to be not prudently smart but ecologically wise, living in harmony and equilibrium with nature because we are not apart from it but part of it.

Sacred cows revisited

Predictions of the devastating effects of global warming, including glacial retreat and rising sea levels, have obliged green activists and national governments alike to make drastic reassessments of their priorities. Although sceptics still abound, the broad consensus that climate change is real, urgent and potentially catastrophic demands a level of intergovernmental cooperation that is far beyond anything that has previously been achieved. To date, the international will to meet this challenge has been pitifully inadequate. At the same time, environmentalists have begun to doubt the sanctity of various sacred cows. As the need to cut emissions threatens to trump all other priorities, many greens openly question the wisdom of continued opposition to nuclear power, at least as an interim solution while adequate renewable energy technologies are developed. Others have proposed a central role for capitalism, traditionally seen as the evil engine driving the consumerist growth economy that lies at the root of environmental problems. Given a proper system of carbon taxing, in which producers incur the full cost of the damage they cause to the environment, might not market forces be the surest means of squeezing carbon out of the global economy?

One of the most influential elaborations of this kind of 'deep ecology' is the Gaia theory, first proposed by the British independent scientist James Lovelock in his 1979 book *Gaia: A New Look at Life on Earth*. Lovelock's central idea is that life on earth maintains the conditions necessary for its own survival: our 'stable planet made of unstable parts' is kept in a state of equilibrium by gigantic feedback mechanisms that are driven by the combined regulatory activity of all its living and non-living components. Humans may be parts and partners of the whole, but they are 'just another species, neither the owners nor the stewards of this planet'. The lesson of Gaia is that the health of our world depends on taking a planetary perspective. The ominous implication is that the earth is likely to survive, however badly we treat it, but that its survival does not necessarily include us.

the condensed idea
Healing the cleavage

24 Fascism

Comparisons are sometimes drawn between the vicious fascist regimes that sprang up in Europe in the 1920s and 1930s and the Stalinist dictatorship that terrorized Russia in roughly the same period. It is perhaps hard to make any very strong moral distinction, as unimaginable suffering and death were visited on millions of people as a direct consequence of both communist and fascist regimes.

But while the Soviet horrors can fairly be attributed to an aberrant tyrant rather than to communist ideology – there is certainly nothing in orthodox Marxism–Leninism to justify Stalin's atrocities – the fascist reign of terror was, to an extraordinary degree, a thorough and methodical implementation of an explicitly articulated political doctrine.

Of those responsible for expounding this doctrine, one of the most significant was Benito Mussolini, the leader (*il Duce*) of the Italian Fascist Party and the first fascist dictator to consolidate his rule in Europe. In 1932 Mussolini put his name to 'The Doctrine of Fascism', an essay that formed part of the entry on fascism in the *Enciclopedia Italiana*. While much of the piece is believed to be the work of Giovanni Gentile, the self-proclaimed 'philosopher of fascism', it remains one of the seminal documents on fascist ideology.

The totalitarian state The various incarnations of fascism differed markedly from place to place – a fact that sometimes perplexed contemporary commentators – and their leaders were always more than ready to mould their policy and presentation to suit local conditions. However, it is clear from Mussolini's writings that the overriding motivation behind fascism was, and always remained, extreme nationalism: a virulent and violent passion, inflamed by

timeline

1917	1919	1922	1933
Russian Revolution spreads fear of communism through Europe	Discontent caused by Treaty of Versailles lays seeds of future fascist regimes	Mussolini becomes prime minister following March on Rome (dictator from 1925)	Adolf Hitler appointed Chancellor of Germany

prejudice, patriotism and propaganda, that was focused narrowly on a fetishized conception of an all-powerful state.

The aim of the fascist state was not merely to create a new kind of society but to forge a new form of human to populate it. To this end, the state's power was absolute, its right to intervene in every sphere of life unquestioned: 'We are . . . a state which controls all forces acting in nature. We control political forces, we control moral forces, we control economic forces.' Fascist domination was so complete that a new term – totalitarian – was coined to describe it: 'everything in the State, nothing against the State, nothing outside the State'. One aspect of this absolutism was the powerless citizen, or at least a citizen whose individuality was obliterated and whose sole purpose was limited to the communal, transcendent life of the state; total immersion in the state offered 'a higher life, founded on duty . . . in which the individual, by self-sacrifice, the renunciation of self-interest, by death itself, can achieve that purely spiritual existence in which his value as a man consists'. Fascism's success in achieving this goal, not just in Mussolini's rhetoric but in chilling reality, is confirmed by the English diarist Harold Nicolson, who was living in Rome in January 1932: 'They certainly have turned the whole country into an army. From cradle to grave one is cast in the mould of *fascismo* and there can be no escape . . . It is certainly a socialist experiment in that it destroys individuality. It also destroys liberty.'

It is a short step from utter veneration to state cult. A spiritual dimension develops in which the state takes on the characteristics of a sentient being or deity (it is 'wide awake', according to Mussolini, 'and has a will of its own'); and it becomes the font and focus of all moral value (outside the state, 'no human or spiritual values can exist, much less have value'). Once sanctified in this way, the state cult quickly assumes the trappings of religion, including an elaborate system of symbols, ceremony, ritual, purification and sacrifice. Much of fascist practice across Europe can be understood in these terms.

> **❛The keystone of the Fascist doctrine is its conception of the State, of its essence, its functions, and its aims. For Fascism the State is absolute, individuals and groups relative.❜**
>
> **Benito Mussolini, Italian fascist dictator, 1933**

1933
Fascist Falange founded in Spain (part of Franco's ruling party from 1937)

1945
Deaths of Mussolini and Hitler bring 'era of fascism' to an end

1975
Last of fascist dictators, Francisco Franco, dies in Madrid

A toxic brew

Mussolini's view of fascism as a cult centred on the state was shared by the founder of the Spanish fascist Falange, José Antonio Primo de Rivera, who in 1933 declared: 'Fascism was born to inspire a faith not of the Right (which at bottom aspires to conserve everything, even the unjust) or of the Left (which at bottom aspires to destroy everything, even the good), but a collective integral, national faith.' What Primo de Rivera also suggests is the extent to which fascism was a mongrel creed – an eclectic dogma that borrowed from ideologies that it viscerally detested, including communism and democratic liberalism. The idea of Nazism parasitizing its enemies was expressed by no less a figure than Hermann Göring, future head of Hitler's Luftwaffe, who observed in a speech in 1933: 'Our movement took a grip on cowardly Marxism and from it extracted the meaning of socialism; it also took from the cowardly middle-class parties their nationalism. Throwing both into the cauldron of our way of life there emerged, as clear as a crystal, the synthesis – German National Socialism.'

Fall and redemption A common foundational myth within cults is the story of redemption following a fall. For fascist myth-makers, an opportunity to fuel popular yearning for national rebirth was offered by the tragically unsatisfactory denouement of the First World War. In several countries that fell prey to fascist regimes, the treaty signed at Versailles created a sense of resentment and victimhood, much of the blame for which was attached to the weakness and incompetence of incumbent liberal democratic governments.

In Italy, the success of Mussolini's March on Rome in 1922 and the subsequent rise of one-party dictatorship were largely attributable to popular discontent with the country's existing liberal institutions and in particular to the government's failure to secure expected territorial gains in the postwar negotiations. In Germany the humiliation of defeat and grievances over confiscated territories were exacerbated by an economic crisis brought on by crippling war reparations and hyperinflation that rapidly ruined the livelihoods of ordinary people. In both Italy and Germany, fascist propagandists exploited the many slights to the nation's pride to create, over time, a full-blown myth of national decline and humiliation. Thus Mussolini, for instance, could fancifully portray the Italian people as a race that had laboured under 'many centuries of abasement and foreign servitude'.

The remedy for decline was national regeneration: reconstitution of the state and return to a largely fabricated golden age. Ultra-nationalist parties offered the hope of wiping away the stain of shame. An important part of the myth, especially in Germany, centred on the supposed corruption of the blood purity of the national stock. Bolstered by much bogus scientific theory, obsession with purification led eventually to nightmarish racial and eugenic policies of compulsory 'euthanasia' and mass extermination.

Fear of shadows Another aspect of victimhood was a sense of persecution and paranoia, and fascist propagandists were skilful in creating an atmosphere in which fear was endemic. Within the state, liberals, socialists, trade unionists and other dissidents were ruthlessly targeted, while fears of a malevolent conspiracy abroad were carefully nurtured. Jews were a particular, though not exclusive, obsession within Nazi Germany, while for fascists generally, the most fearsome bogeyman was communism. In this case, it was fear of events, not events themselves, that mattered. As the Italian writer Ignazio Silone observed, fascism was, in many respects, 'a counter-revolution against a revolution that never took place'. Following the Russian Revolution of 1917, consternation at the supposed threat of communism was exploited incessantly by fascist leaders, whose rhetoric and propaganda painted the most lurid picture of the Red Peril looming in the East. Such dangers called for iron discipline and popular sacrifice and for a strong and resolute leader. It was men such as Mussolini and Hitler who answered the call.

The future refusing to be born

The name 'fascist' was derived from the Latin *fasces*, the bundle of rods and an axe carried before Roman magistrates to symbolize their power. As well as symbolizing the unbridled power that characterized the right-wing authoritarian parties of Mussolini and other fascist leaders, the name also hints at fascism's fixation with a mythically great past, lost but soon to be recovered – in the Italian case, the fallen greatness of ancient Rome. This tendency to look backwards was so marked that fascism has sometimes been described as a reaction against modernity. As the British politician Aneurin Bevan put it in 1952, 'Fascism is not a new social order in the strict sense of the term. It is the future refusing to be born.'

the condensed idea
Everything in the state, nothing outside the state

25 Fundamentalism

The essence of fundamentalism is certainty. Through some form of divine revelation, religious fundamentalists of all kinds believe that they have privileged access to certain elemental truths which are true beyond any question or doubt; and because their beliefs are correct beyond doubt, those of others that contradict their own must be incorrect beyond doubt. Moreover, the beliefs concerned are so supremely important in the minds of those who hold them that they generally consider it morally justified, indeed a duty, to impose them on those who do not share them. Tolerance is no virtue when you are right and the will of God is defied.

The amount of attention paid to Islamic fundamentalism since the 9/11 attacks has tended to draw attention away from other kinds, but there are in fact countless ideologies and orthodoxies that are no less extreme in their world-view. Over the last half-century all the major religions, including Christianity, Judaism, Hinduism and Buddhism, have witnessed the emergence of fundamentalist groups. Unshakeable belief in the unique truth of their own cause has led extremists to carry out many atrocities, from major terrorist attacks and indiscriminate suicide bombings to narrowly targeted attacks on individuals and institutions that have in some way offended them.

Though principally religious in origin, fundamentalisms typically refuse to recognize a clear separation between religion and other domains. Totalitarian in their outlook, they seek to gain political power in order to radically reshape society in conformity with their own principles. The process of secularization that has fashioned Western democracies since the 18th century is generally held accountable for erosion of religious belief and is thus one of the principal causes

timeline

early 20th century	1920
Protestant fundamentalism emerges in the USA	C.L. Laws coins the term 'fundamentalist'

of the resurgence of fundamentalism. For the same reason, liberal and democratic values are usually prime targets of fundamentalist activities and the first casualties when fundamentalist regimes gain political control.

Fundamentalism in the home of the free The 'war on terror' led by the United States in the wake of the 9/11 attacks was presented as a conflict between the liberal and democratic values of the West and the dark and repressive forces of fundamentalist Islam. Such a presentation is misleading, at least to the extent that it conceals the political and popular strength of fundamentalist views within the USA itself. Indeed, the term 'fundamentalist' was originally coined to describe an extreme reactionary movement among American Christians – a movement which remains an uncompromising and ideologically driven manifestation of the phenomenon.

Like other religious movements to which the term has since been applied, the fundamentalist movement that sprang up among evangelical Protestants in the United States in the early years of the 20th century was initially a reaction

A force to be reckoned with

'Heave an egg out of a Pullman window, and you will hit a Fundamentalist almost anywhere in the United States today.' What was true of 1920s America, as recorded by the satirist H.L. Mencken at the birth of Protestant fundamentalism, is no less true today. Recent surveys suggest that some two-thirds of adults in the USA believe that Genesis gives a true and accurate account of the creation of the world and all the plants and animals that inhabit it, a process of manufacture that was supposedly completed in six days at a date within the last 10,000 years. In other words, the majority of those who constitute the most powerful nation on earth reject, at least by implication, the basic principles of geology, cosmology, the theory of evolution, and much else besides, as they are understood by 99 percent of today's scientists. And in democracies at least, numbers equate to power. In 1990 the Reverend Pat Robertson, multimillionaire televangelist and founder of the far-right Christian Coalition, announced, 'We have enough votes to run this country.' It was no idle boast; and it remains a truism that no US presidential candidate can afford to alienate the religious right or to disregard its deeply conservative agenda.

1960s	mid-1990s	September 2001
Evangelical radio spreads across the USA	Taliban seize control of Afghanistan	9/11 attacks and start of 'war on terror'

> 6 **Every fundamentalist movement I've studied in Judaism, Christianity and Islam is convinced at some gut, visceral level that secular liberal society wants to wipe out religion.** 9
>
> Karen Armstrong,
> commentator on religions, 2002

against modernity. Religious conservatives were moved to take a stand against 'liberal' theologians who sought to interpret the Bible and the gospel miracles symbolically or metaphorically, in ways that would sit more comfortably with recent social, cultural and scientific trends. Disgusted by such doctrinal compromise, which seemed to threaten the centrality of divine revelation, leading conservative theologians asserted the primacy of certain 'fundamentals' of their faith, including the virgin birth and physical resurrection of Jesus, the strict veracity of the miracles, and the literal truth (inerrancy) of the Bible. It was Curtis Lee Laws, editor of a Baptist journal, who, in 1920, first applied the name 'fundamentalist' to those 'who still cling to the great fundamentals and who mean to do battle royal' for their faith.

Unwavering in the service of God(s) The reverence shown by traditionalist evangelicals towards ancient scripture is common to other religious fundamentalisms. Although each group reveres a different sacred text or set of texts, they show a similar certitude that their favoured text expresses the literal word of God (or gods) and hence gives a final and authoritative statement of his (or their) wishes. Scriptural teachings are not open to interpretation, and the moral injunctions that they contain are to be followed to the letter. The will of God as revealed in sacred texts is regarded as timeless and unchanging, so a logical feature of fundamentalism is extreme conservatism. This generally entails an unquestioning commitment to established traditions, rejection of all forces of social change, and often a desire to revive a supposedly superior former state – usually an imagined and idealized past.

Extremely conservative in both social and moral matters, fundamentalists of all hues categorically reject most of the civil and political rights that have been hard won in the West over the last three centuries. Cherished notions of Western liberalism, including cultural and religious tolerance, free speech, gender equality and gay rights, are roundly condemned. The uncompromising nature of such convictions was shown by US fundamentalist firebrand and founder of the Moral Majority, Jerry Falwell, whose immediate response to the 9/11 attacks was to blame 'the pagans, and the abortionists, and the feminists, and the gays and the lesbians . . . all of them who have tried to secularize America'.

In bed with the devil

Nowhere has fundamentalism's ambivalence towards modernity been clearer than in its tortured relationship with modern technology. American Christian fundamentalists denounce many aspects of science and technology as the devil's work. In the area of medical science, euthanasia, abortion, surrogacy and stem-cell research (among many other things) have been abominated, usually on the grounds that they contravene some principle such as the sanctity of life. Yet such condemnation has been matched by a remarkable resourcefulness on the part of fundamentalists in exploiting the fruits of technology for their own purposes. So, for instance, a seemingly endless procession of televangelists has used extensive programming on radio, television and now the internet to reach vast audiences who are quickly separated from their money in the cause of God. An even more bizarre coupling of reactionary fundamentalism and modern technology was seen from the mid-1990s in Afghanistan, where the extreme Islamist Taliban coordinated its project of driving Afghan society back to the stone age by means of mobile phones. And from late 2001, after the Taliban had fallen and al-Qaeda had been ousted from its Afghan strongholds, the terrorist group made a highly effective transition to cyberspace. Suddenly the soldiers of Islam were armed with laptops as well as Kalashnikov, and internet cafés became the logistical and planning centres of the anti-Western *jihad*.

Engage or withdraw? Confronted with modernity, fundamentalists have sometimes shown a degree of ambivalence, uncertain whether to withdraw from society or to engage with it in order to eradicate its many perceived faults. Fundamentalisms that are messianic or apocalyptic, anticipating the coming of a saviour and/or the end of the world, may encourage followers to withdraw, confident that non-believers' hold on political power will be short-lived and that their own privileged relationship with God will bring salvation in due course. Other fundamentalists take a more proactive approach and aspire to grasp political power themselves, with a view to imposing a system of government informed by their own beliefs. Rejecting the secular notion that there should be a wall of separation between church and state, they attempt to reinstate religion within the political sphere. Elitist and authoritarian, such fundamentalists typically wish to topple democratic institutions and to establish theocratic rule in their place.

the condensed idea
Faith in certainty

26 Islamism

In the wake of the devastating suicide attacks launched against New York and Washington on 11 September 2001, a wave of Islamophobia swept over the United States and much of the Western world. Responding to the widespread mood of panic and outrage, President George W. Bush declared a 'war on terror' which would not end 'until every terrorist group of global reach has been found, stopped and defeated'.

Whatever initial expectations there may have been, it soon became apparent that this was an altogether different kind of war, in which the enemy was a shadow and the criteria of victory unclear. For the US-led 'coalition of the willing' had gone to war against an idea: Islamic fundamentalism, or Islamism.

The ensuing conflict was perceived by many on both sides as a 'clash of civilizations' – as an ideological and cultural collision that cut across national borders – and perceptions rapidly became polarized and distorted. While the threat to the West posed by Islamist extremists was very real, the Western response to it betrayed insensitivity and lack of understanding. The United States blandly assumed the role of champion of freedom and democracy against a pitiless and fanatical enemy; and from this unnuanced perspective, fear and suspicion of Islamism was projected, often indiscriminately, onto Muslims and Islam as a whole. To many in the Muslim world, on the other hand, the US-led response to 9/11 looked hasty and disingenuous, and nothing that followed eased their suspicions of the West's imperialist ambitions and less-than-pure motives, particularly with respect to its oil interests. Military victories in the 'war on terror' counted for little; more significant was the battle for 'hearts and minds', and here many critics felt that the West was losing and that moderate Muslims were being driven into the arms of the fundamentalists.

timeline

1979–89	1980–8	1990–1
USA supports mujahideen in Soviet–Afghan War	USA supports Saddam Hussein in Iran–Iraq War	US-led coalition defeats Saddam following Iraqi invasion of Kuwait

Returning to the true path of Islam The 9/11 attacks were the fruit of years of careful planning by agents associated with al-Qaeda, a loosely affiliated network of terrorist groups under the leadership of its Saudi founder and soon-to-be world's most wanted man, Osama bin Laden. The attacks were surprising only in the devastation they caused, for they had been foreshadowed by a number of less severe strikes and explicit statements of violent intent. A declaration issued in February 1998 by the World Islamic Front, an association of extreme Islamist bodies, called for a 'Jihad against the Jews and the Crusaders'; it also included a fatwa (religious decree) that stated: 'The ruling to kill the Americans and their allies – civilians and military – is an individual duty for every Muslim who can do it in any country in which it is possible to do it.'

The prime objective of radical Islamists, as stated in a 2008 al-Qaeda webcast, is to 'establish the Shari'a Islamic state that will unite the Muslims of the earth in truth and justice'. According to this view, the current oppressed state of Muslim countries is the consequence of straying from the true path of Islam and the remedy involves strict observance of the teachings of the Qu'ran and (re) implementation of Shari'a, Islamic law as revealed by God. As the one true faith, Islam's scope is universal, so the new (or restored) caliphate will encompass all mankind, everywhere on earth.

Islamist grievances against the West, which are enumerated in the 1998 fatwa, are a cause of resentment in part because they are seen as obstacles to

The false face of Islam

Given the staggering success of the 9/11 terrorist attacks, it was perhaps inevitable, and certainly unhelpful, that al-Qaeda – however nebulous an entity it is in reality – would become the international face of Islamism and that its extreme agenda would wrongly be assumed by many to reflect a commonly held Muslim viewpoint. To make matters worse, the portrait of Islamic fanaticism was fleshed out with gruesome details provided by the Taliban, a fundamentalist Muslim regime which harboured al-Qaeda bases in Afghanistan, where it had seized power in 1996 and proceeded to impose highly repressive theocratic rule on the Afghan people. Terrorist atrocities, near-medieval social repression, suicide bombings, televised beheadings – all have conspired to paint the most lurid picture of Islamic fundamentalism, and by false implication, of Islam itself.

11 September 2001	7 October 2001	19 March 2003
9/11 terrorist attacks kill close to 3,000 in USA	US-led coalition attacks Taliban in Afghanistan	Invasion of Iraq by USA and 'coalition of the willing'

Struggle in the way of god

The concept of *jihad* has done more than any other to cement in Western minds the link between Islam and violence. Yet the interpretation of the word is much disputed by Muslims themselves. The literal meaning of *jihad* is 'struggle in the way of God', which radical Islamists interpret as 'holy war', a religious duty that they believe justifies a range of actions including suicide attacks and targeting of civilians. Moderate Muslims, on the other hand, take the idea of struggle to refer primarily to an internal spiritual conflict. This difference in understanding *ought* to play a significant role in the effort to win over hearts and minds, which both sides agree is a critical battleground in the 'war on terror' that has raged in Afghanistan and Iraq in the wake of the 9/11 attacks. The view of ordinary Muslims that methods involving indiscriminate killing of civilians, including women and children, are un-Islamic and contrary to the true spirit of *jihad* should mean that the radical Islamists are defeated in the ideological battle and become progressively marginalized. Unfortunately, however, the means adopted by the USA and its allies to wage war on Islamic insurgents and extremists have often shown scant regard for Muslim sensibilities and have thus proved no less effective in alienating moderate Muslim opinion. Acting in baffled incomprehension of one another, each side appears bent on losing the battle that really matters.

a return to the true path of Islam. First and foremost among these complaints is US/Western support for 'the Jews' petty state', as the fatwa calls the state of Israel. From the Islamist perspective, alleged Western destabilization of Middle Eastern countries, including conflict in Iraq, is seen as a means of preserving the existence of Israel. Another major grievance is US occupation of 'the lands of Islam in the holiest of places, the Arabian Peninsula', where the Americans are accused of 'plundering its riches, dictating to its rulers, humiliating its people, terrorizing its neighbours'. Particularly offensive was the presence of US military bases, for over a decade after the 1990–1 Gulf War, in 'the Land of the Two Holy Places', i.e. Saudi Arabia, with its sacred sites at Mecca and Medina. Although the Saudi bases were removed in 2003, continuing US military presence in the Middle East, above all in Iraq, is, in the eyes of fundamentalists, a constant and bitter affront to Islam.

Unwanted attentions Islamist resentment at Western insensitivity to Muslim concerns stems from centuries of friction and conflict with the West and, more particularly, from a period of colonial occupation and interference that lasted

> **'Leave us alone to establish the Shari'a Islamic state that will unite the Muslims of the earth in truth and justice. A single word of American protest shall be silenced by a thousand Islamic bombs.'**
>
> **al-Qaeda webcast, 2008**

for much of the 20th century. While Muslim countries are often portrayed in the West as repressive and 'medieval' – backward and opposed to modernity – the chief focus of their fears is what they see as economic and cultural imperialism. The West readily assumes that 'progress' means movement towards its own liberal, secular values, but to many Muslims Westernization is a mark of post-colonial arrogance, an unwelcome imposition that threatens their traditional values and ways of life.

Both radical and moderate Muslims are suspicious of the West's (especially the USA's) motives in its interventions in the Middle East. It is hard to fully refute the charge that a primary US objective in the region is 'plundering its riches' (i.e. protecting its oil interests), while the fact that its preferred method is 'dictating to its rulers' (i.e. exercising control by supporting friendly, if not always savoury, regimes or factions) is a matter of historical record. To take merely the most notorious cases, US support for the Afghan mujahideen during the 1980s Soviet invasion was partly responsible for the emergence of the Taliban, al-Qaeda and bin Laden himself, who fought in an Arab contingent against the Soviets. The other great bogeyman of the Middle East, Saddam Hussein, was likewise supported by the USA in the 1980s Iran–Iraq War, in the hope that his regime would act as a counterweight to the Islamic state led by the radical Ayatollah Khomeini in neighbouring Iran. Such interventions have rarely worked out as US policy-makers intended and have done nothing to win the hearts and minds of ordinary Muslims.

the condensed idea
Struggle for the new caliphate

27 The state

The state is all-pervasive. We are born and die in its embrace, and its arms extend into every aspect of our lives. Like goldfish in a bowl, we are immersed in it, to the extent that for much of the time we are scarcely conscious of its presence. Yet we would know soon enough if the state were not there: there would be no laws to tell us what not to do, no tax to pay – and no roads to drive on, no pensions to sustain us in old age, and nobody to collect the garbage.

'Nothing appears more surprising to those who consider human affairs with a philosophical eye', remarked the Scottish philosopher David Hume, 'than the easiness with which the many are governed by the few.' The simple solution to this riddle is the state, yet the state is much more than just the government of the day. It includes the institutions of government, to be sure, but it also encompasses the courts of law, the civil service, the military services, state schools and universities, social services, public-service broadcasting corporations, and much else besides.

The state is so ubiquitous that we might suppose that it has always been there, but this is not so. As a distinctive type of political organization, the modern state is a relatively recent phenomenon, only emerging in its present form within the last 500 years. So what, exactly, is the state? What is it for, and by what right does it regulate and control our lives?

The monopoly of violence Much modern discussion of the state has been structured around the influential account given in the early decades of the 20th century by the German sociologist Max Weber. In his posthumously published *Economy and Society* (1922), Weber sets out the state's main characteristics:

timeline

1513	1576	1651	1690
Machiavelli credited with first use of 'state' to refer to a territorial sovereign government	Jean Bodin defines sovereignty as state's supreme authority over citizens	Thomas Hobbes's *Leviathan* argues the case for absolute sovereignty	John Locke argues that the state's legitimacy is rooted in popular consent

It possesses an administrative and legal order subject to change by legislation . . . This system of order claims binding authority, not only over the members of the state, the citizens, most of whom have obtained membership by birth, but also to a very large extent over all action taking place in the area of its jurisdiction. It is thus a compulsory organization with a territorial basis . . .

The most salient feature of the state, for Weber, is its claimed 'monopoly of the legitimate use of physical force', which he regards as being 'as essential to it as its character of compulsory jurisdiction and continuous operation'. This monopoly amounts to the state's exclusive right to make rules or laws within its territory and to use violence, actual or threatened, to force compliance with those rules. In Weber's view, it is this means or mode of operation that defines the political character of the state, rather than any particular function or purpose that it may have.

> **The State is a relation of men dominating men, a relation supported by means of legitimate (i.e. considered to be legitimate) violence.**
>
> **Max Weber, 1919**

Territoriality and sovereignty
An obvious feature of the state, prominent in Weber's account, is its territorial basis. Today, virtually every square inch of the earth's land area belongs to, or is energetically claimed by, some or other state. Every bit of land – not to mention the coastal waters that adjoin it, the airspace above it and the minerals beneath it – has been parcelled out into relatively neat and mutually exclusive (though not infrequently disputed) state-based territories. States are ubiquitous for the simple reason that one state abuts another, and there are no spaces between. To be stateless is generally the consequence of political exclusion or expulsion, not of geographical location and certainly not of choice. This is one sense in which the modern state is, in Weber's phrase, compulsory: you cannot 'opt out' of the state system. You are generally a citizen of the state of your birth, and that state demands your allegiance and obedience, requires that you meet certain obligations, and usually prohibits you from assuming the citizenship of another state.

States, then, are exclusive territories – all are discrete and none overlap. The limits of a state's jurisdiction are determined by its borders, and within this area

1762	**1922**	**1990**	**1991**
Rousseau proposes that the state owes its authority to the general will of the governed	Max Weber's *Economy and Society* published (two years after his death)	Single German state formed from East and West Germanies	Former communist state of Yugoslavia begins to split into separate states

it asserts its sovereignty – its supreme power and authority. All states, great and small, recognize the sovereign rights of their fellows, with the result that all are independent, autonomous and formally equal. This principle is crucial in the usual understanding of international relations, where universally recognized national sovereignty implies that there is no political authority higher than the state and hence that states must depend on their own resources ('self-help') to look after their interests and to preserve order (see page 179).

A state's internal sovereignty means that its authority over its citizens is supreme and is not answerable to any higher authority; in all matters relating to the public interest, the state is the final arbiter. Its jurisdiction extends uniformly and directly over all its citizens and, to a significant degree, over non-members present within its territory.

Legitimacy Coercion is not enough; a state could not survive long by force alone. It must justify its claim to sovereignty. Somehow it must convince a majority of its citizens that they should accept, or at least acquiesce in, its authority and management of public affairs. Most of the state's members must recognize, most of the time, that the state's claim to sovereign power is in some sense legitimate and hence that it is not only necessary but right to bow to its authority.

New world order

The idea of states is so powerful, both in fact and in theory, that it is tempting to suppose that the global system which they constitute has always been as it is today. But this is not so. For a state to be a state, its population must be more or less permanent and its institutions must persist through time – they must survive changes of government and leadership – but there is no guarantee that populations will stand still or that institutions will persist, as the recent examples of Yugoslavia and the two Germanies demonstrate. Likewise, the nature of the state's power – centralized, concentrated, penetrating – suggests longevity, but this too is an illusion. A defining feature of the modern state as a system of political organization – the idea that the allegiance of the citizen is due to the state, which is itself transcendent (distinct from both rulers and ruled) – only clearly emerged in the 17th century. Before that time, patterns of government and control were complex, with loosely defined and overlapping domains and hierarchies, and loyalties were often personal, local and transient.

Citizens' acceptance of the state's legitimacy is partly a consequence of how its character and mode of operation are popularly perceived. The state is respected for the same reason that it is not much loved, because it is felt to be detached, impersonal and cold ('the coldest of all cold monsters', according to Nietzsche). Distinct from both rulers and ruled – from both present office-holders and citizens – it is seen as the embodiment of the objective rule of law, not the arbitrary rule of men; as a purveyor of abstract legal principles that are enforced by a neutral (if colourless) bureaucracy and an impartial judicial system. In sum, there is a popular belief, as Weber puts it, 'in the legality of enacted rules and the right of those elevated to authority under such rules to issue commands'.

Not so united nations

The relationship between states and nations is close and sometimes troubled. There is a widely held (or at least widely asserted) aspiration that the two should coincide, to create what would actually be (rather than merely be called) nation-states. Nations – in the sense of large groups of people united by common history, culture, language or ethnicity – often aspire to organize themselves into politically autonomous and self-contained territorial entities (i.e. states). At the same time, many existing states attempt to enhance their unity and cohesion by creating a single unified 'nation' (and with it a sense of nationalism) from the different peoples, sometimes highly diverse in terms of ethnicity and culture, who live within their borders. The consequence is that nation-states are almost never as pure as they claim to be or their name suggests.

Democratic states typically base their legitimacy on the concept of popular sovereignty. According to this view, sovereignty belongs ultimately to the people – the citizens – who voluntarily make over some of their power to the state. The condition of this transfer is that the state should act responsibly and effectively to preserve social order and to further the common good. The existence of the state is justified so long as it enjoys the consent of its members, who may withdraw that consent if it fails to fulfil its obligations. The notion that the state is established on the basis of a tacit 'social contract' between it and its members was elaborated in various ways by the Enlightenment political theorists Thomas Hobbes, John Locke and Jean-Jacques Rousseau (see page 20).

the condensed idea
The monopoly of legitimate violence

28 Constitutions

'We, the people of the United States, in order to form a more perfect union, establish justice, insure domestic tranquillity, provide for the common defense, promote the general welfare, and secure the blessings of liberty to ourselves and our posterity, do ordain and establish this Constitution for the United States of America.'

So begins, with this famously resonant preamble, the world's oldest and most successful written constitution: the Constitution of the United States. Signed by the delegates to the Federal Constitutional Convention on 17 September 1787, this momentous document came into effect ten months later, on 21 June 1788, when the requisite nine states had duly agreed to its ratification.

The idea that the political essence of a nation could be distilled into a set of fundamental principles, rules and procedures was not new in 1787, nor was the use of the word 'constitution' to describe such a distillation. Nearly 100 years earlier, in the year after the Glorious Revolution of 1688, the deposed king James II of England was charged with having violated 'the fundamental constitution of the kingdom'. In the middle of the 18th century, something close to the modern meaning of constitution was given by the political writer Henry St John, Viscount Bolingbroke, in his *A Dissertation upon Parties* (1735), where he defines it as 'that assemblage of laws, institutions and customs, derived from certain fixed principles of reason . . . that compose the general system, according to which the community hath agreed to be governed'. What was new, in the American case, was the idea that the various principles, practices and institutions which together constitute a particular system of government should be summarized and articulated within a single written document.

timeline

1689	1787
Bill of Rights establishes principle of limited government in England	US Constitution signed at the Constitutional Convention in Philadelphia

The long survival of the US Constitution – well over two centuries – is quite unprecedented. No other written constitution has lasted anything like as long. History's second great constitution-maker, France, concocted its first such document in 1791, in the early years of the French Revolution, and has introduced a further dozen or so since. Indeed, the great majority of constitutions in force in the world today were introduced within the last half-century. There are a handful of countries that do not have written constitutions (Britain, Israel and Saudi Arabia are notable examples), but these are exceptional. In general, a written constitution is regarded as a statement of a modern state's legitimacy, or a claim to such status, and as a prerequisite of international recognition.

Hidden meanings On the face of it, a constitution is a relatively straightforward document, with an apparently clear and practical purpose. Most of the words of virtually every constitution, the American one included, are spent on describing how the political system will be set up and function: the procedures to be followed in taking decisions; the distribution of power among the various organs of state; the limits of authority imposed on government officials; the means used to select or elect officers of the state . . . and so on.

> **'The people made the Constitution, and the people can unmake it. It is the creature of their own will, and lives only by their will.'**
> John Marshall, US jurist, 1821

Almost always, however, there is more to a constitution than meets the eye, a meaning hidden beneath the surface of the text. For the effect of a constitution is to impose rules and procedures on those who govern – to limit the powers of governors and in so doing to empower the governed. To tie the hands of those in authority is, necessarily, to enlarge the freedom of those over whom that authority is exercised. But there is no need for such documents in times of political serenity. It is only when governance is seen to be ineffective or unjust that those who feel oppressed are moved to draw up constitutions. The two earliest written constitutions, the American and the French, were both prompted by the perception that the existing government was unjust and arbitrary. Typically, production of a constitution is an act of reform or revolution, and nearly always there is a prescriptive element: it is a demand not only for a constitution but for constitutionalism – a plea for limited government, for the rule of law to exist in place of the whim of a king or despot.

1791

French revolutionaries' first
constitution establishes
constitutional monarchy

1958

Constitution of the Fifth
Republic adopted in France

Towards a more perfect union

The oldest and most influential written constitution in the world is that of the United States of America. Originally consisting of a short preamble and seven articles, it was drafted in 1787, signed in September of that year, and formally came into effect on 21 June 1788, when it had been ratified, as required in its own Article VII, by nine of the thirteen states that existed at that time. Its most general concern, expressed in the brief preamble, is to 'secure the blessings of liberty', an aspiration that reflects the fact that the war in which the United States had opposed the armies of George III, a 'tyrant . . . unfit to be the ruler of a free people', had ended only five years earlier. The preservation of liberty is to be achieved principally by limiting the power of government, and this is effected in the first three articles by the celebrated separation of powers: legislative power is vested in Congress (Article I),

executive power in the presidency (Article II) and judicial power in the courts (Article III).

The remainder of the Constitution comprises 27 amendments, each of which had to be approved according to the formulae set out in Article V. Of these, the first ten together form the Bill of Rights and were adopted jointly on 15 December 1791. The First Amendment protects various freedoms, including freedom of religion, speech, assembly and the press, while the Fifth guarantees the right of witnesses to remain silent if testifying might provide evidence that could be used against them. Of the remaining amendments, particularly noteworthy are the 13th, abolishing slavery (1865); the 14th, providing to all equal protection under the law (1868); the 15th, establishing the right to vote regardless of race (1870); and the 19th, providing women's suffrage (1920).

Written or unwritten? Critics sometimes suggest that a written constitution would be a panacea for the ills of a country such as Britain, with the implication that various political abuses and aberrations can be attributed to the lack of such a document. In reality, however, the British system is not as whimsical as this criticism suggests, nor are the alternatives without difficulties of their own.

A normal feature of a written constitution is that those principles that are thought to be fundamental and indispensable are 'entrenched': they are given a status superior to that of ordinary laws and can only be modified by means of some especially onerous procedure. The keystone of the British political system is the principle of parliamentary sovereignty, which means that parliament can do anything it chooses except bind the hands of its successor. Entrenchment is therefore formally impossible, since it is always possible for a later government to overturn supposedly constitutional statutes enacted by an earlier one. The idea that this necessarily leads to instability and arbitrary government, however, is refuted by history.

The truth of the British constitution is not so much that it is not written but that it is not written down in one place, in a single document. Exactly fitting Bolingbroke's definition, it is a system that has evolved, gradually and imperceptibly, from an 'assemblage of laws, institutions and customs' accumulated over hundreds of years. Many of these are, naturally, matters of convention, and to that extent they can be modified without recourse to law in order to meet changing needs. But such flexibility does not entail weakness. Indeed, the experience of France, for instance, suggests that rigidity in constitutional matters can amount to brittleness. Given the prescriptive nature of French constitution-making – the tendency to detail the content of laws, not merely the procedure by which they should be made – it has generally proved easier to abandon an existing constitution completely and start afresh, rather than adapt it to new political circumstances.

It is certainly true that the existence of a written constitution gives rise to much debate over whether particular political acts are constitutional. A constitution may be set in stone (or ink), but that does not prevent interested parties reading between the lines and finding what they want to find. Written constitutions usually require a system of active judicial review in order to determine constitutionality. A point that is sometimes made in favour of the gradually evolved British system is that it leaves the final decision in the hands of elected politicians, rather than unelected lawyers. If a principal aim of government is political stability, the mere existence of a constitution, written or not, is beside the point. What matters is the willingness of citizens to abide by the rule of law and of those in power to stay within agreed limits, irrespective of how those limits were originally decided. A constitution that does not broadly conform to common expectations of how political life should be conducted will not change behaviour; it will follow innumerable others into extinction.

the condensed idea
The distillation of a nation

29 Presidential system

A crucial feature that distinguishes despotic rule from democratic government is accountability. Modern politicians may have very considerable powers entrusted to them, but in democracies that grant is not unconditional. While an absolute ruler, or autocrat, may do as he pleases and answer to no one for the consequences, those who are elected to govern a country remain accountable for how they choose to do so; at the very least, they have to answer to their electorate for the propriety of their actions.

But who, precisely, should political leaders be accountable to? The answer to this question is important in understanding the differences between the main types of political system found in the world today. In parliamentary systems, such as that of the United Kingdom, the executive – the prime minister and his (or occasionally her) cabinet – is drawn from the legislature, or parliament; it relies on the parliament for support and remains answerable to it for its conduct of affairs (see page 120). In a presidential system, by contrast – most notably, that of the United States – the executive (president) and the legislature (Congress, in the case of the USA) are independent and subject to different selection processes. The president is elected, directly or indirectly, by the people, and it is to them that he is immediately accountable.

Keeping power in check The single most important feature of a fully fledged presidential system is that the president is neither selected by, nor responsible to, the country's legislative body. In contrast to a parliamentary system, where the prime minister is typically a member of the legislature and

timeline

1748	1788
Montesquieu advocates separation of powers in *The Spirit of the Laws*	James Madison advocates checks and balances in *The Federalist Papers*

selected by the majority party from among its members, a president is generally elected directly by the people. In the USA, the president and vice president are chosen by popular vote but at one remove: the process is conducted through an electoral college system, in which the people in each state vote for a list of electors who are pledged to vote for a particular presidential candidate. This system, originally intended to protect the interests of smaller states, is 'winner-takes-all' – the winning candidate in each state takes all the votes for that state – and has been criticized for sometimes allowing a president to be elected even if he does not win a majority of the popular vote. Such a situation happened most recently in the election of George W. Bush in 2000.

The independence of executive and legislature is a cornerstone of the separation of powers – a constitutional arrangement in which discrete powers and responsibilities are given to the different branches of government (executive, legislature, judiciary) in order to prevent concentrations of power in any single branch and thus to protect the people against abuses of authority. Originally developed by the French Enlightenment thinker Montesquieu, the theory of separation was summarized by James Madison, chief architect of the US Constitution, in 1788: 'The accumulation of all powers, legislative, executive, and judiciary, in the same hands, whether of one, a few, or many, and whether hereditary, self-appointed, or elected, may justly be pronounced the very definition of tyranny.' In principle and practice, the activities of one part of government are scrutinized and opposed by others, and their independence from one another is intended to ensure that this takes place without fear or favour. This arrangement of 'checks and balances' is central to the system

If angels were to govern men, neither external nor internal controls on government would be necessary. In framing a government which is to be administered by men over men, the great difficulty is this: You must first enable the government to control the governed; and in the next place, oblige it to control itself.

James Madison, 1788

1885

Woodrow Wilson attacks presidential system in *Congressional Government*

2000

George W. Bush elected US president on smaller share of popular vote

that allows governors to control the governed (as Madison puts it) while at the same time obliging them to control themselves.

Divided government One consequence of the separation of powers is the possibility – not infrequently realized – of divided government: a situation in which the legislature has a different political complexion to that of the presidency and does not support the latter's political programme. This can cause gridlock, a kind of political stalemate in which the president uses his veto to block legislation while his own legislative initiatives meet congressional resistance. In the worst case, such political paralysis may lead one side or other to resort to desperate and unconstitutional measures, even to violence, in order to break the impasse (such crises have occurred, for instance, in several South American countries). Matters do not usually deteriorate to this extent, however, and what critics may call gridlock is seen by others as a benign antagonism that ensures both sides of the argument are fully considered, and excessive or hasty measures avoided. From this perspective, divided government may be seen as an antidote to the radical policy swings that often accompany changes of government within parliamentary systems.

The fact that a president is (more or less) directly elected by popular vote is claimed by some as being more democratic: such a leader has a stronger mandate for his political programme matched by greater accountability, since he cannot hide behind the apparatus of government. Critics, however, turn this argument on its head. As future president Woodrow Wilson warned in 1885, 'the only fruit of dividing power [has] been to make it irresponsible'. Where strict accountability for government actions is not clear, as in a presidential system, it is always possible for one side to blame the other. And as Wilson pointed out, 'how is the schoolmaster, the nation, to know which boy needs the whipping? . . . Power and strict accountability for its use are the essential constituents of good government.'

Fixed terms While a prime minister is continually dependent on parliament for support and can in principle be removed at short notice, a president is normally elected for a fixed term and, short of a major misdemeanour, is immune from removal during his term of office. The knowledge, shared by supporters and opponents alike, that a president's tenure is of a certain and fixed duration may help to foster a climate of political stability. This is especially true when comparison is made with those parliamentary systems that use some form of proportional representation and are accustomed to a situation of often short-lived coalition government.

Two heads better than one?

An obvious difference between presidential and parliamentary regimes is the nature of the head of state. In a parliamentary system, the head of state is usually a ceremonial figurehead (for instance, the monarch in the UK), while real political power is in the hands of the prime minister, the head of government. In a presidential system, on the other hand, the roles of head of state and head of government are combined in the person of the president. In addition to these regime types, there is a third, mixed (hybrid) arrangement in which a president, elected by popular vote for a fixed term, serves alongside a prime minister who is selected by, and answerable to, the legislature (parliament). The best-known example of this so-called 'semi-presidential' system is France. In such a system, both president and prime minister take an active part in the administration of the state, but there is considerable variation in the actual division of powers. Domestic policy, for instance, may be the main responsibility of the prime minister, while the president is active principally in foreign affairs.

The fact that the election date is known in advance and cannot be manipulated by the governing party for party-political reasons, as is the case in some parliamentary systems, is normally held to be a check on executive power. There can be a downside to fixed terms, however. Typically, the constitutional mechanism for removing a president from office – impeachment – is cumbersome and hard to set in train, so it may be very difficult to unseat a president who is ineffective or unsuited to the needs of the moment. It has been suggested, for instance, that the replacement of Neville Chamberlain by Winston Churchill – without which the course of the Second World War would doubtless have been very different – would have been difficult to bring about in a presidential system. As so often in this debate, however, others have argued exactly the reverse, claiming that a president, uninhibited by the need to maintain parliamentary confidence, is able to act more swiftly and decisively in time of emergency.

the condensed idea
Where men are no angels

30 Parliaments

Parliaments are sometimes disparagingly referred to as talking-shops, with the implication that they are places of idle chatter rather than decisive action. It is a curious criticism, in that a talking-shop – or, less pejoratively, a forum for debate – is literally what a parliament is and precisely what it should be. Only autocrats rule without consulting others; debate is the hallmark of open government.

If debate alone were the criterion of democratically governed states, the national assemblies of all modern democracies might aptly be called parliaments. The fact that the term is normally applied more narrowly is due to the government of one country in particular: that of England and (since 1707) Great Britain – the so-called 'mother of parliaments'. Britain at one time presided over probably the most extensive empire that has ever existed, so it is no surprise that the distinctive 'Westminster' style of parliamentary government was adopted by the majority of its former colonies, most of which now belong to the Commonwealth of Nations. However, the prolonged prominence of Britain as a world power and the strength and stability provided by its parliamentary system meant that its political organization was influential well beyond the borders of its own empire and was emulated to some degree by many other countries in Europe and elsewhere.

The Westminster system The feature that most clearly distinguishes the parliamentary system of government from the presidential form found in the USA and elsewhere is that in the former the executive and legislative branches are not fully separated. A president (executive) is elected by the people, in a process distinct from that in which the members of the legislature are elected, and he is not directly accountable to that body (see page 116). A prime minister, by

timeline

1688–9	1788
Glorious Revolution establishes principle of parliamentary sovereignty	US Constitution introduces principle of separation of powers

contrast, is elected in the same manner as other members of parliament (MPs), and is normally the leader of the party that wins the majority of seats in the legislature (parliament). His position as leader is determined by his own party, not directly by the electorate. The prime minister selects a cabinet from the ranks of his fellow parliamentarians (including the second chamber, if there is one). The cabinet is essentially a committee of ministers responsible for formulating government policy, which is then put before parliament, where it is debated and voted on. The central function of parliament is thus to scrutinize, debate and approve laws; not to govern the country as such but to provide the personnel who do so and then hold them to account for their actions.

The particular virtue usually claimed for the Westminster system is its strength and stability. In the presidential system, there can be, and often is, a divided government, in which the executive (president and cabinet) has a policy agenda that is not supported by the majority in the legislature; the result may be gridlock, in which the executive's legislative programme is substantially blocked. In the Westminster system, by contrast, where both prime minister and cabinet are drawn from parliament, divided government in this sense does not occur,

The mother of parliaments

The British parliament, the legislative assembly of the United Kingdom, is usually thought of as a bicameral (two-chambered) system, but there are actually three parts: the monarch and his or her council of advisers (the Privy Council); the Upper House (the Lords Spiritual and Temporal, comprising bishops, archbishops and peers); and the Lower House, or the Commons. The king or queen, now as in the past, is head of state, but today the role is purely formal and ceremonial. A series of reforms in the 20th century altered the composition of the unelected House of Lords, which now contains only a small number of hereditary peers; the great majority are life peers, who are regularly created by the crown from the 'great and the good', on the advice of the government of the day. The same period of reform has seen the powers of the Lords greatly reduced, and today the Upper House can only delay the passage of legislation. Real power is now concentrated in the House of Commons, the body of members of parliament (MPs) who are elected every five years (or less) by popular ballot.

1911, 1949	1958	1999
Parliament Acts radically reduce powers of House of Lords	Life peerages introduced, to be conferred for life on 'the great and the good'	All but 92 hereditary peers removed from Lords by the House of Lords Act

> **'England is the mother of Parliaments.'**
>
> **John Bright, English liberal politician, 1865**

as a prime minister who had lost the confidence (support) of parliament would normally be obliged to request a dissolution and a general election would follow. Within the cabinet itself, the practice of 'collective responsibility' requires that ministers follow the party line, even if they are not personally in sympathy with a particular policy, so once it has been agreed, all are bound to support it. If they cannot do so in good conscience, they are obliged to resign their position. For these reasons, a government with a fair majority is usually able to push through its legislation with little difficulty.

While the Westminster system clearly has the potential to offer firm government, there is a price to pay for such strength. While the separation of powers characteristic of the presidential system is specifically intended to prevent any branch of government becoming excessively strong, the firm executive control enjoyed by a prime minister can become oppressive, allowing government policy

From servant to master

Although the history of the English parliament can be traced back at least to the 13th century, for the first 400 years it was, for the most part, the servant of the monarch, convened sporadically as royal need dictated. It was usually in time of war, when the king's coffers were especially stretched, that it was deemed prudent to assemble the great men of the realm in order to consult and to help smooth the flow of taxes. It was not until the 17th century that the tables were truly turned and servant became master. The Stuart kings' crass handling of parliament led finally to confrontation between crown and parliament in the English Civil War (1642–9), during which the latter began to assert itself and to demand greater powers and privileges. By the time of the Restoration of the Monarchy in 1660, when Charles II became king, parliament had already attained significant powers in matters of legislation and taxation. It was in part James II's failure to follow his brother's conciliatory approach in his dealings with parliament that sparked the Glorious Revolution of 1688–9. It was this bloodless revolution that finally established the principle of parliamentary sovereignty, which obliged all subsequent monarchs to work within constitutional lines and with due regard to the will of parliament. In the course of the following century, as temporary factions began to coalesce into more permanent parties, the machinery of modern government was steadily established. Henceforth it was clear that the monarch's first minister – the prime minister – needed not so much the confidence of the king or queen in order to govern effectively but that of his fellows in the House of Commons.

to be bulldozed through and minority voices to remain unheard. Critics complain that parliament becomes little more than a rubber-stamp for government policy – a fig-leaf of legitimacy to cover the autocratic tendencies of those truly in control. The charge is exaggerated, but the fact that it has some resonance among ordinary people is in itself bad for democracy.

> **'Parliament has really no control over the executive; it is a pure fiction.'**
> David Lloyd George, 1931

Continental variation While all parliamentary systems are indebted to some extent to the British model, at least from a structural perspective, some variants, for instance in Germany and elsewhere in continental Europe, have a clearly distinct character and mode of operation. Most of the time the British system behaves broadly as if it were a two-party system (even though it is not), and this, combined with the first-past-the-post electoral system used in the UK, has generally ensured that one party has had an overall majority and allowed the executive to be drawn from a single party. This fact, more than any other, has been responsible for the traditions of collective responsibility and strong party loyalty on which much of the robustness of the British system depends.

Most European countries that have parliamentary government are multi-party in character and use some form of proportional representation to elect their politicians. With this kind of voting system, it is rare for a single party to win a majority of seats, so governments are normally coalitions of parties that share some goals but not all. Such coalitions are accustomed to negotiation and compromise, with greater tolerance of ministerial independence and less emphasis on collective decision-making. They also tend to be more volatile and break down more frequently. Overall, executive power is weaker than in the British system but accountability is stronger, as coalition leaders are obliged to listen to different views and to respect the mood of parliament. What is lost in durability is gained in accountability, and many would argue that the demands of democracy are thereby better served.

the condensed idea
Forum for debate or talking-shop?

31 Political parties

'A zeal for different opinions concerning religion, concerning government, and many other points, as well of speculation as of practice; an attachment to different leaders ambitiously contending for pre-eminence and power; or to persons of other descriptions whose fortunes have been interesting to the human passions, have, in turn, divided mankind into parties, inflamed them with mutual animosity, and rendered them much more disposed to vex and oppress each other than to co-operate for their common good.'

As James Madison observes in *The Federalist* (1787), there are many and various causes – religion, politics, personal charisma – that draw people into forming parties, so that they can pursue together goals that might be difficult or impossible to achieve on their own. And it has always been so: 'The latent causes of faction are . . . sown in the nature of man.' No friend of party or faction himself, Madison sees it as a principal task of government to regulate and reconcile the 'various and interfering interests' that encourage groups to form and to seek their own advantage at the expense of others.

Today, the nagging anxiety of Madison and other Founding Fathers of the United States about the dangers of faction and party seems excessive, if only because it is almost impossible to imagine the practice of politics in large, modern democracies other than through the medium of parties. Voting for parties that stand for particular values and interests is, for most of us, the most tangible opportunity we have to exercise our democratic rights. And for politicians who succeed at the ballot box, the party system provides the structural framework within which they attempt to realize the values and promote the interests on the basis of which they were elected.

timeline

1787	1828	1830s
James Madison in *The Federalist* warns of the dangers of faction and party	US Democratic Party formed (after split with National Republicans)	British Conservative Party emerges from old Tory Party

One-party systems The dynamics of parties – their character and behaviour – are dramatically influenced by the social and political context in which they operate. At the most general level, the kind of party that exists without competition in a one-party state is radically different from one that competes with others in a multi-party pluralist state. For single, formally unopposed parties, such as the communist parties in the Soviet Union and China, the path to power is typically by way of revolution, involving the violent overthrow of an existing regime. Once established, such parties exercise a monopoly of power, which is used, theoretically at least, to guide the working class (proletariat) to a state of pure communism, at which point all opposition will have been overcome and coercion will no longer be needed. In this pastoral role, the party must be both pragmatic and authoritarian – highly centralized, yet pervasive, infiltrating every layer of society in order to supervise and keep the people in line. To this end, the party remains fiercely ideological, using indoctrination and censorship to maintain orthodoxy and to eliminate dissent.

> **❝Let me . . . warn you in the most solemn manner against the baneful effects of the spirit of party.❞**
> **George Washington, 1796**

Party label and party line In a one-party system, a party does not compete for control of the apparatus of government; to a significant degree, it *is* the apparatus of government. In a multi-party system, by contrast, competing with rivals at the ballot box to win the right to govern is one of a party's essential functions – a recurrent task that takes up much of its energies.

A fundamental difficulty in representative democracy is to give some reality to the claim that the direction of government reflects the will of the people – a problem that is especially acute in a large and diverse country such as the USA. The solution to this problem – a crude one – is periodic elections fought out between competing parties. Belonging to a party is a label that associates a candidate with a more or less well-defined set of values; this gives voters some indication of what a candidate stands for and how he or she is likely to behave if elected. However, the reliability of the inference from label to behaviour depends on the broader political culture. While a green party candidate can be expected to give a high priority to environmental issues, the Democrat or Republican label

1854

US Republican Party formed, initially in support of anti-slavery movement

1906

Foundation of the British Labour Party

attached to a candidate standing in a US election does not in itself give any very clear indication of future voting behaviour. In this case, the candidate is giving little more than a broad expression of sympathy with a particular political tradition. Furthermore, in the US Congress it is normal to vote according to conscience, rather than to adhere to a strict party line. Party discipline, putting pressure on politicians to vote in support of official party policy, is usual in the British system, where it contributes to strong government. It also helps electors to 'read' the party labels but it also tends to limit spontaneity and free thinking.

Two-party and multi-party systems Within pluralist societies, the practice of politics is affected by the kind of party system in use. Countries such as the United States and Britain have so-called two-party systems, although the name may be misleading. In Britain, for example, there is a third party, the Liberal Democrats, which can play an important role in the government of the country, as it did in forming a coalition administration with the Conservatives in 2010. Over the last century, however, the dominant pattern has been set by the two main parties, Labour and Conservative, competing in a first-past-the-post electoral system that usually results in one side or other having a majority of seats in parliament. This has generally occurred even though the majority party, which proceeds to form a government, may have received significantly less than half of all the votes cast. The result is strong government, capable of forcing through its

Listening to the voice of conscience

A central dilemma facing any elected representative is to weigh up the complex and often conflicting loyalties owed to party, constituents and country. And how these should be set against the urgings of one's own conscience. This thorny issue was addressed by the Irish-born politician and political writer Edmund Burke in a speech delivered to the electors of Bristol, where he was elected member of parliament (MP) in 1774. The thrust of his argument is that, in the final analysis, the 'unbiased opinion, mature judgement and enlightened conscience' of an MP should not be sacrificed to local or partisan interests:

> Parliament is not a congress of ambassadors from different and hostile interests; which interests each must maintain, as an agent and advocate, against other agents and advocates; but parliament is a deliberative assembly of one nation, with one interest, that of the whole; where not local purposes, not local prejudices ought to guide, but the general good resulting from the general reason of the whole. You choose a member indeed; but when you have chosen him, he is not a member of Bristol, but he is a member of parliament.

policy agenda, but such robustness is won, arguably, at the cost of democratic fairness.

Outside the Anglo-Saxon world, most democracies use some variant of proportional representation, under which the number of seats won by a party corresponds closely to its share of the vote and which thereby allows smaller parties to survive and prosper. The usual result is a multi-party system in which it is rare for any one party to enjoy an overall majority. Two or more parties must work together and compromise on their policies in order to form a coalition that can command a governing majority. Such coalitions are almost invariably more volatile and less stable than a government drawn from a single party. The kind of discipline that a single party can keep among its members is harder to maintain in a coalition of two or more parties. Such coalitions may often be relatively short-lived, but they can also be dynamic and innovative, drawing on different political traditions and perspectives.

> **'Under democracy one party always devotes its chief energies to trying to prove that the other party is unfit to rule – and both commonly succeed, and are right.'**
> **H.L. Mencken,** US satirist, 1956

Parties in decline? 'The old parties are husks, with no real soul,' declared Theodore Roosevelt on the campaign trail in 1912, and nearly 100 years later it seems to many that nothing has changed. Especially to the young, the major political parties of the United States and Europe appear dull and badly out of touch. Cynicism about the motives of elected politicians, fuelled by not infrequent charges of corruption and hypocrisy, has hastened a decline in party membership, disillusion among party activists and a fall in voter turnout. Loss of popular support has in turn led to a scrabble for the middle ground, and in seeking to please everyone, parties have become anodyne and consensual – short of inspiration and fearful of radical solutions. At the same time, the revolution in communications, especially the internet, has opened up countless new channels for political expression, undermining the traditional monopoly enjoyed by political parties. It may be hard to imagine modern democracies without parties, but faced with popular apathy, they cannot avoid the challenge of reconnecting with new generations of voters.

the condensed idea
Organizing for power

32 Civil service

The civil service is the engine that drives the modern state. From the most senior officials who advise ministers of the day and oversee the implementation of government policy, to the humblest clerk working in a tax office, the agents of the state – the huge body of officials who are responsible for public administration – are the lifeblood that carries the oxygen of public life.

In every country in the world, the civil service is the largest and most fully realized bureaucracy and as such attracts the kind of criticism that is invariably directed at bureaucratic organizations. The usual caricature of the civil servant is harsh and unflattering: a lethargic and self-serving jobsworth who conceals his own incompetence under mountains of red tape manufactured, wastefully and unnecessarily, at public expense. The paradox is that it is the very features that nourish the popular stereotype that make the civil service an essential component of the modern state; its vices are also, to a curious extent, its virtues. The truth is that these often-maligned servants of the state are indispensable, and there are few aspects of our lives that would not become chaotic in their absence.

Loyal servants of the state While the origins of the modern civil service are inseparable from those of the state that it exists to serve (see page 108), the term 'civil service' itself was first used at the end of the 18th century, when it was applied to the civilian (i.e. non-military) activities carried out by 'covenanted servants' – contracted employees – of the British East India Company. Subsequently, the name came to encompass the full range of services provided by publicly paid officials employed in the administration of the affairs of the state, with the principal exceptions of the armed forces, police and judiciary. In principle, there is no reason why those representing the state's interests abroad

timeline

c.1785

First attested use of 'civil service', applied to the British East India Company

should not be called civil servants, but in practice a distinction is usually drawn between the home civil service and the foreign diplomatic service.

Senior civil servants are employed for the most part as permanent and (supposedly) non-partisan advisers to elected or appointed ministers of state. They are expected to bring their experience of public affairs and technical knowledge to bear in assisting elected politicians, necessarily of limited expertise and tenure, to devise and implement effective state policies. In this connection, the UK government issued a document in 1994 in which it defined the values that it expected the civil service to embody; its aim was to create:

> a non political, permanent Civil Service which sets high value on integrity, impartiality, and objectivity, which serves loyally the Government of the day – of whatever political persuasion – and which recruits staff on the principles of fair and open competition on the basis of merit.

These qualities – integrity, impartiality and objectivity – are principal desiderata in most analyses of the modern civil service.

Civil service as bureaucracy In structure and organization, a modern civil service is essentially bureaucratic: a hierarchy in which the chain of command is clear, the division of duties and responsibilities well defined, and decisions reached on the basis of explicit and supposedly objective rules and procedures. The powers given to civil servants are legally limited and exercised not in a personal capacity but by virtue of the position they hold. Given the nature of their work, civil servants may not generally be held in great affection, but so long as their authority is recognized by those over whom it is exercised (i.e. citizens) as impartial and reasonable, they are respected and play a significant role in establishing the popular legitimacy of the democratic state as a whole.

> **The deal that the civil service offers a minister is this: if you do what we want you to do, we will help you publicly pretend that you're implementing the manifesto on which you were elected.**
>
> Tony Benn, English socialist politician

1922	1979–80	2007
Bureaucracy defined by Weber in *Economy and Society* (published posthumously)	Elections of Thatcher (1979) and Reagan (1980) mark rise of the New Right	Global 'Credit Crunch' raises doubts over role of markets in public administration

Following the influential analysis of the German sociologist Max Weber (see box), the civil service, as a model of bureaucratic organization, may be regarded as the most suitable mechanism for managing the complex public affairs of a modern state because it is the most *efficient* such mechanism. Such a bureaucracy, says Weber, has a 'purely technical superiority over any other form of organization'. Such a view may seem paradoxical, however, as a common perception is that public bureaucracies are highly *inefficient*, delivering neither quality of service nor value for money. The kind of specialization that is typical of a bureaucracy may allow roles to be defined and skills to be refined to meet specific tasks, but such focus can make people blinkered and unwilling to work outside their areas of expertise. Hierarchies may give a clear command structure, but they can also encourage excessive caution and a lack of initiative and creativity. Strict rules and regulations may foster continuity and reduce arbitrariness, but slavish adherence to them can result in means becoming ends in themselves and bad practice becoming institutionalized.

Without fear or favour

The modern civil service is often held up as a paradigm or archetype of bureaucracy. Most current views on bureaucracy are significantly indebted to the work of the German sociologist Max Weber, who in the early 20th century developed the idea of an 'ideal type' of bureaucracy – a theoretical model that embraces those features of real-world bureaucracies that work together in a rational and coherent manner to allow certain desired objectives to be achieved.

The structure of an ideal bureaucracy, for Weber, is a hierarchy in which areas of responsibility are well defined and coordinated by a clear-cut chain of command. Decisions are made according to fixed rules and procedures, so like cases are treated alike on a strictly rational and impersonal basis; arbitrary or personal considerations, such as social status and connections, are of no account. If the modern civil service is viewed in this light, the nature of its administration, rationally organized and legally established, contrasts sharply with public administration in the pre-modern period. At that time the conduct of public affairs was typically arbitrary and self-interested, as the influence of the church or the power of a charismatic individual might determine how promotion and other benefits were conferred. The legal-rational operation of the civil service, understood as a Weberian bureaucracy, explains why its authority is recognized as legitimate by citizens of the state.

Rise of the New Right In the last quarter of the 20th century, such doubts about the competence of those responsible for implementing the policies of national governments became crystallized in a dominant political ideology. In the decades of prosperity following the Second World War, many interventionist governments had come to power and introduced a range of welfare and socially progressive policies. From the 1970s, as the boom years came to an abrupt halt, these costly 'big state' policies came under attack from New Right neoliberals, led by Ronald Reagan in the USA and Margaret Thatcher in the UK. And inevitably the big state's loyal foot-soldiers – an army of civil servants whose raison-d'être depended in part on overseeing the implementation of such big-state initiatives – were caught in the crossfire. The fact that civil servants were unelected and stood outside the political process, once regarded as a mark of independence and impartiality, was now seen as evidence of a lack of accountability. The permanence of career civil servants – in contrast to the transience of elected politicians – was once welcomed as a source of continuity and stability; now, it was more likely to be castigated as a cause of intransigence and inflexibility. The success of the civil service in delivering value for money was openly questioned, and its traditional functions were exposed to market pressures. Concerns over the civil service's accountability to its ultimate master – the electorate – led to a sudden outbreak of allegedly democratic initiatives, such as citizen's charters, independent ombudsmen and performance targets for state-controlled institutions.

> **Bureaucracy, the rule of no one, has become the modern form of despotism.**
>
> **Mary McCarthy,** US novelist, 1961

The buzzwords of the neoliberal purge – privatization, downsizing, market-testing, public-private partnerships – have since lost much of their lustre. The turmoil that assailed the global economy in the early years of the 21st century starkly exposed the dangers of unrestrained market forces, and faith in the capacity of the private sector to deliver public services was deeply shaken. Nevertheless, largely unquestioning public confidence in the abilities of state-appointed bureaucrats, potentates and mandarins was gone, never to return. The proper nature of public administration, involving issues of accountability and a complex calculus of quality, efficiency and cost, remained stubbornly unresolved, with profound implications in many areas of policy-making.

the condensed idea
The state's bureaucracy

33 Media

On 11 April 1992, two days after the Conservative Party had defied predictions to win its fourth consecutive election victory, Britain's bestselling daily newspaper, *The Sun*, published across its front page one of its most famous – soon-to-be-infamous – headlines: IT'S THE SUN WOT WON IT.

The paper's boast was based not only on its long-standing support for the Tory Party but also on its relentless attacks on the Labour leader, Neil Kinnock, in the weeks running up to polling day. Whatever the merits of the paper's claim, the defeated Labour Party took it very seriously. Over the following five years, Kinnock's successor Tony Blair busily set about reinventing the party and trying to persuade the press – and in particular, *The Sun* and its proprietor Rupert Murdoch – that 'New Labour' was a horse worth backing. In the end he succeeded: on the eve of the 1997 election the paper renounced its traditional allegiance to the Tories and urged its readers to back Labour. In the event, Labour enjoyed its most successful election result (in terms of seats won) in its history.

The extent to which newspapers and other media are able to influence voting behaviour, and perhaps even to change the outcome of popular elections, has been much debated. While there is little consensus on this question, the enormous impact of the media on the practice of politics and the behaviour of politicians is beyond doubt. Throughout history, only the most autocratic of despots could afford to totally disregard the mood of their subjects, so channels of communication between ruler and ruled have always mattered. But the advent of mass media – first newspapers, then radio and television, and now the internet and various mobile technologies – has brought about a transformation in the practice of politics, allowing politicians to reach vast audiences undreamt of by earlier generations. Today, almost every action of an elected politician is affected to some degree by consideration of how it will be portrayed in the

timeline

1605	1650
First regularly published weekly newspaper appears in Antwerp	First daily newspaper published in Leipzig

media. For a president or prime minister, every public appearance is a media event, meticulously orchestrated by a team of press officers; every meeting or engagement is a potential photo opportunity; every utterance is a potential sound bite to be broadcast over the 24/7 news channels.

Filter and valve The difficulty in assessing claims such as that made by *The Sun* is to determine whether people are influenced in the way they vote by newspapers (or other media), or whether they choose newspapers that reflect their political preferences. Do the media lead public opinion, or do they follow it? While a few voters are bound to be swayed by a partisan press, the current orthodoxy is that the overall impact is seldom sufficient to change the outcome of an election. Unquestionably, however, the media affect political processes in other ways. The media are rarely, if ever, neutral channels or conduits through which information passes between politicians and the public. They also act as a filter, determining what is and is not allowed to pass through, and as a valve, regulating the flow of information. Furthermore, both politicians and media operators, fully conscious of the power and potential of broadcast and print media, are locked in a constant struggle to gain or maintain control of the release and handling of news stories.

Setting the agenda The filtering effect of the media results in some issues being given space and prominence, while others are covered less or not at all. The consequence of this phenomenon, known as 'agenda-setting', is that the public comes to attach particular significance to some issues and not to others. For the most

Nam and CNN

Increasingly critical TV coverage of the Vietnam War is widely credited with having undermined popular support for US involvement in the conflict and having hastened the withdrawal of American forces in the early 1970s. The term 'Vietnam syndrome', coined in recognition of this phenomenon, is often used to refer to the supposed negative impact of the media in other wars. In the 1990s the transmission of real-time satellite pictures from war zones gave rise to what became known as the 'CNN effect'. In this case the complaint was that live reports, backed up by harrowing and highly emotive images of human suffering, were compelling politicians to make snap judgements on the use of military force. Cases where journalists were alleged to have in effect forced politicians' hands in matters of policy include the 1990s US-led interventions in Somalia (Operation Restore Hope) and in the former Yugoslavia.

1920
First radio news programme broadcast in Detroit

1928
First television news programme broadcast in New York

1990s
First newspapers offering online news appear

part, media organizations are commercially driven, so they look to publish or broadcast stories that they believe will be of interest to their audience. Often this means that there is an emphasis on personality over policy and a tendency to focus on 'human-interest' stories. There is, for instance, an over-reporting of crime-related issues, where there is often a simple narrative with easily identifiable villains and victims, while more 'difficult' subjects, such as foreign affairs, which are seen as rather abstract and unengaging, are given relatively little coverage. An exception to this – which clearly proves the rule – is the coverage of wars, which are inherently dramatic and often gruesomely photogenic. Though taking place abroad, such conflicts tend to be treated more like domestic news, with an emphasis on human interest – on the plight of soldiers, refugees or other civilians caught up in the fighting, rather than on broad strategic issues.

One consequence of media agenda-setting is that the public becomes 'primed', or conditioned, to judge politicians largely on the basis of their performance in certain media-selected issues. So, for example, in the run-up to an election, the popular evaluation of politicians may be based on their stated views on crime, even though this is not their area of expertise and is not relevant to their likely role in government. With the agenda effectively out of their hands, politicians are often obliged to follow the media's lead and to prioritize matters that, objectively, warrant less attention. Often this can have a significant impact on policy decisions and distort the political process. For instance, the sad but relatively rare cases of children being attacked or killed by dangerous breeds of dog have led to extensive

Responsibilities of a free press

In liberal democracies, the media's right and duty to scrutinize and, if necessary, to censure government is long and well established. This, however, has not prevented many governments from attempting to gag the media, always in what they suppose or claim to be the national interest. In a landmark case, the Nixon administration tried in 1971 to block publication of *The Pentagon Papers*, a top-secret account of US involvement in Vietnam that had been leaked to the press. In ruling against the government, the Supreme Court opined that 'paramount among the responsibilities of a free press is the duty to prevent any part of the government from deceiving the people and sending them off to distant lands to die of foreign fevers and foreign shot and shell'. These solemn words have been, or should have been, ringing in the ears of many news editors in light of their one-sided and uncritical coverage of the Bush administration's 'war on terror' from September 2001.

media coverage, in response to which the issue has been escalated to the highest levels of government and forced the passage of hasty and poorly drafted legislation.

Framing the issue No less important than the media's role in setting the public agenda is their tendency to 'frame' issues in a particular way. Defined by the *New York Times* in 2005 as 'choosing the language to define a debate and . . . fitting individual issues into the contexts of broader story lines', framing can radically influence the public perception of an issue. It is no surprise, then, that the right to frame politically sensitive news stories is eagerly contested by journalists and press officers alike.

> **The press was to serve the governed, not the governors. The Government's power to censor the press was abolished so that the press would remain forever free to censure the Government.**
> **Supreme Court Justice Hugo Black, 1971**

A notorious case of the media largely caving in to political pressure occurred in the wake of the 9/11 attacks, when much of the mainstream American media virtually gave up their role of analysing and criticizing the US government's military response in Afghanistan and Iraq. Anxious to be seen to rally behind the flag, the media generally fell in step with the Bush administration's aggressive and unilateral stance, accepting most aspects of the government's framing of the situation. There was little public questioning of President George W. Bush's characterization of the crisis as a 'war on terror', which in due course would serve as a justification not only of a military response but also of sweeping domestic powers and harsh treatment of 'enemy combatants'. From the outset, the government wished to suggest that the central issue was the nature of the military response and its timing, not whether it was legally or morally justified in the first place. The debate rapidly became polarized and was often expressed in the rhetoric of a 'clash of civilizations' in which Muslims were the alien 'other', bent on destroying the freedoms of the liberal West. It is arguable that much of what was done would have been done differently if full media scrutiny had not been effectively suspended. In the midst of failure, it was, paradoxically, an impressive demonstration of the media's awesome power.

the condensed idea
Free to censure

34 Propaganda

Campaign managers attempt to sway public opinion in the direction of their candidate, while elected politicians have press officers who 'manage' the news and put a favourable gloss on events. In time of war a government attempts to instil in the population a sense of patriotism and common purpose that is needed to make sacrifices and to overcome the enemy. A military leader tries to intimidate an opposing army by undermining its morale while exaggerating the strength of his own forces. Business people promote the image of their company in such a way as to convince customers that their products are better than those of their competitors.

The common element here is persuasion, and in each case the objective is to modify or reinforce the beliefs, attitudes and behaviour of a particular group or audience. Achieving this objective requires a systematic and carefully planned management of various kinds of information. This process of persuasion, and by extension the information used to achieve it, is called propaganda. We usually think of propaganda as a way of promoting a political cause or ideology, but in principle it is much broader and encompasses any activity aimed at swaying public opinion, including lobbying and commercial advertising.

The negative connotations usually associated with propaganda are due partly to its recent and grim historical associations but also to the methods that it often employs. Propagandists typically rely on the selective use of information, presenting one-sided messages or arguments that are not necessarily untrue but which are misleading or deceptive. Appealing more to emotion and prejudice than to the intellect, propaganda is closer to indoctrination than education, in that it seeks to inculcate ideas, not to explain them. Essentially manipulative,

timeline

1622	1914–18	1930s
Congregatio de Propaganda Fide set up to spread Roman Catholic faith	First World War sees the emergence of first 'information' ministries	Trotsky and other Soviet 'unpersons' erased from historical records

propagandists are usually at pains to conceal their ultimate goals and act to further their own cause, caring little for the interests of the targeted group.

From pyramids to space rockets

Broadly understood, propaganda has existed, in fact if not in name, virtually as long as human societies have lived and fought together. Military commanders have always sought to boost the morale of their own soldiers and to demoralize their enemies; rulers have always set out to convince their subjects that their rule is both inevitable and legitimate. If politics is the art of persuasion, propaganda has been its constant currency. Palaces and pyramids were built, cities named, coins minted, speeches made, poems written: all these, and innumerable things besides, were done by the few to impress and inspire respect and awe in the many, just as in the 20th century armies paraded through Red Square and rockets were sent to the moon.

> **Propaganda does not deceive people; it merely helps them to deceive themselves.**
> Eric Hoffer, 1955

The word 'propaganda' is believed to be derived from the *Congregatio de Propaganda Fide* (Congregation for Propagation of the Faith), a missionary organization set up by Pope Gregory XV in 1622 to spread the Roman Catholic faith. Until the 20th century, propaganda was most commonly employed in religious contexts, where it was used both to propagate the faith and to reinforce existing beliefs. To the extent that teaching the rightness of one set of beliefs implies that beliefs that contradict it are wrong, propagandistic activities such as missionary work must always have been viewed negatively by some people. However, the strongly negative connotations that the term 'propaganda' has today were largely the consequence of the great wars of the 20th century.

Twentieth-century propaganda

Assisted by the rapid development of mass-communication technologies, propagandists emerged as a recognizable type during the First World War, which offered the first clear opportunity for governments to systematically promote their own national cause by denigrating their enemies. This was done energetically on all sides, as a toxic concoction of inflammatory rhetoric, prejudice, xenophobia, half-truths and lies was exploited to discredit opposing nations. Particularly effective were lurid tales of atrocities

1933–45	1957	2003
Goebbels's propaganda machine controls all aspects of German culture	Launch of Sputnik 1 starts the 'space race', history's greatest propaganda battle	Iraq War initiates battle for 'hearts and minds' between East and West

perpetrated by the enemy, which were carried in newspapers and portrayed on posters. Indeed, false or exaggerated reports of the dastardly deeds of the 'filthy Hun' were credited with hastening the entry of the United States into the conflict. Much of this deception and skulduggery was exposed after the war, thereby bringing into disrepute the various 'information' ministries responsible and the business of propaganda in general.

The techniques of propaganda reached their nadir in the hands of totalitarian regimes, communist and fascist, which embarked on a systematic and comprehensive programme aimed at twisting public opinion into a state of conformity with the ruling party's policies and ideology. Hitler's minister of propaganda, Joseph Goebbels, boasted that he had made the Third Reich by propaganda, and the boast was almost literally true. The consummate propaganda machine he created spewed forth its messages of hate through every conceivable medium, including newspapers, radio broadcasts, cinema, mass rallies, and even the Olympic Games, meticulously staged as a showcase for Aryan power and

Not all black and white

Propaganda is sometimes classified as white and black. White propaganda is basically the spreading of true information, the source of which is openly and correctly attributed, in order to further a particular cause. For instance, there is generally not much doubt about the essential veracity, true motivation and source of government information broadcasts intended to promote health or road safety. In contrast, black propaganda uses outright falsehoods or falsely attributed material. Such material is usually provocative and subversive, and intended to embarrass or discredit a particular target. Wartime propaganda, for example, apparently emanating from a respectable source, may falsely accuse an enemy of atrocities that result in a loss of international support, erosion of morale at home, etc. Another influential classification distinguishes between agitation propaganda, which aims to change attitudes, and integration propaganda, which seeks to reinforce attitudes that already exist. In the final analysis, the only distinction that really matters is between what works and what does not. As the US philosopher Eric Hoffer observed in 1951, 'The gifted propagandist brings to a boil ideas and passions already simmering in the minds of his hearers.' The most effective propaganda builds on existing beliefs and prejudices, coaxing the recipient in a direction that he is already minded to follow. Small comfort, then, for those who seek to blame their immoral actions on the malign influence of others.

superiority. By these means Goebbels orchestrated a campaign that saw the German people indoctrinated with bogus racial theories and a sense of national destiny that demanded the subjugation of other peoples.

The cult of the leader An important feature of totalitarian propaganda was the leader cult, the thrust of which was to detach the great one – Hitler, Mussolini, Stalin, Mao – from the common run of mankind. The Hitler myth, presenting the aloof man of action chosen to lead the Fatherland to embrace its destiny, was obsessively managed through the release of a limited stock of approved images, which were given saturation coverage on postage stamps, postcards, cigarette cards and all sorts of press illustrations. The easy assumption that 'the camera never lies' was tirelessly exploited, most notoriously, in the Soviet Union, by the airbrushing-out of 'unpersons' such as Trotsky from photos that he shared with other communist leaders.

> **❝All propaganda is lies, even when one is telling the truth.❞**
> **George Orwell, 1942**

Many elements of the leader cult have been eagerly picked up by less authoritarian regimes. Every US president since F.D. Roosevelt has been conscious of the need to project just the right image to the American people (and beyond), and in the age of television and now the internet, most senior politicians in democratic countries have teams of experts devoted to different aspects of image management. Roosevelt's press secretary maintained tight control over 'photo opportunities' at the White House and in particular was at pains to keep the president's physical disability out of view. A recent instance of such image-tweaking, much criticized since, occurred in May 2003, when George W. Bush was flown onto the USS *Abraham Lincoln* to deliver his infamously premature victory speech in the Iraq War. By choosing to arrive by fixed-wing aircraft, rather than helicopter, the president, who had early been embroiled in accusations of draft-dodging, was able to emerge on the flight deck, not in civilian clothes, but in a military flying suit: to all the world, a warrior among warriors.

the condensed idea
Bending the truth

35 Poverty

Poverty exists because vital resources – the things that make life good and, sometimes, the things that make life possible – are not evenly distributed. Whether such resources could or should be allocated equally, or less unequally, is a key concern of social justice. To the extent, therefore, that politics is the business of creating a fair social order, poverty is, and always has been, an issue of central importance in political theory and practice.

Poverty is usually thought of as a condition in which people are unable to satisfy their basic needs and hence to function normally within society. But what counts as a basic need and what counts as normal? In many developing countries, a significant proportion of the population live at or near the subsistence level: they have barely enough food to keep themselves alive, while provision of shelter, medicine and education is inadequate or non-existent. In the developed world, on the other hand, very few lack the basic things needed to sustain life, but there are always some who do not reach a socially acceptable standard of living and so fall below an imaginary 'poverty line'. Variously and contentiously defined, the poverty line broadly indicates that a household has insufficient resources, usually measured in terms of income, to participate in the social and leisure activities typically enjoyed by other households within the community. Thus, for example, in a society where the possession of a television or a telephone is considered normal and necessary, the fact of being unable to afford them may be taken as an indication of poverty.

Relative and absolute poverty Poverty, then, can mean very different things in different contexts. In economically developed, industrialized countries, poverty is usually considered in relative terms: people are considered poor, not because they lack the basic requirements needed to sustain life and health, but

timeline

The Millennium Development goals

At the United Nations Millennium Summit in 2000, world leaders set forth the Millennium Declaration, the aim of which was to 'free all men, women, and children from the abject and dehumanizing conditions of extreme poverty'. The objective was detailed in the following eight Millennium Development Goals (MDGs), none of which is currently on course to meet its target date of 2015.

1 Eradicate extreme poverty and hunger
2 Achieve universal primary education
3 Promote gender equality and empower women
4 Reduce the child mortality rate
5 Improve maternal health
6 Combat HIV/AIDS, malaria and other diseases
7 Ensure environmental stability
8 Develop a global partnership for development

because they fail to meet a minimum standard that is set relative to others in the community. In developing countries, by contrast, poverty is often measured in absolute terms, as a condition in which people lack the resources necessary for subsistence. In principle, absolute poverty could be eliminated if sufficient resources were made available to the poor, while relative poverty is certain to persist while the distribution of resources remains unequal. Poverty, then, is a critical concern in both global and domestic politics, but it is not a single issue that is susceptible to a single solution.

The crucial point about poverty in the developed world is that it is avoidable. The total wealth generated by an industrialized economy is such that, if it were divided up equally among all members of society, nobody would be poor, in relative or absolute terms. The fact that in these circumstances poverty is *not* eradicated is itself a political decision. Given that no political ideology sees poverty as a good thing in itself, why then is its persistence tolerated and how is its existence justified?

Socialist and liberal views From a socialist perspective, poverty is not tolerated and cannot be justified. The fact that no real-world society is, or ever has been, free of poverty is a matter of blame that socialism seeks to

2000	2005
Millennium Declaration pledges to eradicate extreme poverty by 2015	World Summit discusses progress towards Millennium Development Goals

remove, though – imperfectly realized – it has so far failed to do so. According to the socialist analysis, derived from Marx, poverty is a structural feature of capitalism and a natural consequence of its operation. The capitalist imperative of maximizing profit entails the exploitation of labour through low wages, long hours and minimal welfare provision; in other words, the business of furthering one's own economic advantage encourages policies and attitudes that tend to increase inequality and hence (relative) poverty. Socialism's task, then, is to remedy the iniquities of capitalism and, adhering to Marx's maxim 'to each according to his need', to allocate resources in such a way as to create equality of social and economic conditions and so eradicate poverty.

The classical liberal view also sees poverty as structural, but it shares little else with the socialist analysis. Its central assumption is that the distribution of resources within the state is determined most efficiently by market forces. Within a free market, individuals compete with one another in pursuit of their own interest, thereby producing an economic outcome that is better than any alternative but not equally good for all; there are always winners and losers, and

Double standards, mixed motives

International aid may be more plentiful today than at any time in the past, but in truth it is still painfully inadequate. With few exceptions, developed countries have consistently failed to come close to targets for foreign aid set by the United Nations. Worse still, many foreign-aid initiatives are viewed with suspicion, often justly, by critics within donor and recipient countries alike. International agencies such as the World Bank and the International Monetary Fund (IMF) have often been accused of ideological bias: intent on spreading the gospel of capitalism, they make aid conditional on market-focused reforms (privatization, removal of trade barriers) and in the process saddle recipient countries with levels of debt that actually exacerbate poverty. Few donors are seen to act disinterestedly. Old colonial powers such as Britain and France are suspected of using aid as a means of perpetuating their influence, while others often appear less concerned with relieving poverty than with serving corporate interests and boosting their own exports. Most contentious of all, the biggest donor, the United States, is often charged by its critics with acting out of self-interest: supporting unsavoury but politically useful regimes, protecting vital trade and energy interests, granting aid to those willing to accommodate military bases. In a swirl of accusation and distrust, much of the good work undertaken by international aid agencies is at risk of sinking in a swamp of cynicism.

this is an essential dynamic of the system. The resulting pattern of wealth is a reflection of the talent and skill of individuals; wealth provides the motivation to succeed, while fear of poverty is part of a system of incentives that drives individual effort and enterprise. According to this analysis, the usual socialist measures to reduce poverty, such as redistributive taxation and extensive welfare programmes, are dangerous because they interfere with the proper functioning of market mechanisms and so jeopardize overall prosperity.

The gulf between rich and poor The vast gulf between rich and poor countries in the world today is a daily affront to human dignity. It is estimated that over 80 percent of the world's population live on less than 10 dollars a day; the poorest 40 percent account for about 5 percent of global income, while the richest 20 percent account for 75 percent. Of approximately two billion children who live in the developing world, roughly one-third do not have adequate shelter; one-fifth do not have access to safe water; and one-seventh have no access to health services. Each year over 10 million children under the age of five die of malnutrition and preventable diseases. This situation of vast wealth on one side and abject poverty on the other is both morally abhorrent and politically unstable.

> **Poverty is an anomaly to rich people; it is very difficult to make out why people who want dinner do not ring the bell.**
>
> Walter Bagehot, 1858

Since the end of the Second World War industrialized countries have donated foreign aid on an unprecedented scale, and there have been sporadic successes in promoting economic development and fostering political stability. There have been high-profile humanitarian initiatives in response to natural and man-made disasters, including famine, genocide and war. Immunization programmes and infrastructure projects (providing access to clean water and improved sanitation, for example) have increased life expectancy and reduced infant mortality in some areas. Yet for the most part the gap between rich and poor, both within and between countries, is growing wider. The political will in the industrialized world is too feeble and too dissipated to address the underlying issues with suitable urgency. However, the developing world will not wait: the deep injustices within the global order are bound to cause further fractures that will shake the rich nations out of their complacency.

the condensed idea
A world divided

36 Crime

'Crime is naught but misdirected energy. So long as every institution of today, economic, political, social, and moral, conspires to misdirect human energy into wrong channels; so long as most people are out of place doing the things they hate to do, living a life they loathe to live, crime will be inevitable, and all the laws on the statutes can only increase, but never do away with, crime.'

Writing in 1917, the US anarchist Emma Goldman expresses a view that sounds as relevant today as it did nearly a century ago. She echoes a point made some 12 years earlier by the English writer H.G. Wells, who observed that crime is 'the measure of a State's failure, all crime in the end is the crime of the community'. On any reading, a central purpose of the state is to establish institutions that maintain a condition of social order, by requiring obedience to laws assented to by society as a whole. Crime, carried out in violation of such laws, represents disruption of social order and is a clear challenge to the state's authority. A society is dysfunctional to the extent that it fails to eliminate crime; to a significant degree, the *point* of a state is to impose lawfulness – its legitimacy depends on its ability to do so – so a state characterized by criminality is, literally, pointless.

A crime is, by definition, an offence that extends beyond the confines of private relations into the public domain. Usually defined and prescribed in some kind of penal code, a criminal act is one whose commission is judged offensive or harmful to society and punishable under the law. The apparatus for dealing with criminal activity is set up and managed by the state, and usually involves officials authorized to act in its name (a police force) and a judicial system that is responsible for prosecuting and punishing wrongdoers. The integrity of society

timeline

1789	1891
Bentham argues that 'all punishment in itself is evil'	Oscar Wilde's *The Soul of Man under Socialism* published

depends on respect for the law, which must not only be obeyed but seen to be obeyed. 'If he who breaks the law is not punished,' US psychiatrist Thomas Szasz affirmed in 1974, 'he who obeys it is cheated. This, and this alone, is why lawbreakers ought to be punished: to authenticate as good, and to encourage as useful, law-abiding behaviour.'

Lies, damned lies . . . Crime casts a broad shadow, blighting the lives not only of victims but of many others around them, so the way it is addressed by those in power is an intensely political issue. It is no surprise that in opinion polls it consistently appears at or near the top of voters' concerns. Public perception of crime is largely determined by television and other media, which tend to focus on sensational and extraordinary stories. As a matter of practical politics, elected politicians have to deal as much with this distorted perception as with the more sober reality. Indeed, determining the nature of this 'reality' is itself a complex business, as the information on the basis of which policies are often determined – official crime statistics – is misleading and socially constructed, in the sense that it is significantly shaped by the fears and prejudices of both politicians and ordinary people.

> **❝Poverty is the mother of crime.❞**
> **Marcus Aurelius,** Roman emperor, 2nd century AD

Generally, only incidents that come to the notice of the police are investigated and recorded, so many (potential) crimes are not picked up in statistical reviews. Serious offences such as rape and domestic violence are often not reported, while so-called 'victimless' crimes, such as drug possession and prostitution, are not discovered unless the police make it their business to look for them. It is clear that official statistics greatly underestimate the incidence of crime, probably capturing much less than half of all incidents that would, if reported and prosecuted, be recorded as crimes. Given their severe limitations, such statistics arguably tell us less about the frequency of crime and more about the offences that are regarded by politicians as important and which are actively pursued by the police and lead to successful prosecutions. Ironically, though inevitably, official figures are never more than a record of unsuccessful criminals – those not smart or lucky enough to evade detection. Many types of criminal and many

1905

H.G. Wells's *A Modern Utopia* published

1917

Publication of Emma Goldman's essay 'Anarchism, what it really stands for'

> ❝The idea of justice must be sacred in any good society . . . Crime and bad lives are the measure of a State's failure, all crime in the end is the crime of the community.❞
>
> **H.G. Wells,** *A Modern Utopia*, 1905

types of crime – including corporate and white-collar crimes, such as fraud and embezzlement – rarely appear in official statistics.

Balancing the scales of justice Crime, then, is among the most emotive of issues, and one that requires politicians to tiptoe among the conflicting and sometimes contradictory views of the people they are elected to serve. Political success is gauged by (allegedly) measurable reductions in crime rates, yet extensions of police powers have to take account of popular concerns that civil liberties are being eroded. Unlimited surveillance and stop-and-search powers, for instance, while doubtless they might assist police in catching criminals, would be seen by most as overly oppressive and hence politically impracticable. In a similar way, the issue of punishment needs careful handling in order to maintain an acceptable balance between the abstract demands of justice and the more down-to-earth matter of preserving social order and ensuring public safety.

The task of punishing criminals – and of justifying doing so – presents the state with a considerable burden. In this context alone, the state's normal duty to protect the rights of its citizens is suspended; here alone, it is called upon to inflict harm on its members and to deny them freedom of movement, political expression and so on. Some find the fact of punishment insupportable. Oscar Wilde, for one, wrote in 1891 that society is 'infinitely more brutalized by the habitual employment of punishment than it is by the occasional occurrence of crime'.

A necessary evil? The standard liberal view is that punishment is a necessary evil, justified because the social benefits it brings outweigh the suffering it causes. 'All punishment is mischief,' insisted the English philosopher Jeremy Bentham, 'all punishment in itself is evil.' Uncontentiously, the danger posed to the public by murderers and other serious offenders is sufficient to warrant their imprisonment (other less liberal types would say execution). Another benefit claimed for punishment is its deterrent value, though here the case is less easy to make. Why should someone be punished, not for the crime he has committed, but in order to deter others from offending in a similar way? Such scruples aside, there are also doubts over the effectiveness of such deterrence, as there is good evidence that it is not so much punishment as fear of capture that deters would-be criminals.

Perhaps the most compelling argument in favour of punishment, from the liberal perspective, is the hope that it holds out of rehabilitating offenders – of reforming and re-educating them in such a way that they can become full and useful members of society. In this area, too, however, there are serious doubts over the ability of penal systems – most current systems, at least – to achieve this kind of benign outcome.

An eye for an eye Competing with this relatively humane conception is an older, more visceral view of punishment as retribution. Everybody is under an obligation to abide by society's rules, so those who choose not to do so incur a penalty (a debt or due) which must be paid. A minor offender may literally 'repay his debt' to society, by paying a fine, while in more serious cases a greater price must be paid, in loss of liberty or (in some jurisdictions) loss of life.

More radically, the general idea that 'the punishment should fit the crime' is sometimes taken to imply that that crime and punishment should be equivalent not only in severity but also in kind. Defenders of the death penalty, for instance, often plead that the only proper reparation for the taking of life is the loss of life. The point is less persuasive in the case of some other crimes, and few would suggest that rapists, for instance, should be raped (though in practice many are). The chief difficulty in this approach is to keep a sanitary distance between (supposedly moral) retribution and (morally indefensible) revenge. It may be objected that punishment expresses society's disgust or outrage at a particular act, but when retribution is stripped down to little more than an urge for vengeance, it scarcely appears adequate as a justification for punishment.

the condensed idea
When society fails

37 Security

'*Salus populi suprema est lex*', proclaimed the great Roman statesman Cicero in the middle of the first century BC: 'The safety of the people is the highest law.' The safety of the state and its members, and the safeguarding of its interests, have since remained a central concern – some would say *the* central concern – of politics, in both theory and practice.

Though its significance is beyond doubt, the concept of security – the condition of such safety and the many things that contribute to bringing it about – defies simple definition. In its most basic meaning, a feeling of security is a psychological state – a subjective response to one's physical circumstances that may or may not be warranted by the circumstances themselves. Different people, and communities of people, feel insecure for different reasons, so the causes of insecurity – the vulnerabilities that exist in individuals and societies and the threats to which they are (or feel) exposed – are enormously variable. Broadly interpreted, such causes may encompass anything that endangers our mental and physical well-being, including threats to our health, way of life and material prosperity. War, poverty and disease are among the many threats, natural and humanly created, that may imperil our security.

National security and deterrence Given its subjective character, the understanding of security is closely tied to the perception of threat and so may vary considerably from one time to another. Historically, the scope of security studies has been limited mainly to activities undertaken to protect the nation-state and its territorial integrity from threats from beyond its borders. A fundamental assumption of this view is that the international system of states is 'anarchic', in the sense that it is composed of independent states that are autonomous and sovereign and so do not recognize any higher authority that is competent to enforce agreements and laws between them. In such a system, the

timeline

*c.*52 BC	1651	1919
Cicero's *De Legibus* (On Laws) asserts supreme importance of people's security	Hobbes's *Leviathan* affirms role of state in provision of security	League of Nations set up to prevent war through collective security

state is regarded as the principal actor: the most effective means of providing national security, both through its own resources (mainly military) and by its ability to form strategic alliances and agreements with other nations. The general assumption is that each state's prime motivation is its own self-interest, and above all its own preservation. Starting from the premise that the 'natural' outcome of unrestrained interaction between states is conflict, the task of the security analyst is to look at means and mechanisms by which the risk of war can be minimized.

Short of actual military engagement, a nation's security against external threats generally depends on some form of deterrence: convincing a would-be aggressor that the benefit to be gained through an act of aggression is outweighed by the cost that would be incurred by committing it. On the face of it, the simplest form of deterrence is provided by defences sufficiently robust that they discourage realistic hope of successful attack, but a well-known dilemma arises in this connection. A state may increase its armament purely with the intention of deterring attack, but – assuming that its attacking capabilities are also thereby

Solitary, poor, nasty, brutish, and short

As security depends on being and feeling protected from harm, creating a secure environment has always been recognized as one of the primary purposes of the well-ordered state. Most centrally, freedom from fear – for instance, of harm that might be inflicted by others – is provided by the hierarchical structure of authority that is integral to the state and which most clearly distinguishes it from the anarchical order that exists between states. The horrors of life without the security provided by the state are graphically painted in the most famous passage from Thomas Hobbes's *Leviathan* (1651):

> There is no place for industry, because the fruit thereof is uncertain: and consequently no culture of the earth; no navigation, nor use of the commodities that may be imported by sea; no commodious building; no instruments of moving and removing such things as require much force; no knowledge of the face of the earth; no account of time; no arts; no letters; no society; and which is worst of all, continual fear, and danger of violent death; and the life of man, solitary, poor, nasty, brutish, and short.

August 1945	October 1945	1991	11 September 2001
Explosion of atomic bomb at Hiroshima, Japan, marks beginning of nuclear age	United Nations comes into being to maintain global peace and security	Dissolution of Soviet Union signals end of Cold War	Islamist attacks on USA highlight dangers of international terrorism

> ❝Since, in the main, it is not armaments that cause wars but wars (or the fears thereof) that cause armaments, it follows that every nation will at every moment strive to keep its armament in an efficient state as required by its fear, otherwise styled security.❞
>
> Salvador de Madariaga, Spanish writer, 1974

enhanced – other states will feel obliged to take this new offensive potential into account and so to enlarge their own arsenals. The likely consequence is some kind of arms race and an escalation of tension and suspicion that may result in war. Thus, paradoxically, fear and insecurity may be more likely than aggression to cause conflict, even where there are no aggressive intentions on either side.

For much of the 20th century, an important model of deterrence was collective security, which was the underlying principle first of the League of Nations, then of the United Nations. Instead of depending on regional alliances to maintain a balance of power, collective security relies on global cooperation between the international community of states, who agree to treat aggression against one state as aggression against all. While straightforward in theory, recent history has shown that the conditions that have to be met for collective security to be effective in practice are very challenging. Conflicting interests on the part of the often optimistically named 'international community' have led to disagreement over definitions of aggression and tended to undermine commitment to concerted action.

The diversification of threat Over the last quarter-century, the scope of security studies has broadened rapidly. The end of the Cold War marked the start of a transition from a bipolar globe dominated by two nuclear superpowers to a highly variegated world exposed to many new (or newly prominent) dangers. The forces of globalization, driven by a revolution in communications and especially the internet, made national borders both porous and fuzzy, so the line between internal and external threats became ever more blurred. Swift movement of people and capital across borders brought new opportunities and new dangers, including transnational fraud and other crime. At the same time, international terrorism – especially after the 9/11 attacks – presented a threat to security that could not be excluded by, or contained within, national borders and that called for an unprecedented level of international cooperation.

A MAD world

In the latter half of the 20th century, during the period of the Cold War, the focus of security analysts and politicians alike was narrowly trained on relations between the Soviet-led Warsaw Pact and US-led NATO, where the agenda was dominated by the ever-present threat of nuclear war. The prevailing theory of deterrence current at the time was mutually assured destruction, or MAD, which was predicated on the practical unusability of each side's nuclear arsenal. According to the terrifying logic of MAD, a stable if tense peace would be maintained by the unimaginable destructive force of nuclear weapons, which meant that their use by one party would trigger a retaliatory strike that would ensure the annihilation of both. It then became a fevered preoccupation on both sides to ensure that they had a force robust enough to survive a first strike with sufficient remaining capacity to inflict unacceptable damage in return. The resulting security, if it could be so described, was of a very peculiar kind, for it was shot through with the most agonized insecurities over the dangers of uncontrollable escalation and accidental first use.

A notable expansion of the traditional scope of security has occurred in issues relating to the environment, broadly conceived. Though complex and controversial in detail, so-called environmental security is based on the recognition that a wide range of 'non-conventional' (non-military) threats can dramatically degrade the quality of life and, in particular, play a role in fomenting or exacerbating violence and conflict. The many sources of environmental stress raised in this connection include scarcity of vital resources, such as water and oil; degradation of the environment due to global warming, pollution, soil erosion, desertification, forest destruction and loss of biodiversity; uncontrolled population growth; epidemics of infectious diseases; and natural disasters such as floods and earthquakes. The link between global security and the environment remains contentious but is now clearly among the most pressing issues on the international agenda, as US secretary of state Warren Christopher emphasized in 1996: 'Environmental forces transcend borders and oceans . . . Addressing natural resource issues is frequently critical to achieving political and economic stability.'

the condensed idea
Threats and vulnerabilities

38 Intelligence

'Know the enemy and know yourself; in a hundred battles you will never be defeated.' The wisdom of the Chinese soldier and strategist Sun Tzu, first set forth over 2,300 years ago, still captures the central insight that informs the work of today's intelligence services. Reliable information about those who have aggressive or malign intentions towards the state and its interests can be of the utmost value in combating potential dangers and preserving national security.

In the popular imagination, fed on a diet of novels and films, the business of intelligence is conducted in a sinister world of adventure and intrigue, populated by an exotic cast of spies, moles and double agents. Historically, indeed, there has been no shortage of strange plots and plans, sometimes successful, to gain information of an enemy's intentions. However, while the use of spies – espionage – has always played a part in intelligence gathering, the adventures of a Mata Hari or a James Bond are extremely rare. The task of gathering, analysing and disseminating useful intelligence is often highly skilled, calling on specialized techniques and technology and commanding massive budgets, but for the most part the work requires not a licence to kill but a very deep reserve of patience and perseverance.

Strategic and tactical Until recent times, efforts to obtain intelligence were for the most part ad hoc and rough-and-ready. Such activities were conducted mainly in the context of military operations, in order to ascertain details such as an enemy's battlefield strength and deployment. It was only in the 20th century that governments began to turn an essentially military function into dedicated peacetime intelligence services.

timeline

4th century BC	December 1941	1947	1973
Importance of military intelligence stressed in Sun Tzu's *The Art of War*	Japan launches surprise attack on US naval base at Pearl Harbor	CIA established to coordinate US intelligence activities	Chilean president Salvador Allende ousted in CIA-backed coup

The principal task of such agencies is to collect and evaluate data – primarily military, political and economic – on countries or other groupings that are considered to pose a threat to national security or some other more specific interest. The information is then passed to relevant decision-makers, who use it to guide them in forming policy. At a strategic level, intelligence on the capabilities and intentions of particular nations helps to define relatively broad policy positions. Tactical intelligence, by contrast, is more narrowly focused on the needs of military commanders making operational decisions in the field.

Eyes in the sky, eyes on the ground Much of the popular image of intelligence work was moulded in the era of the Cold War, in an ideologically divided world where the stakes were so high that any price seemed worth paying to obtain good intelligence. In the East and West, vast budgets were dedicated to intelligence services that recruited the brightest minds and harnessed the latest technology to penetrate the obsessively guarded secrets of their opponents. Then, as now, the great majority of intelligence data was gathered not directly by human

Between diplomacy and war

The most controversial task usually entrusted to intelligence agencies has very little to do with intelligence. Many aspects of intelligence work call for secrecy and discretion, so when a government needs to cast a shroud over its activities abroad, it often looks to exploit the peculiar talents of those who are in the habit of keeping things dark. Covert action, according to a view given by the South African government in 1995, is 'activity abroad intended not to gather information but to influence events, an activity midway between diplomacy and war'. Such undercover actions, always unacknowledged at the time, range from attempts to destabilize governments and to sway election results to full-scale paramilitary operations. The most energetic sponsor of such activities is the US government through its Central Intelligence Agency (CIA). Lasting controversy has hung around many of the CIA's operations, including its role in undermining the Allende government in Chile in 1973 and in providing military and financial support for the mujahideen in their guerrilla war against the Soviets in the 1980s.

1980s	1991	11 September 2001	March 2003
Afghan mujahideen supported by US in war against Soviets	Collapse of Soviet Union marks end of Cold War	9/11 attacks on USA represent major intelligence failure	US-led war against Iraq launched on basis of poor intelligence

spies but by a variety of technical means. Both sides relied heavily on signals intelligence, which involved bugging (electronic eavesdropping) and intercepting and deciphering radio and other kinds of electronic communication. Equally important was imagery intelligence, which was obtained by aircraft and satellites taking photographic, infrared and other kinds of images of installations and other features on the earth's surface.

As these technical surveillance methods became ever more sophisticated, they came to overshadow so-called 'human intelligence' gathering, though it was still the latter that continued to fascinate creative artists and their audiences. Human intelligence, typically gathered in situ in foreign countries, is mostly obtained from foreign officials or others in positions of trust who are induced to reveal secret information that has been entrusted to them. These so-called human 'assets' are handled by intelligence or 'case' officers, who often work under diplomatic cover, attached to an embassy, or have some kind of non-official cover, presenting themselves as (for instance) academics or businesspeople.

Counterintelligence All nations are engaged to some degree in a never-ending battle to gather information on their rivals and competitors, so one of the main functions of intelligence agencies is counterintelligence – the business of blocking and disrupting an opponent's efforts to obtain valuable information about one's own country. One aspect of counterintelligence is

Missed dates of infamy

It is the inevitable fate of intelligence agencies to be remembered more for their failures than for their successes. The FBI and CIA's inability to anticipate the 9/11 attacks in New York and Washington has been called the greatest failure in the history of US intelligence. This catastrophic lapse was swiftly followed by a defective assessment of Iraq's capacity to develop weapons of mass destruction – faulty intelligence that was used as the principal justification of the 2003 Iraq War. The 9/11 attacks that precipitated US president George W. Bush's entire 'war on terrorism' were themselves repeatedly likened to an earlier, equally traumatic intelligence failure: the Japanese attack on Pearl Harbor in December 1941, the event that brought America into the Second World War. In both cases, the problem was not so much the quality of the intelligence available but the inability of different agencies to coordinate their efforts and to take appropriate action. Both brought deep soul-searching and reassessment among the US intelligence community.

denial of information: keeping secret (classified) information from falling into the wrong hands, by implementing robust security procedures, encrypting and limiting access to sensitive data and so on. The more proactive side of counterintelligence involves thwarting rival espionage operations, in order to prevent foreign spies infiltrating the government, armed forces or intelligence agencies. Disrupting adversaries' ability to analyse and evaluate data they have managed to obtain can sometimes be achieved by introducing double agents, or 'moles', into their intelligence service, or by planting false or misleading information.

New challenges In the context of the Cold War, where safeguarding state secrets became a neurosis, the clandestine intelligence-gathering methods used by agencies such as the US CIA (Central Intelligence Agency) and the Soviet KGB (Committee for State Security) allowed a flow of information that helped to maintain a state of long, if tense, superpower stability. Most of the time it was pretty clear who the enemy was, and information was always precious, because it was scarce and hard won. All that changed after the collapse of the Soviet Union in 1991.

The prominence on the world stage of many non-state actors, some of them fundamentalist and ready to resort to terrorist methods, has presented an array of new threats. At the same time, the revolution in global communications, especially the internet, means that most countries are more open to scrutiny than ever before. While a large amount of intelligence has always been 'open source' – painstakingly gleaned from newspapers, broadcasts and other public sources – most high-value information was procured through covert operations. Increasingly, in an unfamiliar world awash with information, the problem is not so much how to get hold of intelligence but how to avoid drowning in it. Some states, it is true, remain closed and demand attention, but much of the burden has now shifted from procurement to filtering: the task of coping with a tsunami of data and extracting gems from mountains of dross. Few seriously doubt that the business of intelligence will continue to thrive into the future, but equally it is clear that many of its traditional functions and methods must be reconsidered and that it needs to forge a new role in a rapidly changing world.

the condensed idea
Knowing your enemy

39 Political violence

Politics presupposes violence. Violence, or the threat of it, is one of the principal concerns that motivates people to form societies in which government is entrusted to a central authority – the state. And it is for this reason that the state claims a 'monopoly on the legitimate use of violence' – an exclusive right to exercise physical force against external enemies and its own citizens, when they break its rules.

Such, at least, is the view of a political tradition that goes back to Thomas Hobbes, John Locke and others in the 17th century and remains influential to this day. If people did not live in politically organized societies, Hobbes suggests, they would live in a 'state of nature', a terrifying condition in which individuals existed without social restraint: driven by lust for power, caring for and trusting in no one, stalked by 'continual fear, and danger of violent death'.

The principal difference that distinguishes political violence from other forms of violence is that, from the perspective of the perpetrator, the former is always legitimate. There is truth in the cliché that one man's terrorist is another man's freedom fighter. Every state, of course, regards acts of violence against itself as illegal, and this is formally true (in the same sense that violence against the Nazi state was illegal). But a justly constituted society should provide legal channels through which its members can voice their dissent. Where no such channels exist, it is reasonable for people to question the legitimacy of the state and sometimes to challenge it. Such challenges can take many forms. Some – most notably, Mahatma Gandhi and Martin Luther King – have insisted on non-violent protest, in particular 'civil disobedience', in which the laws and regulations of an offending state are deliberately and systematically flouted. Most, however, would allow that recourse to violent means is justified if all else fails.

timeline

1914	1916	1933
Assassination of Archduke Franz Ferdinand at Sarajevo	Irish rebels embrace blood sacrifice at Easter Rising	First concentration camp at Dachau foreshadows Nazi genocide

Such means include acts that the targeted state would call terroristic and might extend, in extreme circumstances, to outright revolution.

Civil war The most comprehensive and widespread expression of political violence, and generally the most costly in human life and suffering, is civil war. Typically, such conflicts are sparked by discord over political control of a state, or of territory within a state, and involve government forces on one side and a rebel group or groups on the other. The latter often belong to minority communities that suffer discrimination on the basis of ethnic, cultural or religious differences and which demand rights to proper political representation, greater autonomy or full independence. The eruption of civil conflict may expose deep social divisions that have existed for many generations and which persist long after the formal resolution of war. It has been estimated that there were over 100 such conflicts in the second half of the 20th century, with an aggregate loss of life that far exceeded the casualties of 'conventional' international wars in the same period. In recent decades some of the most serious civil wars have taken place in African countries, including Angola, Congo, Rwanda, Liberia, Sudan and Somalia; but there have been numerous conflicts elsewhere, in places as far afield as Afghanistan, East Timor, Chechnya, Sri Lanka and the Balkans.

Genocide and 'ethnic cleansing' To be sustained for any length of time, a civil war requires some kind of parity of power between the opposing forces. Where such balance does not exist or has been destroyed in the course of fighting, another equally deadly form of political violence may manifest itself. Especially where the cause of conflict is ethnic, cultural or religious – often a pretext deliberately exaggerated by one side or other – social discord may escalate into pogroms and state-sponsored murder. Whereas in civil war women and children often get caught up in the fighting as innocent victims, in campaigns of genocide, where a claim of racial distinctiveness is explicitly made, such non-combatants may be specifically and deliberately targeted.

In terms of numbers of victims, the 20th century saw more state-inflicted genocide and mass killing than had occurred in the history of the world to that date. The most notorious case of a population selected on the basis of cultural and religious

1947	**1992**	**1994**	**2001**
Indian independence marks culmination of Gandhi's campaign of non-violence	Beginning of 'ethnic cleansing' in former Yugoslavia	Genocide in Rwanda sees death of over half a million Tutsis	9/11 Islamist attacks mark climax of 'new' terrorism

difference was that of the Jews in Europe before and during the Second World War, when the explicit policy of the Nazi state was to 'cleanse' all the territory it occupied by forcibly removing and exterminating undesirable elements (a term which also included gypsies and many others considered inferior or corrupt, such as homosexuals, the disabled and the mentally ill). Since 1945 over 50 cases of genocide or politically inspired mass killing have been recorded around the world; infamous recent cases occurred in Rwanda and the Darfur region of Sudan.

In a gruesome terminological twist, from 1992 onwards the phrase 'ethnic cleansing' came to be applied to the policy of mass killing, deportation and internment used principally by Bosnian-Serb paramilitaries against rival ethnic groups in the former Yugoslav republic of Bosnia-Herzegovina. Their aim was to create 'racial homogeneity' in disputed areas that had previously been ethnically diverse in order to bolster their claim to sovereignty over those territories. Critics saw use of the term, in the mouths of both politicians and diplomats, as a cynical euphemism for genocide intended to sanitize the actions of the perpetrators and to excuse the unwillingness of the international community to intervene as the gravity of the case warranted. While it is clear that genocide is an extreme form of ethnic cleansing, it is unhelpful to see the terms as synonymous, as there are means of ethnic cleansing, such as forcible expatriation, that clearly fall short of genocide. Application of the term retrospectively to events prior to 1992 remains contentious.

Blood sacrifice

Perpetrators of political violence naturally regard their actions as legitimate and worth the cost, in suffering and lost life, paid by themselves and others. Few, however, have embraced the prospect of death with such relish as the leaders of the 1916 Easter Rising against British rule in Ireland. The signatories of the Proclamation of the Irish Republic – the public reading of which marked the start of the rebellion – all agreed that Ireland must prove its worthiness by 'the readiness of its children to sacrifice themselves'. The most fervent worshipper at the alter of blood sacrifice was rebel leader Patrick Pearse, who wrote mystically of bloodshed as 'a cleansing and sanctifying thing' and of the 'old heart of the earth' being 'warmed by the red wine of the battlefield'. The rebels felt, rightly as it turned out, that a grand gesture – one that might bring on their own deaths – would revitalize the spirit of revolutionary nationalism in the Irish people. Within three weeks of the start of the rising, Pearse himself and 14 of his fellow rebels had been tried and executed by firing squad. They died as martyrs, however, and the march to Irish independence was unstoppable.

> **❝Violence appears where power is in jeopardy, but left to its own course it ends in power's disappearance . . . Violence can destroy power; it is utterly incapable of creating it.❞**
>
> **Hannah Arendt**, German political theorist, 1970

Terrorism The label 'terrorist' is never neutral. An act of terrorism is, by definition, something illegal and morally indefensible, so political actors are called terrorists only by their opponents, never by themselves. Such acts are invariably politically motivated and usually carried out by sub-state actors or groups united by some common concern or ideology. The actions of states may sometimes be described as terroristic, but such statements are rhetorical and accusatory, with the implication that the relevant behaviour is (amongst other things) unworthy of an entity that calls itself a state. States are sometimes accused of 'sponsoring' terrorism, usually with the implication that they are involved in giving financial or other indirect support to those committing violent acts in other countries. There is often a whiff of hypocrisy in such charges, however, as in the 1980s, when the Reagan administration in the US accused Libya of sponsoring terrorism while simultaneously supporting violence against constitutional governments in Nicaragua and elsewhere.

International interest in terrorism has remained at an unprecedented level of intensity since the Muslim fundamentalist attacks against New York and the Pentagon on 11 September 2001. This atrocity was seen by many analysts as the worst, though not the first, instance of a new brand of terrorism marked by fanaticism and rejection of compromise. These 'new' terrorists, most notably the Islamist group al-Qaeda, are driven more by extreme religious beliefs than by any earthly concern. Ultimately accountable only to God, they are quite willing to sacrifice their own lives in order to maximize the deaths of their enemies, including non-combatants. As such they remain incomprehensible to their enemies, presenting a threat that has not yet been fully understood, let alone adequately countered.

the condensed idea
When is it right to fight?

40 Welfare

"Tis not enough to help the feeble up, but to support him after,' says Shakespeare's Timon of Athens, and it might serve as a motto for the welfare state. Only the truly blessed get through life without ever needing the support of others. Unemployment; family breakdown, violence and abuse; illness and disability of body or mind; delinquency and drug addiction; old age: almost everyone, at some time or another, is unable to cope on their own with the problems that life throws at them. What, then, could be more benign than the picture of the state as safety net, to catch us when we fall into difficulty or hardship?

The picture is certainly familiar. The scope and organization of welfare services may be enormously varied from one country to another, but virtually every state provides some level of support to its citizens. Many, indeed, would unhesitatingly agree with Samuel Johnson that 'A decent provision for the poor is the true test of civilization.' Providing for the social and economic security of a country's entire population demands investment in a huge infrastructure and a vast array of benefits, which may include unemployment and sickness pay, pensions, free healthcare and subsidized housing. Setting up such a system requires that the better-off give up some of their wealth to improve the lot of their fellow citizens. Consent to taxation and redistribution of wealth on this scale betokens, many would say, a social consciousness that is the mark of a properly constituted civil society; such sentiment fosters inclusivity and contributes to a sense of common purpose, even of national identity. To this extent, the emergence of the nation-state as the pre-eminent political form has been linked to the concurrent development of the welfare state.

timeline

1930s	1942	1949
Roosevelt's New Deal introduces unemployment relief, old age pensions etc. in US	The Beveridge Report proposes comprehensive social insurance scheme in Britain	Truman's Fair Deal programme includes extensive welfare provisions in US

This reassuring picture of welfare as the key to social cohesion is deceptive, however, for the issue of welfare lies squarely on a major ideological fault line. Writing in 1994, the US politician and social scientist Daniel P. Moynihan neatly summed up the level of hostility: 'Welfare became a term of opprobrium – a contentious, often vindictive area of political conflict in which liberals and conservatives clashed and children were lost sight of.' Supporters value welfare as an essential corrective to the unjust and socially divisive effects of market forces: a bulwark against the iniquity and exploitation that would follow from unrestrained capitalism. Critics, on the other hand, fear that welfare, if not strictly limited, interferes with the operation of the market, introducing inefficiencies, stifling initiative and removing incentives to work. The consequence, they say, is a nanny state, a dependency culture in which recipients of welfare are discouraged from taking proper responsibility for their own lives.

> **Power has only one duty – to secure the social welfare of the people.**
> Benjamin Disraeli, 1845

From cradle to grave The main impetus behind modern welfare services was public concern over the appalling conditions of overcrowding, filth and epidemic disease that arose in the wake of the incipient Industrial Revolution in the early decades of the 19th century. Enlightened Victorian industrialists rejected the view that poverty reflected a moral failing in the poor themselves; recognizing that various kinds of hardship were a natural product of industrialization and the operation of capitalism, they founded numerous charities and philanthropic societies that were the basis of today's welfare services.

The first modern welfare states developed in the period after the Second World War, at the instigation of socialist or social democratic governments in northern Europe, notably in Sweden and the United Kingdom. These pioneering systems were all-embracing, aiming to protect citizens at every stage of life 'from cradle to grave', and offered access to (at least) a basic level of such essentials as health services, education and housing. Much early assistance was directed at those unable to work through unemployment, disability or sickness, so funding for welfare has historically come, in part at least, from insurance contributions paid by workers who would thereby build up their own level of entitlement. Today, most welfare systems are structurally complex, relying on a 'mixed economy' of

1965
Lyndon B. Johnson's Great Society programme introduces Medicare and Medicaid in US

1973, 1979
Drastic increases in oil price (oil shocks) trigger global economic crises

1980s
Reagan and Thatcher regimes in US and UK undertake restructuring of welfare

state, private and voluntary provision in which government agencies, commercial operations and charitable bodies work alongside one another.

Boom and bust In the period following the Second World War a broad consensus in favour of comprehensive welfare provision prevailed in Western European industrialized countries. In the United States, meanwhile, welfare principles were embodied in Franklin D. Roosevelt's New Deal, which was followed by Harry S. Truman's Fair Deal and various welfare programmes pioneered by later presidents. In the 1970s, however, a number of factors conspired to bring an end to the status quo. Sustained postwar growth and prosperity ground to a halt as the supply of cheap energy was cut off in the 1973 oil crisis ('oil shock'). Rising unemployment then combined with budget deficits in high-spending socialist-governed countries to bring about severe recession. Changing patterns both in the workplace and within society at large only served to make matters worse. The shift of income from young to old, always implicit in the welfare state, was accelerated as the proportion of elderly people – net consumers of social services – increased. At the same time decades of prosperity led people generally to expect a higher standard of living and better social services. In the matter of healthcare, for instance, new treatments and more

A culture of dependency

Concern that state assistance may breed dependency in those receiving it is nothing new. In a memorandum written to the British prime minister William Pitt the Younger in 1795, the Irish politician and political theorist Edmund Burke warns of the dangers of attempting 'to feed the people out of the hands of the magistrates'. He goes on to explain how 'having looked to Government for bread, on the very first scarcity they will turn and bite the hand that fed them. To avoid that evil, Government will redouble the causes of it; and then it will become inveterate and incurable.' In recent decades similar concern has centred around the role of welfare in the development of a social underclass: a section of the population that is permanently excluded from mainstream society and characterized by joblessness, broken and single-parent families, drug abuse, gang culture and criminality. There has been much scholarly disagreement over the precise nature and cause of such an underclass – whether its social exclusion can be explained in terms of the attitudes and behaviour of its members, or whether deeper structural inequalities within society are to blame.

effective drugs became available, but the cost was high. Suddenly it was necessary to make choices and to set priorities.

Against this turbulent background there was a political shift as neoliberal governments, including Ronald Reagan's in the USA and Margaret Thatcher's in the UK, came to power. Political discourse became polarized, as free-marketeers decried the culture of dependency that had (allegedly) grown up under socialist regimes and demanded that government cut back expenditure in key areas such as health, education and social security. Yet, in spite of the rhetoric, the rolling-back of the state – and the welfare state with it – was never more than partial. While there was a show of toughness – eligibility rules were tightened and the rigours of the market were trumpeted – there was little appetite for anything more than refining and restructuring.

> **❝Welfare's purpose should be to eliminate, as far as possible, the need for its own existence.❞**
> **Ronald Reagan, 1970**

Sacred cows and turkeys Since the 1980s, the social and economic pressures on welfare services have in no way let up. Indeed, since the 1990s, the forces of globalization have created a culture of highly mobile – and highly fickle – capital investment which has eroded nation-states' control over their own economic destiny. High wages and high social-security costs are now a luxury that threatens to undermine a country's global competitiveness. Yet, within democracies, cutting or abolishing social-service programmes remains electorally unpalatable. Even if voters are opposed in principle to high taxation and public spending, they are reluctant to vote against services from which they themselves benefit. Writing in 1991, the US political humorist P.J. O'Rourke made the point exactly:

> Social Security is a government program with a constituency made up of the old, the near old and those who hope or fear to grow old. After 215 years of trying, we have finally discovered a special interest that includes 100 percent of the population. Now we can vote ourselves rich.

So long as democracy survives and turkeys refuse to vote for Christmas, welfare states are likely to remain safe from the abolitionary ambitions of elected governments.

the condensed idea
Securing society

41 Racism

Some ideas take on a life of their own, however bad they may be. In the minds of educated people, few concepts have been so thoroughly discredited as racism. Science has shown that it has no intellectual substance; history that it has no place in civilized society. Yet racism's biological unreality has not prevented it having a thriving political life.

In every modern society belief in race, in some form or other, lingers on. This is the idea that human beings belong to a number of discrete biological groups (races) that are exclusive and exhaustive – everyone belongs to one and one only. Each race is thought to share distinct physical features, such as skin colour, and it is usually assumed that these are attended by characteristic psychological attributes, such as temperament and intelligence. This set of beliefs and the prejudice that it spawns (racism) are the cause of deep inequalities and injustices at every level, political, social, economic and cultural. Even though racial theory itself is no longer given much credence, many of the power structures and institutions that it helped to create and was once thought to justify are still in place and constantly reinforced by powerful interest groups.

The word 'race' has long been applied, with little precision, to groups of people who are linked, or believed to be linked, in some way – sharing a common ancestry, perhaps, or coming from a particular geographical region. In other contexts, such groups might be called nations, or peoples, or communities. It is only over the last three centuries that the more precise meaning of race evolved that underlies the term 'racism'.

Origins of race The idea of race and the racist world-view can be traced to the growth of European colonialism in the 17th century, and in particular to the

timeline

1641
Slavery first legalized
in American colony of
Massachusetts

1865
Slavery abolished in the USA

emergence of slavery and the slave trade (see box). In the centuries that followed, the sense of racial 'otherness', at first largely intuitive and barely conceptualized, was reinforced by successive waves of discriminatory legislation and by the theorizing of both intellectuals and scientists. Thinkers such as Kant and Voltaire explicitly endorsed the view that 'savages' or 'primitives' were racially inferior, while the energies of scientists were channelled into identifying the supposed racial divisions of the human species. Some even went so far as to propose that other racial groups constituted different species – in effect, that they were not human, or fully human, at all. At any rate, by the early years of the 20th century, after many decades of habituation, an essentially racist understanding of the world was generally accepted as biological and anthropological fact. The idea that there were natural differences between human groups that followed racial lines had become fully ingrained in most societies around the world, and with it the assumption that such differences justified differential social and political treatment.

Race and slavery

For the first English colonists settling in North America at the beginning of the 17th century, life was unimaginably tough. In this dog-eat-dog world, it must have seemed quite natural – a matter of brute survival – to exploit those with whom they came into contact: first the Native Americans, then the black Africans who arrived shortly afterwards. Over time, however, what had been driven by economic necessity nurtured a habit of mind, and by the end of the 1600s half-formed notions of cultural and moral superiority had begun to coalesce into a full-blown rationalization of a mainstay of their hard-won prosperity: the institution of slavery. The common view that these non-European peoples belonged to different races and were on that account inferior was gradually reinforced by philosophers and scientists alike. At the time of the birth of the USA in 1776, slavery had been legalized in the American colonies for over a century, and for the first 89 years of its existence the self-proclaimed 'home of the free' and bastion of liberty depended on slave labour. Many aspects of the discriminatory treatment that slavery entailed lasted for a hundred years after its formal abolition in 1865, and the legacy of racism that it created is still very much alive today.

1933	1964	early 1990s
First anti-Jewish racial policies implemented in Nazi Germany	Civil Rights Act outlaws racial segregation in the USA	Apartheid system brought to a (legal) end in South Africa

Racism and rac(ial)ism The racist view of the world is essentially ideological. It is based on a system of beliefs and attitudes about humankind and its relationships. Certain physical characteristics (skin colour, skull shape etc.), which can naturally be explained in biological terms, are assumed to be indicative of deeper biological differences that are markers of racial identity. Dependent as they are on the unique biology of the race concerned, these differences are believed to be genetically determined and thus hereditary, innate and permanent.

Racism of this kind (sometimes called 'racialism') does not lead to any clear moral or political conclusions. There is no contradiction between a belief that people belong to biologically distinct races and that everyone should be treated equally and granted equal rights. A common adjunct to the racist world-view, however, is that the races supposed by the theory are unequal in terms of qualities such as mental capacity and moral worth and hence that it is possible in principle to rank them according to their relative superiority.

It is the idea that some races are superior to others that explains racism as it is popularly understood. Typically, this is a crude and non-intellectualized contempt for those who are different from oneself in physical appearance, geographical

Apart or a part?

An important factor in the postwar dynamics of racism in Western Europe was the influx into countries such as Britain and France of immigrants from former colonies in Asia, Africa and the Caribbean. Many migrants were encouraged to settle in the boom years of the 1950s and 1960s, generally to fill unwanted and low-status vacancies in the labour market, only to become targets of racist resentment and abuse when harder economic times followed in the 1970s. Since that time, the issue of how best to integrate ethnic minorities into the dominant host community has never left the political agenda. Politicians have had to walk a tightrope, with the legitimate social and political aspirations of immigrant groups on one side and the anxieties of sections of the 'white' population on the other. The countries concerned have tried very different strategies, from the strongly assimilationist approach of France, which insists that newcomers broadly conform to traditional French norms, to the multicultural approach of Britain, where it is expected that groups of different ethnic origins will retain many of their native ways and customs. There is nothing like consensus on which approach is more effective – if either.

> **❝I refuse to accept the view that mankind is so tragically bound to the starless midnight of racism and war that the bright daybreak of peace and brotherhood can never become a reality.❞**
> **Martin Luther King Jr, 1964**

origin and so on. In individuals, such contempt may express itself in aggressive or violent behaviour. More significantly, the assumptions of the racist world-view can be, and have been, used by politicians and legislators to justify discriminatory policies and institutions in society at large. Most notoriously, in South Africa, until its abolition in the early 1990s, the system of apartheid, or 'separate development', formally sanctioned a range of discriminatory measures against the non-white majority population, who were segregated and cordoned off in certain designated areas, restricted to low-status jobs, and denied access to most political and economic opportunities and privileges.

The slow death of race Up until the 1970s politicians seeking to advance racist agendas could still claim the theoretical support of many scientists. This scientific orthodoxy soon began to crumble, however, under the weight of evidence – first of blood group patterns, and then of DNA and various other genetic markers – that failed to show any correlation with the conventional racial categories. Today, the biological conception of race is almost universally rejected by scientists. It is generally understood that the idea of race is a social construction, of relatively recent origin, that can only be understood in the context of specific historical, cultural and political circumstances. Unfortunately, if inevitably, it is certain to take much longer to eradicate this destructive notion from the minds of ordinary people.

the condensed idea
The starless midnight of racism

42 Corruption

'Corruption is not a new problem . . . It's a human problem, and it has existed in some form in almost every society . . . It is painfully obvious that corruption stifles development – it siphons off scarce resources that could improve infrastructure, bolster education systems, and strengthen public health . . . In the end, if the people cannot trust their government to do the job for which it exists – to protect them and to promote their common welfare – all else is lost. And this is why the struggle against corruption is one of the great struggles of our time.'

On a visit to Kenya in 2006, Senator Barack Obama, soon-to-be 44th president of the USA, made a frank speech about the corrosive effects of widespread corruption on every aspect – political, economic, social – of a country's life. As Obama implies, no age or place has been free of corruption. For almost as long as humans have organized themselves socially into political hierarchies, there have been questions over the proper use of power and the role of virtue in public life; the temptation to abuse one's status and position of power to enrich oneself has always existed, so the conditions for corruption to thrive have always been present.

'Among a people generally corrupt, liberty cannot long exist.'

Edmund Burke, 1777

The effects of corruption run far beyond the damage it inflicts on the internal health of a country. In today's globalizing world, the destiny and well-being of every nation is inextricably linked with that of every other. Countries that suffer, or are perceived to suffer, from high levels of corruption and lack of transparency in the way they do business are bound to be at a disadvantage in global markets, where trading partners and outside investors are easily alarmed and quick to look elsewhere.

timeline

1944	1993
Foundation of World Bank	Transparency International founded to raise awareness of corruption

Framing the problem The damage caused by corruption, locally and globally, is now widely recognized. While no country is immune, its impact is most acutely felt in developing countries, where political institutions are typically more vulnerable and official procedures and safeguards less robust. In such circumstances, it is relatively easy for a culture of fraud, bribery and extortion to take root. It may become routine for illegal 'facilitation' payments – various kickbacks and backhanders, big and small – to be made in order to gain preferential treatment from bureaucrats. Cumulatively, this can mean that a significant share of public funds and resources gets diverted into private pockets, thereby exacerbating poverty among the general population and generating widespread cynicism about political processes. For these reasons the task of tackling corruption has become a high priority for supranational bodies such as the World Bank and for several non-governmental organizations such as Transparency International.

The challenge is daunting, not only because the scale of the problem is almost impossible to quantify (corrupt dealings are by their nature secretive), but because there has long been little consensus even at the level of definition. Traditionally (and currently, too, in popular usage), corruption has been seen as a perversion of a political system or the vice of an individual; to say that a person is corrupt is to make a negative evaluation of his character and integrity. The difficulty with such assessments is that they are deeply value-laden and cannot be properly understood outside the moral and cultural context in which they were made.

Progress on the ground in tackling corruption calls for objective (or less subjective) analysis and meaningful comparison of empirical data obtained from

❛Corruption . . . erodes the state from the inside out, sickening the justice system until there is no justice to be found, poisoning the police forces until their presence becomes a source of insecurity rather than comfort.❜

Barack Obama, 2006

1999

OECD Anti-Bribery Convention
comes into force

2006

Barack Obama addresses issue of
corruption on visit to Kenya

An opportunistic infection

Corruption is often portrayed primarily as a problem of non-Western, developing countries. It is true that levels of corruption are much higher in (say) sub-Saharan Africa than in Scandinavia, but the reality is that corruption is opportunistic, springing up wherever conditions allow. The lower incidence in Western countries can largely be attributed to the strength of the safeguards in place: more robust institutions, greater transparency in procedures, and less inequality in incomes and hence less temptation to bend the rules. Corruption has more opportunities in fledgling democracies and non-democratic regimes, but there is no room for complacency anywhere and – as history has repeatedly shown – no country is immune. What is beyond dispute is that the West must bear a large share of the responsibility for the parlous situation of developing countries. For many of the bribes – and almost all the biggest bribes – are offered by Western companies and giant multinationals seeking to win major leases, concessions and contracts. Indeed, it was not until 1999 that any effort was made to introduce sanctions against bribery in international business transactions, when the Organization for Economic Cooperation and Development (OECD) established a convention that required signatories to criminalize the act of bribing foreign public officials.

a wide range of different contexts. To this end, Transparency International has adopted a neutral definition of corruption as 'abuse of entrusted power for private gain'. Power is granted to officials, by the people or otherwise, on condition that it is used for the benefit of society as a whole, so to use it for personal gain is an illegal breach of trust. Corruption, according to this view, is interpreted merely as an illegal exchange – a preferential grant of a benefit from an official to a recipient, in return for some sort of bribe (monetary or other). On this basis, data from different nations can be gathered and analysed, thereby allowing the scale and nature of the problem to be better understood.

The cost of corruption The insidious way in which corruption seeps into the fabric of a country ensures that its effects are never restricted to the economic sphere. The richest pickings are to be had in the area of military procurement and in high-profile, big-budget projects such as dams and power plants, so public funds tend to be diverted into these areas even when there is a far greater need for essential (though less newsworthy) infrastructure projects such as schools and hospitals and the supply of energy and water to rural areas. Popular disaffection prompted by such wasteful and self-serving decisions readily turns to political apathy and distrust of government. In a culture where corruption is commonplace, people quickly become cynical about the motives of elected politicians and lose faith in the political institutions in which they serve. Where political leaders are seen to be unaccountable and 'on the make', it is almost impossible for democratic institutions and respect for the rule of law to take root.

The heavy cost incurred by a country for the corrupt practices of its officials can stretch far into the future. The routine offering of bribes is sometimes seen as an efficient and relatively harmless way of 'getting business done' in systems that are bound up in miles of bureaucratic 'red tape'. This may sometimes be true, though most recent research strongly suggests that systemic corruption breeds inefficiency in the long term. However, regulations and procedures that are dismissed by an impatient businessman as red tape may include measures that are essential in protecting public health and the environment. Bending or disregarding the rules has allowed developed countries to export their pollution, in the form of toxic and nuclear waste, to nations desperate for income. Meanwhile logging and mining concessions (for instance), granted not in the public interest but for private gain, have seen reckless short-term exploitation of natural resources. The landscape is scarred, the earth's riches despoiled, forest cover stripped away. And as ever, it is ordinary people who bear the brunt of the damage, as local communities are displaced, soils eroded and climatic patterns disturbed.

> **The accomplice to the crime of corruption is frequently our own indifference.**
> Bess Myerson, Miss America 1945 and New York politician

the condensed idea
Something rotten in the state

43 Political correctness

In 2006 a number of British newspapers gleefully ran a story on two children's playgroups that had mirthlessly assumed the straitjacket of political correctness. Consumed with misplaced paranoia about causing racial offence, they had rewritten the traditional nursery rhyme 'Baa Baa Black Sheep', changing 'Black' to 'Rainbow'. In the same joyless spirit, it was reported, the shattering fate of Humpty Dumpty had been altered to avoid trauma to young minds, while the seven dwarfs had been evicted from Snow White in order to cushion the sensibilities of the vertically challenged.

'Political correctness goes mad at the nursery,' as one tabloid put it. Except it hadn't. The charity responsible for the two playgroups at the centre of the media storm explained that their action had nothing to do with political correctness or avoiding 'racially offensive' language. A variety of descriptive words had been introduced into the traditional nursery favourite in order to turn it into an action rhyme: 'They sing happy, sad, bouncing, hopping, pink, blue, black and white sheep etc. This encourages the children to extend their vocabulary.' Needless to say, newspapers did not let the truth get in the way of a good story, especially when there was an opportunity to mock the latest excesses of the 'Loony Left'.

A good thing gone bad? Political correctness *ought* to be a good thing. After all, on the face of it, one of its main aims is to create a fairer world and to correct past and present wrongs. Politically correct (PC) people believe that differences – especially differences over which we have no control, such as gender

timeline

1960s

Concept of political correctness first appears in feminist literature

and skin colour – should not only be tolerated but respected. Everybody, they feel, should be treated as individuals, never as stereotypes; people should be judged on their own merit, and they should never be patronized, belittled or mocked because they are black, female, gay, fat or disabled. Political correctness is also socially progressive. It aims to reform and improve society by moving beyond conventional attitudes and traditional prejudices. Talking and acting sensitively, in a way that does not give offence to others, is a statement about how we see the world and what kind of world we want to live in.

Yet the reality is that political correctness generally gets a thoroughly bad press, and it is not only on the pages of British tabloid newspapers. The most vociferous critics may be conservative, right-wing commentators, but they are not alone. There are plenty of others who shake their heads in disbelief at the latest absurdity of the earnest and po-faced PC brigade: Christmas banned for fear of giving offence to non-Christians; a menu listing a 'ploughperson's lunch'; the black market renamed the parallel market; the disabled becoming differently abled. Surveys repeatedly show that a large majority of ordinary people are simply fed up with the antics of the PC lobby. And often laughter turns to real indignation, even anger, at these self-appointed vigilantes, these control freaks, who take it upon themselves to watch our every word, to tell us what to think and how to behave.

> **❝The phrase "political correctness" was born as a coded cover for all who still want to say Paki, spastic or queer, all those who still want to pick on anyone not like them, playground bullies who never grew up.❞**
>
> **Polly Toynbee,** British journalist, 2009

The backlash against all that is labelled 'politically correct' is now so complete that to be called 'PC' is almost always to be criticized, not praised. Conversely, to be politically incorrect, or non-PC, is usually seen as a badge of honour: an indication that someone is unconventional, outspoken, prepared to stand up for common sense against the tyrannies of the thought police. How, then, did it ever become normal to mock and pillory those whose mission is apparently to bring more fairness into the world and to reduce the amount of gratuitous offence?

1978

Supreme Court ruling implies that affirmative action is constitutional

from 1980s

US 'culture wars' begin – 'the struggle to define America'

PC: a vertically challenged herstory Today, the term 'political correctness' is to be found in all sorts of contexts; it is more often encountered in newspaper headlines and everyday conversation than it is in more rarefied debate. This present currency is surprisingly recent, however. Largely confined to the pages of radical feminist literature for the first two decades of its life, the concept rose to notorious prominence from the mid-1980s, when it took centre stage in the US 'culture wars' – the simplistic title given to a complex ideological struggle between liberal left and conservative right that raged, initially at least, over the issue of progressive teaching methods and new curricula in American universities.

The background to this struggle was a newly emerging liberal critique of Western civilization that painted its history (or herstory, as some feminists preferred) as the story of 'dead white males' who dominated and repressed other groups (women, non-whites) and denied them a political and cultural voice. The chief antidote to this tale of oppression, from the liberal perspective, was 'affirmative action', a policy that was based on the view that it was not sufficient merely to eliminate the causes of past injustices; it was necessary to correct them by actively promoting women, racial minorities and other historically disadvantaged groups. When applied to university admissions, this policy called for a quota system in which a proportion of places was reserved for black and other minority students. In the same spirit, university curricula were modified to reflect a new multicultural outlook, in which non-Western traditions and cultures were

The language battleground

Some of the fiercest fighting in the PC wars has been fought in the field of language – what we can say and how we should say it. And it is here, too, that the virtues and vices of the movement are most clearly on display. On the one hand, there is the sheer absurdity of a US television reporter, desperate to describe the black African Nelson Mandela as black without using the word 'black', finally opting to call him 'African American'. Some proposals – 'herstory' for 'history', 'womyn' for 'women' – are deliberately provocative (and etymology-defying), while others are daft and can scarcely be used without tongue firmly in cheek ('cerebrally challenged' for 'stupid', 'non-waged' for 'unemployed'). On the other hand, there is much that only the most reactionary curmudgeon could object to. Even such a person would, presumably, sense the oddity in calling a male flight attendant an 'air hostess', even if he (and it is likely to be a he) felt that it was no job for a man.

celebrated. Courses on Western civilization were downgraded or mothballed, while the great classics of Western literature were shelved, to be replaced by recent works written by women, blacks and other minorities.

Predictably, this radical programme of reform was deeply repugnant to the right, not least because it appeared to ride roughshod over the principle of equality of opportunity which was a cornerstone of the American political system. It was as part of the right's attack on this programme that conservative critics took up the phrase 'political correctness' and turned it, with conscious irony, on those who had created it. One target of the right was the apologetic world-view of the PC lobby, who were apparently so racked with post-colonial guilt and self-loathing that they would embrace other cultures while disdaining their own. The main thrust of their attack, however, was reserved for the hypocritical intolerance of the call for toleration. In their anxiety to overthrow traditional attitudes and conventions, the zealots of political correctness seemed to be unaware of, or indifferent to, the fact that they were seeking to replace the old system of beliefs with a new and rigid orthodoxy of their own. This dogmatic insistence that there was one 'correct' way of viewing things was branded by critics as 'liberal fascism': an unbending and illiberal outlook that was both self-righteous and quick to chastise heresy or dissent in others.

Good causes, lost causes A movement that was at first largely confined to academia soon spread further afield, in the US and elsewhere. Before long it had come to encompass a wide range of liberal positions on everything from environmentalism and animal rights to the importance of breastfeeding and the dangers of competitive sport. In their choice of issues, as well as the stridency with which they have sometimes been presented, it is hard to deny that the champions of political correctness have tended to play into the hands of their opponents. Artless and provocative by turn, they have frequently and defiantly defended the indefensible, or what seems so even to impartial observers. The irony is that, amidst a good deal of nonsense and distraction, there is much that is eminently defensible and, indeed, badly needs defending – a fact that is often lost in all the political rancour and posturing.

the condensed idea
Liberal fascism?

44 Realism

'We [the Athenians] have done nothing extraordinary, nor contrary to human nature, in accepting an empire that was offered to us and refusing to give it up again. In this we are constrained by three of the most powerful motives: honour, fear and self-interest. Nor are we the first to act in this way – it has always been the way that the weaker must bow down to the stronger. We feel that we are worthy of our power, as did you Spartans, until thought of your own interest made you speak of right and wrong. Talk of justice never deterred anyone from seizing by force whatever he could.'

The speech of which these words form a part was supposedly made in 432 BC, shortly before the outbreak of the Peloponnesian War, by Athenian envoys attempting to dissuade their main rivals, the Spartans, from making a stand against their city's rising power and aggressive imperialism. Written over 2,400 years ago by the Greek historian Thucydides, the tone of the speech is worldly and cynical, its message thoroughly pragmatic and uncompromising. For the Athenians, political interaction between different peoples is ultimately a struggle for power, and in this struggle the prime motivations are fear for one's security and self-interest. They have no time for moral scruples, for in the end all agree that might is right; the battle for domination is rooted in human nature and everyone would act as they do, given the same opportunities.

Thucydides' Athenians speak the language of realpolitik, or political realism. Moral or ideological considerations count for little, and neither justice nor any other sentimental or idealistic consideration is allowed to cloud hard judgements of national interest. Unerringly isolating its key components – concern for security and the struggle for power – Thucydides has sometimes been called the

timeline

5th century BC	1532
Thucydides expresses realist attitudes in his *History of the Peloponnesian War*	Machiavelli's *The Prince* gives classic account of realist 'power politics'

father of political realism, an approach to international relations that came to the fore in the mid-20th century and is still prominent today.

The failure of optimism The recent emergence of realism as a theory of international relations was largely a reaction to the perceived failures of what had immediately preceded it. Between the world wars, the dominant perspective on global politics was idealism, which was founded on a utopian belief in an underlying harmony of interests between countries; its basic contention was that war and other improper uses of power could be averted by establishing effective international laws and organizations. The inadequacy of such assumptions was cruelly exposed by the demise of the League of Nations, the naked aggression of Hitler and other fascist leaders and their shameless flouting of international law. The failed policy of appeasement, symbolized by the Munich Agreement of 1938, was the catalyst for a more hard-headed approach to world politics, in which actors on the global stage were seen for what they were, not for what deluded dreamers might wish them to be. The time was ripe for a new era of realism in international relations.

Predictably, given the context in which they formed their ideas, the generation of political realists who emerged during and after the Second World War, subsequently known as classical realists, shared a somewhat pessimistic view of the nature and conduct of international relations. According to their analysis, the primary concern of statesmen is the national interest, interpreted,

Safer to be feared than loved

Historically, the most celebrated realist is the Florentine political theorist Niccolò Machiavelli, who in *The Prince* (1532) famously counsels rulers that it is better to be feared than loved and that effective use of power depends on their readiness to disregard conventional morality. In a similar vein to his 20th-century successors, Machiavelli makes a powerful case against the idealism of his contemporaries:

> It being my intention to write a thing which shall be useful to him who apprehends it, it appears to me more appropriate to follow up the real truth of the matter than the imagination of it; for many have pictured republics and principalities which in fact have never been known or seen, because how one lives is so far distant from how one ought to live, that he who neglects what is done for what ought to be done, sooner effects his ruin than his preservation.

1938
British and French appeasement of Nazis at Munich symbolizes failure of idealism

1939
E.H. Carr gives first expression of realist outlook in *The 20 Years' Crisis, 1919–1939*

1979
Kenneth Waltz develops neorealist approach in his *Theory of International Politics*

> **❝Utopia and reality are . . . the two facets of political science. Sound political thought and sound political life will be found only where both have their place.❞**
>
> **E.H. Carr,** *The 20 Years' Crisis,* **1939**

minimally, as survival or preservation of the state, which once secured may permit domination or control over others. The means to achieve these ends is power, and hence the 'struggle for power' – the urge to maximize the state's capabilities, broadly interpreted – is the driving force of all political activity.

As state power is both relational (exercised over somebody else) and relative (measured relative to the power of others), the early realists supposed that it could only be increased at the expense of other states. In global interactions, there are always winners and losers; in the later language of game theory, the system of states is a zero-sum game, in which gains in one area are necessarily matched by losses in another. In such an analysis, the business of satisfying national interests (by winning greater power) is always intrinsically competitive and conflictual. And because classical realists shared the view that the struggle for power was an essential part of the human condition – it was an inevitable expression of more or less immutable human nature – they held out little hope of change or improvement in the future. For the realist, then, conflict and war are the default, and the main task is to analyse how they can be regulated or reduced through diplomacy and strategic alliance.

Neorealism Realism established itself as the dominant approach within the study of international relations in the decades following the Second World War. In particular, it became the leading paradigm in analysing threats and framing policies in the context of the Cold War, in which two superpowers confronted each other across the global stage. In a polarized world living under the threat of nuclear annihilation, there was a strong appeal in the stark clarity of the realist world view, with its unbending focus on security. From the 1960s, however, elegant simplicity began to look like oversimplification, and moves were made to add greater conceptual definition and theoretical sophistication.

Neorealism shares many of the assumptions of its classical precursor. It adheres to the central claim that the behaviour of individual states is essentially competitive and best explained in terms of the distribution of power among them. It also continues to place the sovereign state at centre stage, treating it as a coherent actor that behaves rationally in pursuit of its own interests. The key development, prominent in the neorealist analysis, is the idea that the conflict at the heart of the international system is a consequence, not of immutable laws of human nature (as classical realists typically suggest), but of the structure of the system itself. Being sovereign, the states that constitute the system are formally equal with one another and so do not recognize any authority higher than themselves; the system is thus 'anarchic', in the sense that it lacks any supreme authority to enforce laws and agreements between its members. In such a system, each state is obliged to operate on the principle of 'self-help': in its dealings with other nations, it cannot count on their goodwill but must rely on its own resources to protect its interests.

Complex interdependence Realism, in its neorealist or 'structural' form, remains a highly influential perspective within the study of international relations, not least for the copious and constructive criticism that it has generated. The attractions of realism, especially its simplicity, are, for its critics, its weaknesses. In particular, it is suggested that its state-centred view of the world fails to capture (if it ever did) the complexity and interconnectedness of global relations as they are today. The forces of globalization, economic and other; the influence of transnational and non-state actors (multinational corporations, international organizations, terrorist groups etc.); the decline and fragmentation of state power; the proliferation of complex threats (terrorist, environmental); the diminished role of conventional military forces: all have conspired to render the realist view anachronistic at best. Equally strident have been criticisms of realism's lack of a moral grounding, as evidenced by its insistence on conflict as the essential dynamic within the international system. To all of this, the realist, ever wary of utopianism, would probably reply in much the same way as he would have done more than half a century ago: look at the world as it is, not as we might wish it to be.

> **Political Realism has at all times insisted that the nature of politics is fundamentally determined by the struggle for power.**
> John Herz, *Political Realism and Political Idealism*, 1951

the condensed idea
The struggle for power

45 War

'There is an urge and rage in people to destroy, to kill, to murder, and until all mankind, without exception, undergoes a great change, wars will be waged, everything that has been built up, cultivated and grown, will be destroyed and disfigured, after which mankind will have to begin all over again.' Writing in May 1944, the 14-year-old Jewish German Anne Frank expresses a despair shared by many. Of all creatures, the human species alone appears to be bent on destroying and killing its own kind. War has never been long absent from any place at any time, so it is tempting to suppose, with the young diarist, that it is an ingrained and chronic feature of human nature.

A swift response to the question of war's permanence is given by the Prussian military theorist Karl von Clausewitz: 'War', he asserts, 'is the continuation of politics by other means.' So long as humans remain political animals hungry for land and other resources, there will be disputes about which group lives where and which group tells others what to do. And very often these disputes will be beyond resolution by other, peaceful means, and violent conflict will be the inevitable consequence. In contrast – and the experience of history notwithstanding – others have stubbornly clung to the hope that a future without war is possible; that warfare may be in some way cultural, a consequence of social practices that could in principle be reformed or removed.

Fighting the good fight Views may differ on whether or not war is woven into the fabric of human nature, but few would disagree that some disputes are worse than others and that not all violence is equally bad. 'War is an ugly thing,'

timeline

4th century BC	5th century AD	13th century
Sun Tzu writes *The Art of War*, the world's first work of military theory	St Augustine develops the Christian doctrine of just war	Aquinas refines the principles of just war

wrote the Victorian philosopher John Stuart Mill, 'but not the ugliest of things: the decayed and degraded state of moral and patriotic feeling which thinks that nothing is *worth* a war, is much worse.' Mill was among the most humane of men, yet he believed that sometimes it is necessary to fight the good fight. On occasion the motive may be so compelling, the cause so important that recourse to arms is morally justified. In these special circumstances, war may be the lesser of two evils: war may be just war.

> **'There never was a good war, or a bad peace.'**
> **Benjamin Franklin, 1783**

The origins of the notion of just war go back to St Augustine, who attempted in the fifth century AD to reconcile the early Church's pacifism with the harsh realities of imperial rule. Augustine's musings were refined in the 13th century by the theologian Thomas Aquinas, who was responsible for the now-canonical distinction between *jus ad bellum* ('justice in the move to war', the conditions under which it is morally right to take up arms) and *jus in bello* ('justice in war', rules of conduct once fighting is underway). Much of the current debate over the ethics of war is structured around these two ideas.

Conduct unbecoming

It is possible to fight a just war unjustly, and an unjust war justly: it is one thing, in other words, to embark on a war for the right reasons, another to conduct oneself in a morally appropriate manner once the fighting has started. This second aspect (*jus in bello,* according to usual terminology) encompasses a wide range of issues, including the use of particular types of weapons (nuclear, chemical, mines, scatter bombs etc.) and the behaviour of individual soldiers in their relation both to the enemy and to civilians. One crucial point is that the means chosen to achieve a particular end must be proportionate: most, for instance, would consider no military objective sufficiently important to justify a nuclear attack. A second point is that combatants and non-combatants must be strictly distinguished. It is generally considered immoral, for example, to target civilians, however effective it might be in military terms. The aerial bombardment of cities, by both Axis and Allied bombers, in the Second World War is often given as a case of such illicit failure to discriminate.

1832

Publication of Clausewitz's highly influential *On War*

1862

American Civil War prompts J.S. Mill to extol the notion of just war

A lesser evil . . . Most authorities agree that there are a number of conditions all of which must be met to justify a move to war. First and foremost, there must be 'just cause'. In earlier times this was often a religious justification. However, such a reason would now generally be dismissed, in the secular West at least, as ideologically motivated, and modern theorists tend to limit the scope of just cause to defence against aggression. Uncontroversially, this would cover self-defence against a violation of a country's basic rights – an attack on its political sovereignty and territorial integrity – and most would extend it to include assistance given to another country suffering such aggression. Just cause is not enough on its own, however. It must be accompanied by 'right intention'. The sole motivation behind any action must be to right the wrong that was caused by the original act of aggression. The claimed just cause cannot be a fig leaf for some ulterior motive, such as national interest or territorial expansion.

> **❝Anyone who has ever looked into the glazed eyes of a soldier dying on the battlefield will think hard before starting a war.❞**
> Otto von Bismarck, 1867

A further condition is that a decision to take up arms should only be taken by the 'proper authority'. For most of human history, the situation was as described by the poet John Dryden, who declared at the end of the 17th century that

The sovereign disinfectant

War has never lacked its enthusiasts, quick to extol its invigorating or ennobling qualities. Writing in 1911, three years before the outbreak of the 'war to end all wars', the Prussian military historian Friedrich von Bernhardi wrote glowingly of 'the inevitableness, the idealism, and the blessing of war'. In an essay written at the start of the same ghastly conflict, the English poet and critic Edmund Gosse praised war as 'the sovereign disinfectant' whose 'red stream of blood . . . cleans out the stagnant pools and clotted channels of the intellect'.

Less surprisingly, we find war eulogized by fascists such as Mussolini, who drools over war that 'imposes the stamp of nobility upon the peoples who have the courage to make it'. Predictably, it is most often war's veterans, such as Eisenhower, who understand its true nature: 'I hate war as only a soldier who has lived it can, only as one who has seen its brutality, its futility, its stupidity.' Or as the Dutch humanist Erasmus put it: 'War is delightful to those who have no experience of it.'

'War is the trade of kings'. Within 100 years, however, the French Revolution had ensured that the right to declare war would thenceforth reside with whatever body or institution of the state held sovereign power. The concept of proper authority raises, of course, tricky questions about legitimate government and the appropriate relationship between decision-makers and people. For instance, few would deny that the Nazi governors of 1930s Germany lacked not only just cause but also basic legitimacy to declare and wage war.

... and a last resort A country should only resort to war, even a just one, if it has a reasonable prospect of success: there is generally no point in sacrificing lives and resources in vain. Others, though, would argue that it is right (and certainly not wrong) to resist an aggressor, however futile the gesture may be. Furthermore, a sense of proportionality must be observed. There must be a balance between the desired end and the likely consequences of getting there: the expected good, in terms of righting the wrong that constitutes the just cause, must be weighed against the anticipated damage, in terms of casualties, human suffering etc.

War-war or jaw-jaw?

Most political theorists today subscribe to some version of the just war doctrine, but it is not the only perspective. Two other significant views are realism and pacifism. Realists are sceptical about the whole business of applying ethical concepts to war. For them, war is an essentially natural outcome of the interaction of independent and autonomous states on the global stage; international influence, national security and self-interest are the key concerns. Pacifists, in contrast, ardently believe that morality must hold sway in international affairs; military action, in their view, is never the right solution – there is always a better way of resolving a problem. Or, as Winston Churchill observed in 1954, 'To jaw-jaw is always better than to war-war.'

'To subdue the enemy without a fight is the supreme excellence,' according to the Chinese general Sun Tzu, the world's first great military theorist. Military action must always be the last resort and is only ever justified if every other peaceful, non-military option has failed. As the British politician Tony Benn once pointed out, there is a sense in which 'all war represents a failure of diplomacy'.

the condensed idea
Politics by other means

46 Nationalism

'A country is not a mere territory; the particular territory is only its foundation. The country is the idea which rises upon that foundation; it is the sentiment of love, the sense of fellowship which binds together all the sons of that territory.' Writing in 1860, Italian politician Giuseppe Mazzini here describes the sense of patriotism – the love of country – that inspired him to become one of the architects of Italian unification.

Few would doubt the sincerity of the sentiment expressed by Mazzini. At moments of crisis, patriotism can be the mainspring of heroic sacrifice and selfless resistance to oppression; at quieter times, love of one's native land may inspire a deep and lasting sense of community and social cohesion. But setting a high value on one's own country generally means devaluing those of other people. Patriotism's close cousin, nationalism, often demands a fierce devotion that excludes others and may nurture a sense of superiority over them. The national character which nationalism cherishes may be, as the German philosopher Arthur Schopenhauer observed in 1851, 'only another name for the particular form which the littleness, perversity and baseness of mankind take in every country'. An 'infantile sickness . . . the measles of the human race', in Einstein's opinion, nationalism was the principal cause of two world wars in the 20th century and has recently been deeply implicated in horrendous violence and grotesque 'ethnic cleansing' in places as far apart as Rwanda and the Balkans. Indeed, nationalism has aroused such passion and fury over the last two centuries that it must bear a large share of responsibility for the dire conflict and strife that have scarred the world during those years.

The struggle for statehood Nationalism goes beyond the love of country – the pride in its successes and concern for its well-being – that is the basis of patriotism. More focused and more intellectualized than this simple emotion,

timeline

1775–83	1789–99	c.1870
The USA, forged in the American Revolution, inspires liberal nationalism	French Revolution fought for 'Liberty, Equality, Fraternity'	Italian state created after half-century of nationalist endeavour

> **6Patriotism is a lively sense of collective responsibility. Nationalism is a silly cock crowing on its own dunghill.9**
>
> **Richard Aldington, English novelist and poet, 1931**

nationalism often has a political or ideological component, combining patriotic feeling with an active programme for change or recognition. Typically, the central aspiration of such a nationalist programme is to win statehood, a new status that implies independence and sovereignty for a community whose members have some grounds for believing that they constitute a 'nation'. Once this primary aim has been achieved, the objectives of nationalism are to promote the nation's well-being and to defend those values and characteristics on which a shared sense of identity and destiny were originally constructed. In pursuing these various goals, nationalists believe that the object of their endeavours – the nation-state, aspirant or realized – has the right to the loyalties of its members above other loyalties and that its interests trump other interests.

The genius of a nation What, then, is the nation on which nationalists build their hopes and dreams? The long-term survival of a state doubtless depends on having a recognized territory with strong borders, but every nationalist would agree with Mazzini that land alone is not the issue. In his *Table Talk* of 1830, the poet Samuel Taylor Coleridge is close to the true meaning: 'I, for one, do not call the sod under my feet my country. But language, religion, laws, government, blood – identity in these makes men of one country.'

But even this is not enough. It is characteristic of nationalists to believe that their own country is unique (and hence that it is superior to others); to have a conviction that there is a peculiar character or identity, a 'genius of a nation', as Emerson put it, 'which is not to be found in the numerical citizens'. Common origin and ethnicity; a single language; a shared fund of myths and memories; traditional values and customs: some or all of these factors – historical, geographical, cultural – mystically conspire to form something that is greater than all of them: the distinctive and unique national character. To sense this quality is

1871	**1922–45**	**1991–2001**	**1994**
Germany formed into nation-state under leadership of Bismarck	Fascist dictators pursue extreme nationalist policies in Europe	Nationalist hatreds fuel war in Balkans	Nationalist-inspired genocide in Rwanda

Inventing the past

Today, nationalism and national self-determination are widely accepted as legitimate political aspirations. One aspect of this legitimacy is the belief that the nation, as a unit of political organization, is of great antiquity – a belief that is much bolstered by nationalist folklore, which traces the nation's historical and cultural roots back into the immemorial past. In reality, however, nation-states are essentially modern constructions, and the picture of unbroken historical continuity is a largely fictitious product of 'retrospective nationalism'. This is not to suggest that people throughout history have not always been attached to the land of their birth and to customs and traditions handed down by their ancestors. But the patterns of allegiance in the pre-modern world were essentially different. The primary loyalty was not to the state as such but usually to a divinely sanctioned monarch; and beneath the monarch there was a complex hierarchy of localized loyalties that were owed to feudal lords or aristocratic elites. And at the base of all other beliefs was the notion that every human belonged to an overarching religious community that aspired, ultimately, to encompass all mankind. Only when these ancient ties began to loosen, in a process that began with the turmoil of the American and French revolutions, was it possible for the forces of modernity – secularization, popular sovereignty, the concept of human rights, the scientific revolution, industrialization – to shape the nation-state. And from the beginning, for better or for worse, the constant companion of the nation-state has been the nationalist fervour that it inspires.

more a matter of feeling than knowing, more instinct than intellect: 'Nations do not think,' wrote Mark Twain in 1906, 'they only feel. They get their feelings at second hand through their temperaments, not their brains.'

The existence of such a mystical quality is by the nature of things hard to disprove (though the onus should be on those who wish to prove that it does exist). Undoubtedly, however, the grounds that are usually adduced to show that a nation is some kind of coherent and privileged community are extremely shaky. The usual 'glue' of nationhood is ethnicity, supported by a variety of historical, cultural and other factors. The reality, though, is that ethnic groups have been intermingling for thousands of years and that no present-day population of any size is ethnically homogeneous. Even if there were such ethnic groups, the evidence suggests that common ethnicity has rather little to do with community bonding and integration when compared with factors such as shared language and religion.

Nationalisms, liberal versus authoritarian The origins of nationalism as a modern political phenomenon are necessarily tied to the birth of the nation-state around which its ambitions form (see page 108). While the manner in which nationalism has expressed itself has been highly variable, reflecting widely different conditions of time and place, from early in its development two quite distinct strains were apparent: one liberal and progressive, the other authoritarian and backward-looking.

Deeply patriotic though they were, the Founding Fathers of the United States shared a nationalist feeling that was essentially liberal and forward-looking. Adopting a universal outlook based on reason, they saw themselves blazing a trail for mankind as a whole in its march towards greater liberty and equality. The vision of the new American nation was a direct inspiration, just a few years later, for the nationalism of the French revolutionaries, who expressed their universal aspirations in their famous slogan: 'Liberty, Equality, Fraternity'. In both America and France the formation of the new nation was an act of self-determination willingly undertaken by its members.

Partly as a reaction to the excesses of the French revolutionaries and the subsequent depredations of Napoleon Bonaparte, the German nationalism that evolved in the first half of the 19th century took on a very different complexion. Romantic and inward-looking, it favoured instinct over reason; tradition over progress; authority over freedom. Rejecting universalism and the idea of the brotherhood of nations, this version of nationalism was at once self-absorbed and exclusive, fabricating a national history that emphasized difference and superiority. It was this conception of the nation and the kind of nationalism it inspired that were exploited by the fascist dictators of the 20th century.

the condensed idea
The dangers of infantile sickness

47 Imperialism

The word is relatively new, but the practice of imperialism is almost as old as history itself. From the earliest times, people who succeeded in forming strong political communities would look to gain control over weaker ones, usually by force of arms, and to exploit their land, labour and other resources.

The successive civilizations of ancient Mesopotamia and the Mediterranean basin form a continuous narrative of imperial domination, from the Babylonian and Assyrian empires to the Persian empire of Cyrus the Great, the naval empire of Athens, and the vast Macedonian empire of Alexander the Great. It is the fate of empires to rise and fall, and in time the remnants of these mighty empires gave way to what would soon become one of the greatest and longest-lasting of all: the expansive land empire of the Romans, which at its peak stretched from Britain to northern Africa and the Middle East. Aptly, then, the words 'empire' and 'imperialism' are both derived from the Latin word imperium. The basic meaning of this word is 'power to command' or 'authority', either of a civilian magistrate or of a military commander, and it highlights the essence of empire: power.

At its first appearance in the middle of the 19th century, the term 'imperialism' signified no more than a system of government headed by an emperor, sometimes with the negative suggestion that such government was arbitrary or despotic. Before long, however, in the peak years of the British empire, the word gained a more positive sense, indicating a policy – and advocacy of a policy – which aimed to extend a state's power and influence, usually through force of arms and colonization. Today, 'imperialism' is almost always used in this latter sense, but a century of two world wars and much (initially) communist-inspired invective have completely changed the connotation. In the 21st century imperialist ambitions are almost invariably nefarious ambitions.

timeline

mid-6th century BC	478–404 BC	336–323 BC	3rd century BC
Persian empire established in the Middle East by Cyrus the Great	Alliance of Greek states against Persia is transformed into Athenian empire	Alexander the Great of Macedon conquers a huge empire extending to India	Beginnings of Roman empire as Rome's power expands beyond Italy

> **‘Imperialism, sane Imperialism, as distinguished from what I may call wild-cat Imperialism, is nothing but this – a larger patriotism.’**
>
> **Lord Rosebery,** British Liberal politician, 1899

Where might is right Superior power has always been the necessary condition of empire, and it is only in the last 100 years that the right to use such power to the full has been seriously questioned, either by conquerors or by conquered. The idea that might is right – that it is the right of the powerful to subdue the weak – is explicitly expressed by the Greek historian Thucydides in his history of the Peloponnesian War. He tells how a delegation of Athenians, addressing the Spartan assembly in 432 BC in an effort to avert war, seeks to justify Athens's imperial rule over other Greeks by insisting that they are only doing what anyone else would do in their place: 'It has always been the way that the weaker must bow down to the stronger.' Justice, they add, has nothing to do with the matter and 'never deterred anyone from taking by force as much as he could'. All that counts is political expedience and power.

Where need meets opportunity The power that lies at the heart of empire is essentially unequal power that opens up the opportunity for exploitation of one country by another. Throughout history inequality of this kind has often arisen when one state has gained a particular advantage in weapons or techniques for waging war. For instance, the development of an improved stirrup, which allowed the Mongols to use their bows more effectively on horseback, is credited with helping them win a vast empire that stretched from the Pacific coast of China to the shores of the Black Sea. Likewise, the use of gunpowder and, later, self-loading rifles and machine guns permitted Europeans to seize large empires in Asia, Africa and the Americas.

Where opportunity coincides with need, communities that are sufficiently empowered may look to expand and seize resources beyond their borders. Sometimes the motivation may be a sudden and unforeseen event, such as famine or drought; or it may be more gradual, such as a growing population that demands

13th century AD	**15th–19th century**	**1920s–1945**	**2001**
Mongols conquer a vast empire across Eurasia	European colonization of the Americas, India etc.	Fascist dictators initiate a new phase of aggressive imperialism	War on terror introduces a new phase of American imperialism

more land for settlement and farming. Often there may be an economic motive: a desire to control exotic or valuable commodities (minerals, spices, narcotics), to harvest tax and tribute, to gain access to cheap or slave labour, or to win and control markets for domestic products. Imperialist ambitions are generally complex, and the glory of conquest may be a motive in itself, perhaps in order to win popular support for a regime or to distract attention from domestic issues.

The White Man's burden In the modern era the most active and unapologetic phase of empire-building was the so-called 'new imperialism' that occurred in the half-century before the outbreak of the First World War in 1914. A huge land-grab – including, most spectacularly, a frantic 'scramble for Africa' – was pursued with such vigour that by 1914 roughly four-fifths of the earth's land surface was under the dominion of a handful of colonial powers. At the forefront of this activity were Britain, Germany, France and various other European powers, which were later joined by Japan and the USA.

From the outset, the dominant tone of new imperialism was triumphalist and patronizing. Central to this was the myth of the 'civilizing mission', in which the nations of the West saw it as their duty, as the British statesman Lord Palmerston airily put it, 'not to enslave but to set free'. The view that the blessings of civilization and culture were bestowed, rather than imposed, on subject peoples was shared by many of Britain's political and intellectual elite. With magnificent

The American empire

Imperialism is far from dead; it has merely multiplied its means. Or so, at least, enemies of America would argue. Chastened by the failure of military muscle to deliver in Vietnam in the 1970s, successive US administrations began to explore a range of less formal means to ensure that American influence would continue to be felt around the world. Most effective of these was the huge clout delivered by the United States' powerful economy, which allowed Washington policy-makers to spread the message of freedom (and free trade) and democracy (and anti-communism) by dangling vast carrots in the form of American investment and loans. The visible symptoms of global US economic and cultural penetration were signs and billboards that sprouted all around the world, courtesy of the McDonald brothers and the Coca-Cola Company. Confidence in military means gradually returned, however, and the sheer might of the American empire was displayed at last in the wake of the 9/11 terrorist attacks of September 2001, as the war on terror was waged in Afghanistan and Iraq.

condescension, the supposed 'virtues of empire' were set forth by Rudyard Kipling in a poem called 'The White Man's Burden' (1899), in which he urged his readers to dutifully accept their god-given imperial vocation.

A virtue no more The smug assurance of the new imperialists took a ferocious battering in the course of the First World War, and in the immediate aftermath it was pounded further by a barrage of communist rhetoric. In a pamphlet written in 1917, Lenin finessed the Marxist interpretation of imperialism, arguing that it was the inevitable 'highest stage' of capitalism – the crisis point at which industrialized capitalist economies are forced by declining domestic profits to pursue new overseas markets in order to dispose of their surplus production; and as such, he concluded, it could only be defeated by revolution. The communist critique set the prevailing tone for the decades that followed, and in Soviet propaganda 'imperialist' became a term of abuse virtually interchangeable with 'capitalist'.

This is not to suggest that imperialism lacked its supporters in the years after 1918. Indeed, in Hitler and Mussolini it found two of its most vocal and active enthusiasts. For them, imperial domination was part of the natural order; it was human destiny that the strong would prevail over the weak. But these fascist leaders were essentially nostalgists, forever harking back to a mythical past, and their eventual defeat naturally did nothing to rehabilitate the idea of imperialism. In the postwar years the negative sense had become so well established that Cold War propagandists on both sides could readily call each other 'imperialist', a term of abuse now largely drained of significant meaning. More pointedly, 'imperialist' appeared in post-colonial rhetoric, where, in the mouths of the formerly oppressed, it could comprehend the past and present sins of the ousted colonial powers. At the end of the century, in a world dominated by a single superpower, the charge of imperialism (or neo-imperialism) was most frequently levelled at the United States, as it attempted, often clumsily and with mixed success, to protect its interests around the world.

the condensed idea
Burden or benefit?

48 Isolationism

No good comes from looking for trouble. It is always a sensible plan – other things being equal – for a country's leaders to steer clear of other countries' problems. And the safest way of staying out of other people's quarrels is to avoid entering into commitments that would necessarily limit your freedom of action and lock you into decisions you might not otherwise want to make.

Unfortunately, in the real world other things are never truly equal. Every country is bound to others by historical links – political, social, cultural – that cannot easily be set aside, and few nations could prosper for long without trade that is built on a network of commercial ties. Often, too, a country's security is dependent on alliances that allow the weaker to act collectively to deter the aggressive intentions of the stronger. Central to the idea of a state's sovereignty is its right to determine its own destiny and to act independently of others in pursuit of its national interests. For most states, some loss of national sovereignty – some sacrifice of autonomy – is a price worth paying for prosperity and self-preservation.

At various times and for various reasons, certain countries have chosen to cut themselves off, to a greater or lesser extent, from the outside world. China and Japan are historical examples, while North Korea is well known today for its deep political and cultural isolation. The last of these might qualify as a paradigm case of an isolationist policy imposed on a country's citizens, on ideological grounds, by its political leaders. Often, however, the term 'isolationist' is applied quite narrowly, in political discourse, to describe a current of thought that played a prominent and distinctive role in 20th-century US politics.

timeline

1793
Washington makes
Proclamation of Neutrality

1801
Jefferson warns against
'entangling alliances'

1920
US Senate blocks
American participation
in League of Nations

Against foreign adventures 'Isolationism' and 'isolationist' are of relatively recent coinage, their first known usage dating back to the early years of the 20th century. Although US politicians to whom the labels might accurately be applied first appeared only a short time earlier, this is not the way the politicians concerned would have seen the matter. Typically, they regarded themselves as conservative and traditionalist, advocating a creed in the 20th century which they believed had been widely and wisely practised in the 19th and before.

The set of attitudes and policies that defined the isolationist position came to the fore in the years between the two world wars, when the USA – an emerging superpower with rapidly growing political, economic and military might – was struggling to come to terms with its new eminence in the world. In opposition to politicians of a more interventionist bent, isolationists, who at that time formed a significant political constituency, were deeply suspicious of attempts to embroil the United States in various kinds of foreign adventure. The manner in which the United States had been drawn into the First World War was seen as a cautionary tale illustrating the perils of getting entangled in foreign wars, especially in Europe. In general, isolationists were averse to the kind of permanent military alliances that might necessitate such interventions, and by extension they were opposed to joining international organizations, such as the League of Nations, that aimed to maintain peace by the collective action of their members. Their overriding concern was not the pacifist belief that their country should refrain from warfare; merely that it should jealously guard its national autonomy – its freedom to act independently, unilaterally and on its own initiative.

> **'Tis our true policy to steer clear of permanent alliances with my portion of the foreign world.**
> George Washingston, 1976

Entangling alliances with none In making the case for isolationism in the 20th century, its advocates would frequently appeal to the words and example of the Founding Fathers, and in particular George Washington and Thomas Jefferson. The first champion of American neutrality, Washington

1934–7	1941	1945
US neutrality laws prevent loans and arms sales to belligerents	Japanese attack on Pearl Harbor deals fatal blow to isolationists	UN founded to maintain global peace through collective action

made a Proclamation of Neutrality in 1793 which stipulated that the US should adhere to 'a conduct friendly and impartial' towards the various belligerents in the European revolutionary wars. Three years later, in his Farewell Address, he explained that the primary reason why his countrymen should 'steer clear of permanent alliances' was a lack of common purpose and interest: 'Europe has a set of primary interests which to us have none or a very remote relation.' The desired policy – cooperation without commitment – was definitively expressed by Jefferson in his inaugural address of 1801, in which he recommended the goal of 'peace, commerce and honest friendship with all nations, entangling alliances with none'.

The 20th-century isolationists' nostalgia for the ways of the Founders was largely misplaced. Jefferson's wariness of 'entangling alliances', shared by a succession of later presidents, was a prudent response to the circumstances of the newly created USA. Having recently escaped the clutches of an overbearing European power, the new country was economically and militarily weak; distant from the mainstream of world events, neither threatening to others nor threatened by them on account of its geographical remoteness. In such circumstances it was common sense not to meddle in other countries' affairs, and it remained a guiding principle of US foreign policy through much of the 19th century. But the emphasis was always on remaining neutral and autonomous, never on isolation as such. Indeed, during this period the United States remained open to the world,

Eastern exclusivity

Isolationism may be most familiar as a phenomenon within US politics, but the most thoroughgoing historical examples are to be found in Japan and China. For over two centuries, from the 1630s, Japan under the Tokugawa shogunate implemented a policy of national seclusion (sakoku, meaning 'closed country'), which prevented Japanese from leaving the country and largely denied entry to foreigners. A measure intended initially to keep out Christian missionaries, the seclusion order coincided with an unprecedented period of peace, but it had a severe impact on trade and is credited with creating a culture of chauvinistic insularity. In China under the Ming and Qing dynasties, a 'sea ban' (haijin) – an embargo on maritime activities – was imposed intermittently between the 14th and 17th centuries. Its precise purpose is disputed – elimination of piracy was at least part of the reason – but its main effect was to damage trade and to bring hardship to coastal communities.

literally and on an unprecedented scale, as it welcomed millions of immigrants – the 'huddled masses yearning to breathe free' – to a new life, and busily extended the global network of commercial ties that would in due course make it an economic colossus.

New realities The high-water mark for US isolationists was reached in their successful opposition to the internationalist ambitions of two presidents. First, they managed to thwart Woodrow Wilson in his attempts to bring the US within the League of Nations, which was a critical component in his stated aim of making the world 'safe for democracy'. Then, in the 1930s, they doggedly opposed Franklin D. Roosevelt as he tried to give practical expression to his growing sympathy for European states in their struggle against the rise of fascism. Between 1934 and 1937 a series of neutrality laws were introduced that greatly restricted the kind of assistance, in the form of arms and loans, that could be given to countries at war. However, as global stability was rocked by fascist victories in Spain and Italy, the imperialist ambitions of Japan, and the growing menace of Nazi Germany, the viability of isolationism was increasingly questioned. The fall of France in June 1940 ratcheted up American feelings of insecurity; the Japanese surprise attack on Pearl Harbor in December of the following year plunged the isolationists into full retreat.

Since the end of the Second World War, the awesome ascent of the United States has seen it established as an unrivalled military superpower with full global reach and an economic powerhouse at the epicentre of world trade. It led the way in setting up international bodies such as the United Nations (UN) and the North Atlantic Treaty Organization (NATO), and then proceeded to direct and dominate their agendas. Time and again – in Korea, Vietnam, Latin America, Afghanistan, Iraq – America has intervened in affairs of other countries, sometimes successfully, sometimes in collaboration with others. Nevertheless, in a country that is so fully engaged in global politics, isolationism still holds some of its allure. At times of trauma – in the wake of the Vietnam debacle, for instance, and of the 9/11 terrorist attacks – there are always prominent voices that call for a withdrawal into fortress America. Today, however, such cries are tinged more with nostalgia than realism.

the condensed idea
Avoiding entanglement

49 Globalization

The world has shrunk. Mobile phones, text-messaging, email, social networking, instant bank transfers, satellite information systems: each new technological development has enhanced the reality of rapid global communication. And this shrinkage in virtual space has been matched by the contraction of real space. A voyage to the other side of the globe that a century ago would have taken weeks can now be completed in hours. Places that were once impossibly remote have been opened up to millions of tourists by cheap international flights. Wherever we go, increasingly we wear the same clothes, eat the same foods, watch the same sports and television programmes. We even contract the same diseases.

These developments are all aspects – some causes, some symptoms – of what is currently one of the most voguish political buzzwords: globalization. In spite of its ubiquity, the concept is hard to capture. Straightforwardly, it is a movement towards globalism: a world-view that is just that – a way of looking at things primarily from a global, rather than a local, perspective. Beyond this, it evades easy definition, partly because it has so many facets – social, political, economic, cultural; and partly because it is clearly related to, though distinct from, other equally slippery concepts, such as modernization, westernization and cultural homogenization.

One theme that links the various aspects of globalization is the manner in which the sovereignty of nation-states is being eroded. National borders that could once be jealously guarded are permeable and porous, offering little defence against a barrage of traffic, real and virtual – an unstoppable avalanche of ideas, information, goods and people. The change in focus from national to global

timeline

1962

The idea of the global village appears in McLuhan's *The Gutenberg Galaxy*

1971

The first Asian McDonald's opens, in Tokyo, Japan

has opened up new opportunities. In the world of business, giant multinationals have expanded to exploit new global patterns of production and consumption. Politically, a will to look beyond narrowly national interests has spawned international organizations, most notably the United Nations and its many affiliated agencies. And with globalism has come a sharpened awareness of the world as a unified whole and of global dangers, from AIDS to climate change.

Prophet of the global village . . . The apparent compression of distance and time that drives the process of globalization was famously explored in the 1960s by the Canadian media theorist Marshall McLuhan:

> Electric circuitry has overthrown the regime of 'time' and 'space' and pours upon us instantly and continuously concerns of all other men. It has reconstituted dialogue on a global scale. Its message is Total Change, ending psychic, social, economic, and political parochialism ... Ours is a brand-new world of allatonceness. 'Time' has ceased, 'space' has vanished. We now live in a global village.

At the time McLuhan wrote this, 'electric circuitry' did not go much beyond televisions and telephones, but every subsequent innovation of the information age has served only to confirm his prescience.

McLuhan was generally enthusiastic about the prospect of life in the global village and many since have shared his optimism. An influential disciple is the American right-wing philosopher Francis Fukuyama, who speculated in 1992, in an ecstasy of post-Cold War euphoria, that the collapse of authoritarian rule in the Soviet Union and elsewhere might

globesity

Always a favourite target of anti-globalists, McDonald's and the other colossuses of Western fast food are not only held accountable for a dreary homogenization of the world's diets; they are now implicated in the creation of a new horror: 'globesity'. As a consequence of deteriorating global food habits (more meat, fat, processed sugars etc.), the World Health Organization projects that by 2015 some 700 million adults worldwide will be obese. Yet these giants of cultural imperialism are not all bad, it seems. They have also been credited with the emergence of polite waiters in Moscow, queuing in Hong Kong, and cleaner public toilets throughout the world.

1988

Debord ridicules McLuhan in *Comments on the Society of the Spectacle*

2015

World population of obese adults set to reach 700 million (according to WHO)

mark 'the end point of mankind's ideological evolution and the universalization of Western liberal democracy as the final form of human government'. In this worldwide triumph of liberalism, Fukuyama suggested, a 'true global culture has emerged, centering around technologically driven economic growth and the capitalist social relations necessary to produce and sustain it'.

> **❝The new electronic interdependence recreates the world in the image of a global village.❞**
>
> **Marshall McLuhan, 1962**

In company with many other pro-globalists, Fukuyama bases his argument on a largely unquestioned assumption of the benign impact of Western-style liberal market economics. The swift and unfettered movement of money and goods over the globe, he supposes, will bring great efficiencies and benefits for all: more and cheaper commodities to already rich countries; more and better-paid employment to currently impoverished ones. In the case of the latter, growing prosperity will lead in due course to improved education and greater political sophistication; and if history is our guide, this in turn will lead to liberalization and democracy.

. . . or village idiot Not everyone is so upbeat about the prospect of life in the global village. Most trenchantly, the French avant-garde thinker Guy Debord, writing in 1988, scathingly dismisses McLuhan as the 'most convinced imbecile of the century'. Dazzled by the glitzy and shallow attractions offered by the global village, the 'sage of Toronto', Debord notes, has failed to appreciate the sheer vulgarity of village life: 'Villages, unlike towns, have always been ruled by conformism, isolation, petty surveillance, boredom and repetitive malicious gossip about the same families.'

Conformism and boredom lie at the heart of the anti-globalist critique. As national borders begin to break down, the flow of commodities and ideas is inevitably strongest from the economically and politically dominant regions, above all from the United States. Critics are appalled as the highly commoditized popular culture of America and other Western countries starts to swamp local practices and customs. The onward march of this new cultural imperialism sees local cuisines rudely snuffed out by Ronald McDonald and Colonel Sanders; the authentic statements of indigenous film-makers drowned out by the shrill din of Hollywood's latest blockbuster. And behind the superficial consumerism lies a soulless array of aggressive and cynical multinational corporations: vast businesses that 'swindle the West and exploit the rest', by snatching jobs from Western workers and replacing them with slave labour in Third World sweatshops.

Plus ça change

Is globalization a radically new phenomenon, or is it merely the continuation of an historical process? Well, probably neither – quite. A process akin to globalization is certainly recognizable in the past. The imperialists, missionaries and traders of earlier centuries aspired to extend their power, faith and commerce as widely as possible across the globe, and they deposited a great weight of cultural baggage, willy-nilly, wherever they went. In a sense the landing of Columbus in the New World in 1492 (for instance) represents a classic case of globalization: the coming together of two continents and two worlds after which neither side would ever be the same again. What is new today is the astonishing scale and speed of the transformation, political, economic and cultural. In that respect, we are indeed in new territory – in several senses.

Staying rooted These views are extreme. The truth, predictably, is that globalization is much more nuanced than either its opponents or its proponents allow. The global culture that is welcomed on one side and condemned on the other is in fact largely fictitious. The voluminous research into globalization reaches the clear conclusion that it is almost never a one-way process. When different cultures meet, it is not the case that one simply dominates and displaces the others; rather, there is a subtle process of cross-fertilization in which something new and distinct emerges – something that may have an enriching effect on all sides. However curious people may be to experience new things, they seem to retain a strong sense of belonging to a particular locality and of sharing in a complex system of local customs and beliefs. Humans being humans – and being animals too – are naturally territorial, not cosmopolitan. Any account of globalization that fails to acknowledge the importance of human rootedness will remain inadequate.

the condensed idea
Living in the global village

50 United Nations

The United Nations (UN) is the largest and most successful international organization that has ever existed. Its greatest triumph, of course, is that there has been no global conflict – no Third World War – over the last half-century and more. But this is only a fraction of its achievements: human rights have been promoted throughout the world; the effects of devastating diseases have been mitigated; the social and economic systems of developing countries have been nurtured; the most pressing issues of the day – global terrorism, the trade in narcotics, international organized crime, climate change – have been addressed and put firmly on the agenda.

Or so, at least, the UN's many supporters would have us believe. There is a very different view, most clearly elaborated by (though not limited to) right-wing conservatives in the US. According to this analysis, the UN is a deeply flawed body: largely impotent and marginalized for the first 45 years of its existence; and since the end of the Cold War, an undemocratic forum for anti-Western (especially anti-American) intrigue and lobbying. At best, an irrelevant and costly talking-shop; at worst, a breeding ground for dissent and conflict.

Even its critics might concede that the UN represents an impressive vision. Forged in the awful inferno of the Second World War, the UN's lofty Charter is an appeal for global cooperation: a plea for nations to work together in order to resolve their differences peacefully and to make the world a better and safer place by smoothing a path towards social justice and respect for human rights. The problem, critics argue, is that this ambition is just pie in the sky, a vision that totally fails to grasp the hard realities of global politics. National interest is the driving force that animates states on the global stage, and – for all its high-minded

timeline

June 1945

UN Charter signed at San Francisco
(promulgated Oct 1945)

1971

Communist People's Republic of
China takes seat of Republic of China
(Taiwan) on Security Council

pieties – the same is true of the actions of states within the hallowed portals of the United Nations. In a real sense, then, debate over the role of the UN is a debate over the nature of international politics. Is the idea of global governance – a system in which international relations are conducted collaboratively under the rule of international law – a realistic prospect or a dangerous delusion?

Charter for peace The failures of the UN's predecessor, the League of Nations, were manifest all around in the ruins of war, so well before fighting was at an end plans were underway for a new international body to take its place. Intensive negotiations were led by the leaders of the three major undefeated Allied powers: Franklin D. Roosevelt (USA), Winston Churchill (UK) and Joseph Stalin (Soviet Union). A serious area of disagreement, foreshadowing future problems for the fledgling organization, concerned the balance of power and influence between the 'Great Powers' and other states.

The UN Charter, the formal basis of the new organization's activities, was signed by representatives of 50 states at a meeting in San Francisco on 26 June 1945 and came into force on 24 October of the same year. The UN's central insight, prominently set forth in the Charter, is that the task of maintaining international peace and security cannot be separated from broader considerations of social justice and human rights. Thus, in the Preamble to the Charter, 'the Peoples of the United Nations' declare their determination:

- to save succeeding generations from the scourge of war . . .
- to reaffirm faith in fundamental human rights . . .
- to establish conditions under which justice and respect for the obligations arising from treaties and other sources of international law can be maintained
- to promote social progress and better standards of life in larger freedom.

The 111 articles of the Charter then proceed to set out the purposes and principles of the organization and to outline its structures, tasks, finances and procedures.

1991
Russian Federation takes place of Soviet Union on Security Council

2008
UN mobilizes more than 12 billion dollars for humanitarian relief efforts

2009
Number of UN member states stands at 192

Veto and gridlock Criticism of the UN usually starts from its patchy and often poor performance, especially in the first half-century of its existence, when global politics followed the grim logic of the Cold War. Most of the UN's failures at this time can be attributed to compromises and contradictions that were allowed to impair its original structure. In particular, the division of powers between the Security Council and the General Assembly often paralysed the UN in carrying out its stated mission of keeping the world at peace.

The General Assembly is the UN's main representative body, where every member country has a seat. It has many functions, particularly in relation to budgeting and election of members, and it is the principal forum for debate on important issues that are brought before it. However, while the General Assembly passes resolutions concerning threats to the peace, it has no power to force any wrongdoer to comply with them. It is with the Security Council, according to the Charter, that the 'primary responsibility for the maintenance of international peace and security' rests. This body has the authority to make decisions that are binding on all UN members, but for structural reasons it has often been ineffective. Of its 15 members (originally 11), 10 are non-permanent, elected for a two-year term by the General Assembly. Then there are the 'big five' – the five

Poles apart

The seemingly unbridgeable gulf between the UN's supporters and its critics is well illustrated by a contrasting pair of essays published in the *Oxford Companion to the Politics of the World* (2001). The case for the defence is made by Lloyd Axworthy, Canadian statesman and twice president of the UN Security Council:

'How many more lives would have been lost to conflict, disease, and starvation if there was no United Nations? And can we say that we would have avoided a third world war without it? . . . No longer can the nation-state, not even the most powerful, go it alone. International cooperation is essential . . . A robust United

Nations should occupy a central position in that system, for it has great potential to address the complex problems of today's world.'

The prosecution case is made by John R. Bolton, and former US Ambassador to the UN:

'There may in fact simply be no "solutions" to the UN's current problems. It may be that the inherent internal contradictions in the UN Charter make it impossible for the UN to function any more effectively than it now does . . . Thus, the most likely future role for the UN will be an approximate continuation of its muddled, incoherent, and marginally important present status.'

permanent members: USA, UK, France, Russia (Soviet Union until 1991) and the People's Republic of China (Republic of China/Taiwan until 1971). Each member of the Security Council has one vote, but the permanent members each have the power of veto and so can block any decision.

The consequence of this system during the Cold War was almost total gridlock in the many cases where two or more of the 'big five' were involved. Before 1966, at a time when the Soviet Union tended to see the UN as an instrument of Western imperialism, it vetoed over 100 resolutions. Between 1966 and the collapse of the Eastern bloc in 1989, a period during which the US increasingly saw the UN as a hotbed of hostile communist and Third World groupings, it vetoed some 67 resolutions. Since the end of the Cold War there has been a significant thaw, and in the last decade of the century the UN launched roughly three times as many peacekeeping operations as it had in its history to that date. Even so, its record was still patchy, with notable failures, or failures to act, in the former Yugoslavia from 1992 to 1995; during the Rwandan genocide in 1994; and in Iraq in 2003, when the UN was sidelined by the Bush administration.

Towards a better future Critics, inevitably, focus on the UN's shortcomings and gloss over its considerable successes. From its headquarters in New York City, the UN of the 21st century oversees and coordinates the work of a network of specialized agencies whose task is to tackle a vast array of economic, social, cultural, humanitarian and environmental problems. The so-called United Nations system – the UN itself together with its specialized agencies – includes many of the most powerful and highest-profile bodies in the world: the Food and Agriculture Organization (FAO), the United Nations Educational, Scientific and Cultural Organization (UNESCO), the International Labour Organization (ILO), the International Court of Justice, the World Health Organization (WHO), the International Monetary Fund (IMF), the World Bank. They may have been faltering and scarcely adequate, but such steps as mankind has taken in recent decades to better itself – to improve global health and nutrition, to expand the scope of education, to eliminate poverty, to obliterate 'the scourge of war' – are mainly due to the efforts of the United Nations.

the condensed idea
Avoiding the scourge of war

Glossary

absolutist Describing a regime in which the ruler's (occasionally, rulers') power is unlimited, though legally exercised; often contrasted with constitutional (where power is legally restricted) and tyrannical (where power is unlimited and illegitimate).

American Revolution The political and military struggle, ending in 1783, in which North American colonists freed themselves from British control.

autocratic Describing a regime in which all power is concentrated in the person of a single ruler.

authoritarian Describing a style of government in which unquestioning obedience is demanded of the ruled, at the expense of personal liberty.

autonomous Of a person or state, self-governing.

bureaucratic Describing a system of administration in which decisions are made by permanent, usually unelected officials, who are organized hierarchically and act in according with a strict code of rules.

constitutional see under absolutist.

despotic Describing a ruler or regime in which absolute power is exercised, usually in a cruel or oppressive manner.

dictator A ruler who exercises total power, usually obtained by force, over a state; originally, an ancient Roman magistrate granted absolute power in a time of emergency, for a limited period.

Enlightenment The 'Age of Reason', the period of Western thought, beginning in the late 17th century and driven by the Scientific Revolution, in which the power of reason was elevated over the authority of religion and tradition.

federalism A system of government in which power is vested in a group of constituent bodies (often called 'states'), not in a central body set over and above them.

feudalism The dominant social system in medieval Europe, in which the crown granted lands to the nobles in exchange for military service; the lower echelons of the social hierarchy were filled by vassals and peasants (serfs).

French Revolution The overthrow of the absolute monarchy in France, achieved with escalating bloodshed between 1789 and 1799; sometimes considered the first modern revolution, because it transformed the nature of society and introduced radically new political ideologies.

geopolitics An approach to the analysis of international politics in which particular weight is given to geographical variables such as size and location.

Glorious Revolution The replacement on the English throne, in 1689, of the Catholic monarch James II by his Protestant daughter Mary and her husband William of Orange; the bloodless coup marked the end of absolutism and the beginning of constitutional government in England.

ideology A coherent set of ideas and beliefs that forms the basis of a political or economic theory and which provides a distinctive explanation of the way the world works.

Industrial Revolution Social and economic transformation of agrarian societies into industrial, urbanized ones. Beginning in 18th-century Britain, the process was driven successively by the development of steam power, the advent of factory production and the construction of railways.

laissez-faire An economic doctrine according to which markets perform best in the absence of intervention (interference) by government.

left and right A theoretical spectrum of political orientation, widely but imprecisely used; today, the left wing is generally associated with a broadly socialist agenda, while the right wing is typically conservative and concerned with such issues as economic liberalization (free trade etc.).

lobbying Activity undertaken by particular interest groups in order to inform politicians of their views and to persuade them to vote or draft laws in support of them.

Marxist Relating to the thought of the German political philosopher Karl Marx (1818–83), the founder (with Friedrich Engels) of modern communism.

medieval Relating to the Middle Ages, the period of European history extending from the fall of the Western Roman Empire in the 5th century AD to the start of the Renaissance in the 1400s.

meritocracy A social system in which power or status is granted in proportion to merit (talent and effort), rather than as a consequence of class, gender, age etc.

modern Relating to the period of Western history extending from (roughly) the 15th century to the present day; the earlier part of this period, until around 1800, is often referred to as 'early modern'.

natural law The idea that there is an order in nature from which humans can rationally derive standards or rules of human conduct; it is generally supposed to provide the permanent foundation of humanly constructed laws.

neoliberalism An economic and political theory, prominent from the 1970s onwards, that combines aspects of classical liberalism (especially the omnipotence of free markets) with an enthusiasm for personal liberty and shrinking the state.

populist Describing a political movement that claims to prioritize the views and preferences of ordinary people; often consciously anti-intellectual and purporting to represent the 'small man' against the machinations of the state and powerful elites.

progressive Of politicians or their policies, favouring innovation and reform. A taxation system is said to be progressive if the proportion of income taken in tax rises with the level of income, with the result that the rich pay relatively more than the poor.

rationalism Broadly, the insistence that action and opinion should be based on reason and knowledge; the usual contrast is with faith or belief founded on religious revelation or tradition.

Reformation A religious movement in 16th-century Europe calling for reform of the Roman Catholic Church and leading to the emergence of Protestantism.

Renaissance The revival of European art and literature, extending from the 14th to 16th centuries, inspired by rediscovery of classical models.

separation of powers A doctrine according to which political power is divided among several different bodies (usually legislature, executive and judiciary) as a safeguard against tyranny.

sovereignty Vested in a person or an institution, sovereignty is the claim to supreme political authority within the state; the right to make laws and political decisions and to require everyone else in the state to abide by them.

totalitarian Describing a system of government in which every aspect of private and public behaviour is controlled by the state; in such a regime, the interests of citizens are totally subservient to those of the state.

tyrannical see under absolutist.

Index

Quercus Publishing Plc
21 Bloomsbury Square
London
WC1A 2NS

First published in 2011

A catalogue record of this book is available from the British Library

UK and associated territories: ISBN 978 1 84916 254 8
US and associated territories: ISBN 978 1 84866 083 0

Designed by Patrick Nugent
Printed and bound in China

10 9 8 7 6 5 4 3 2 1